# SOUND EFFECTS

# SOUND EFFECTS

## YOUTH, LEISURE, AND THE POLITICS OF ROCK 'N' ROLL

### SIMON FRITH

PANTHEON BOOKS
NEW YORK

Library of Congress Cataloging in Publication Data
Frith, Simon.
Sound effects.
Bibliography: p.
Includes index.
1. Sound recording industry—United States.
2. Rock music—History and criticism.
ML 3790.F74       784.5'4       81-47195
ISBN 0-394-50461-5          AACR2
ISBN 0-394-74811-5

Grateful acknowledgment is made to the following for permission to reprint previously published material:

Straight Arrow Publishers, Inc.: Excerpt from interview with Pete Townshend by Jann Wenner from *Rolling Stone*, September 28, 1968. By Straight Arrow Publishers, Inc. Copyright © 1968. All rights reserved. Reprinted by permission. Also, excerpt from interview with Keith Richards by Robert Greenfield from *Rolling Stone*, August 19, 1971. By Straight Arrow Publishers, Inc. Copyright © 1971. All rights reserved. Reprinted by permission. And, excerpts from a two-part interview with John Lennon by Jann Wenner from *Rolling Stone*, January 21, 1971, and February 4, 1971. By Straight Arrow Publishers, Inc. Copyright © 1971. All rights reserved. Reprinted by permission.

Chappell & Co., Inc.: Lyrics from "Nice Work If You Can Get It" by George Gershwin and Ira Gershwin. Copyright © 1937 by Gershwin Publishing Corp. Copyright renewed, assigned to Chappell & Co., Inc. International copyright secured. All rights reserved. Used by permission.

National Lampoon, Inc.: Lyrics from the song, "Art Rock Suite." Copyright © National Lampoon, Inc. Lyrics by Sean Kelly and Christopher Guest. Used by permission.

Book designed by Kathleen Westray
Manufactured in the United States of America
9876

# CONTENTS

# ACKNOWLEDGMENTS

This book is the result of years of talking, writing, and arguing about rock music. For their friendship, encouragement, and inspiration at various times I would like to thank Lester Bangs, Bob Christgau, Iain Chambers, Simon Clarke, James Donald, Gill Frith, Charlie Gillett, Dave Laing, Greil Marcus, Dave Marsh, Angela McRobbie, Richard Williams, and Wendy Wolf.

# ONE

# ROCK
# MEANINGS

# CHAPTER 1

# INTRODUCTION

This book began as an academic text in a British series on "communication and society." It was a solid and generally sober work. I was determined to take rock seriously. I had one eye on my sociological colleagues, still ignoring music in their accounts of the mass media, and the other on my fellow rock fans, still making sense of their music with loose political assumptions left over from the 1960s. I armed my book with footnotes and statistics: everything *I* said was properly documented, every assertion "proved." My approach, cautious objectivity, reflected my position—I was an academic sociologist as well as a rock journalist; but it reflected, too, a wider set of British assumptions about rock and its significance.

When I went to college in 1964 I assumed that I'd reached the end of my teenage bopping days, and I didn't even take my records with me. Rock 'n' roll was heard then, by me too, as youth music—and as working-class music at that; it was time now for me to grow up. Three years later, in 1967, I had an Oxford degree, my entrance ticket to bourgeois culture, and I didn't feel particularly eccentric setting out for California under the inspiration of a pop song, Scott McKenzie's "San Francisco." My use of music hadn't changed after all, and even in England, pop's power was now publicly realized. In Berkeley I found a culture in which rock and politics, music and the Movement, pleasure and action were inextricably linked. They have been so for me ever since, and by the time I came back to England again, in 1969, I was sure that rock was the most interesting and most encouraging of the contemporary mass media.

In the heyday of the counterculture and student organization, this was a widely shared (if rarely examined) assumption. In Robert Christgau's mocking words: "Why is rock like the revolution? Because they're both groovy!" But in the 1970s sociologists turned their attention back to traditional academic matters, and the learned tomes on rock that once seemed likely to appear never materialized. The decline of serious interest in rock was particularly obvious in Britain, where the music had never achieved much cultural respectability anyway. Its status had been as a news event, and the arts editors of the quality press, with a sense of relief, soon shuffled the few rock critics off their pages again. Complacency, rather than disillusion, set in: rock was, after all the alarums, only a matter of fleeting academic concern—just another youth culture quirk.

In order to pursue my musical interests I had to lead a double life: on one hand, going through the paces of an academic sociological career—doing respectable research on youth as a social phenomenon; on the other hand, ringing the changes as a semiprofessional rock writer, contributing my obstinate prejudices and enthusiasms to the thousands of words that accompany the release of every new rock record, the discovery of every new rock star.

My two careers were rarely good for each other: rock writing is not considered suitable for inclusion in an academic curriculum vitae; and "sociology" is a term of abuse among rock writers. However, I didn't lose the convictions that linked my two worlds: rock is a crucial cultural practice and sociological analysis is needed to make sense of it. But I couldn't avoid being defensive either. Nagging questions were always at the back of my mind: Is this topic suitable for sociology? Is this approach right for rock?

My belief in the social importance of rock was sustained by the sales statistics. By the mid-1970s well over $4 billion was being spent annually in the world on musical products, and in America music had become the most popular form of entertainment—the sales of records and tapes easily outgrossed the returns on movies or sports. The British record industry had tripled its output between 1955 and 1975; the collapse of Decca and EMI in 1979 was less a reflection of declining sales than of managerial inability to deal with any situation that wasn't actually a boom. It took the recession to bring home to people how big a business music had become. The difficulties the record industry faces in the 1980s are difficulties derived from success.[1]

The question is: What do such sales figures mean? Sociologists couldn't ignore the record players, tape recorders, and transistor radios found in just about every household by the 1960s, and so records became included in textbook lists of mass media. But this is usually the only mention that records get. Media analyses on both sides of the Atlantic continue to be dominated by terms and problems derived from studies of television and the press; records cannot easily be fitted into the subsequent arguments. The figures I've cited are certainly those of a profitable industry, but they don't directly establish records as a mass *medium*. To determine the social power of rock I had to go beyond the account books and sales returns. I had to work my way through definitions of mass communication.

Some aspects of the argument were straightforward. Records are the result of complex organizations. While in live musical experiences the musicians and their audiences are joined by the immediacy of sound, in recorded music they are linked by an elaborate industry. Between the original music and the eventual listener are the technological processes of transferring sound to tape and disc and the economic processes of packaging and marketing the final product; like the other mass media, records rely on capital investment, specialized technical equipment, and on the organization of a variety of skilled roles. The basis of any sociological analysis of records must be an analysis of the record industry, and this will be my focus in Part Two. But the immediate question about record production is this: Are records directed at a large audience? In light of the sales statistics, this may seem a silly question; but it is, in fact, crucial to an understanding of rock as *mass* culture.

"Large" is a relative term in media studies. Mass media have large audiences relative to other media and relative to the number of communicators involved; there is not a given size of audience to which a communication must be addressed to reach mass status. But the position is especially complicated in the case of records because of the relationship between the record industry as a whole and its products, individual records. The record industry is geared to capital accumulation, and its profits depend on the number of records sold. Initial recording costs are once-only expenditures, unaffected by the number of records eventually produced, while the costs of manufacture and distribution are proportionately reduced as the number of records involved increases. The record business is ruled by the logic of mass production, and a large market is its overriding aim.

This market is, however, made up of different audiences buying different records and listening to different musics. And the sales of a particular record can be anything from the handful for an avant-garde recital to the millions for the latest platinum smash from Fleetwood Mac. Should we assume that all records, whatever their genre or sales, are directed at a large audience? Or should we assign some (random?) sales figure that a record must reach before it can be classified as mass communication?

Both approaches are wrong. We can, more constructively, make a distinction between music conceived with no reference to a mass market and music that is inseparable from the mass market in its conception. The former category includes classical music, folk music, and most jazz; the latter category is pop music. Pop music is created with the record industry's pursuit of a large audience in mind; other music is not (and, as we will see, one of the contradictions of rock revolves around this distinction). That classical or folk music can be listened to on records is accidental for its form and content; it is only pop music whose essence is that it is communicated by a mass medium. This is true even though some classical records sell tens of thousands of copies and most pop records are bought by nobody. Pop music is created, however successfully, for a large audience and is marketed accordingly by the record industry; pop records get the bulk of the attention of the advertisers, distributors, and retailers. The assumption is that a pop audience can be *constructed* by the record industry itself. The audiences for classical, folk, and the other "special" forms are, by contrast, not only relatively small (classical music accounts for about 10 percent of record sales in the UK), but also believed to be relatively autonomous— their tastes are "given." The music business can service these tastes but it can't manipulate them.

Pop music doesn't actually have to be on record by this definition—Tin Pan Alley was marketing songs for mass consumption long before the recording industry was flourishing. But at least since World War II pop music has meant pop records. To define "pop" as music aimed at a large market is also, these days, to define it as music aimed at record sales.

Once a record has been issued, there is nothing to stop anyone from listening to it except its price or the (increasingly rare) lack of playback equipment. Radio stations can ban a record from the air-waves, but they can't stop people from buying it: the Sex Pistols' "God Save the Queen" topped the British sales charts despite the banning efforts of the BBC, commercial radio, and even the record shops themselves. Record distributors can't control consumer choice as effectively as can, say, film distributors. Pop records, indeed, have a wider public than any other medium because their availability is not limited by considerations of literacy or language. They can and do cross all national and cultural boundaries. Elvis Presley in the 1950s, the Beatles in the 1960s, Abba in the 1970s were mass media phenomena in nearly every country in the world, and there is a continuous interplay between English, American, and Continental European pop. If anything, Anglo-American mass music dominates the world more effectively than any other mass medium.

It follows that the record-buying public is heterogeneous, coming from a variety of social conditions. This brings me to the central peculiarity of records as a medium: though pop interest is not exclusive to any country or class, to any particular educational or cultural background, it does seem to be connected specifically to age— there is a special relationship between pop music and youth.

The importance of this youth connection becomes clear when we consider the "simultaneity" of record listening. In general terms, the pop public is dispersed: people may listen to the same records, but they do so independently of each other. In what sense, then, is their listening simultaneous? The importance of this concept for other mass media is obvious. Radio listening and television watching are exactly simultaneous activities, and even reading newspapers and magazines can be judged as approximately simultaneous—most people read Tuesday's paper on that Tuesday. But there are no technological or topical reasons why record listening should be so time-bound. People can listen to their records when they choose, and the value of their records is not obviously limited to a particular date. Records can be used with pleasure over and over again (unlike films or many books) and wear out slowly. There are, nevertheless, good economic reasons why records should be time-bound. The record industry depends on constant consumer turnover and therefore exploits notions of fashion and obsolescence to keep people buying.

British record companies issue about 3,000 singles and 3,000 pop albums every year; the American figures are 7,000 singles and 5,000 albums. While a certain proportion of these are rereleases or repackages of old recordings, the majority are new. A good part of the record business involves persuading consumers to buy a record at the moment of its release, to get bored with it after a few weeks, to discard it for a yet newer release, and so on. Pop records are released with a fanfare of publicity, advertising, plugging, and hype. They are produced specifically for the hit parade, which symbolizes simultaneous listening by listing the records that attracted the most purchasers the previous week. The chart's suggestion of continuous musical sensation and change is reinforced by the music press and pop radio, which, by turning pop music into news, make the dating of records even more precise.

As a result, records have a limited active life (for singles it's 60 to 180 days, depending on success) during which time they can be heard on the radio, on jukeboxes, in discotheques. After that they're considered "out-of-date" and cease to be played; they're deleted, only to be revived as "oldies," their appeal then resting on their precise nostalgic connection with a particular date in the past. Individual consumers, encouraged by market pressures, novelty, and fashion, echo this pattern in their own listening. They will give a record a brief active life by listening to it incessantly before sending it to the bottom of the pile when something new comes along; they will bring it out again later only to revive memories.

Only 7 to 8 percent of a year's record releases are hits of this sort—they appear in the charts, get played on the radio, turn up on jukeboxes; but the vast majority of records sold each year come from the Top 30. Records that aren't hits, in other words, don't sell at all. The pop audience buys and listens to the same few records at the same brief moments. The series of apparently individual decisions about what records to buy thus takes on a collective force—everyone makes the same decision. For pop fans themselves, the resulting musical dating process—each sound linked to a specific time—seems so natural that the conservatism of other musical cultures seems inexplicable to them: How can Ernest Tubb fans enjoy exactly the same country show, decade after decade after decade?

But it is the "stimultaneity" of pop record buying and listening that needs explaining. Are pop fans simply the victims of a commercial process? What are the cultural effects of the patterns of pop collective behavior?

In Britain it is quite clear that the "collective" part of the pop audience is youth. They buy the chart records, read the chart music papers like *Smash Hits* and *Record Mirror*, listen to the national chart stations Radio 1 and Radio Luxembourg. "Old pop," middle-of-the-road, is produced for a mass market but, by and large, lacks young pop's accoutrements—hit parades and magazines and jukeboxes. It takes the form of "standards" with "timeless" appeal. "Quality" pop is broadcast on Radio 2, Britain's easy-listening station, and is featured on the bills of workingmen's clubs and TV variety shows. It is eternal film-score music and background music and difficult to date. Easy-listening music, by definition, neither reflects the historical moment in which it was made nor carries an active sense of its audience. Its "qualities" are negative or, at best, passive.

The distinctions between chart and easy-listening pop are not clear-cut. Easy-listening stars like Barry Manilow do get onto the hit parade; chart toppers like the Beatles make "standards" like "Yesterday"; musicians move from one type of music and audience to the other. And, of course, the chart audience is not exclusively young, nor is the easy-listening audience exclusively old. Nonetheless, the relationship between chart pop and youth has always been taken for granted, not the least by the record business itself, and this relationship lies at the heart of pop music's cultural importance. In most respects, pop consumers make up just another impersonal and anonymous mass public—the music marketplace is not, in any organized sense, anything more than a collection of individuals. But *young* consumers have a sense of being part of a common audience, whether a generation or a cult. Pop stars since Elvis Presley have been, from whatever distance, a part of this community—they are also young. It is with reference to youth that we have to examine the issues of manipulation and its meaning: the sociology of rock is inseparable from the sociology of youth.

In Britain, certainly, it is easier to justify the sociology of rock in terms of youth culture than in terms of mass culture. Britain's few academic theories of rock have emerged from studies of youth, and this reflects a general cultural point: music is integrated into youth cultures in Britain in ways that it isn't in America (punk is only the most recent example of this use of music as a subcultural sign). The history of British pop audiences has always been a history of British youth styles.

The same point can be made the other way around: America has an adult music audience of a sort unknown in Britain, where, throughout the 1970s, people still stopped buying new records at the age of twenty-five. America has a visible rock generation, weaned on rock 'n' roll and still serviced by new music as it moves into affluence and parenthood. The contrast between audiences is obvious in the music press. America's *Rolling Stone* has grown with its readers, its consumer tips becoming steadily more middle-aged. The British music papers, by contrast, are written for an ever-changing audience of the same teen age. Hence, the contrasting treatments of punk: *Rolling Stone*, detached, grudging, patronizing; *New Musical Express*, half cynically, half joyously, leaping into the maelstrom itself.

For all this, there is obviously a special relationship between music and American youth cultures, too, but the social significance of rock is not *defined* in terms of youth in America as it is in Britain. Rather, youth itself is defined differently, as an ideological and not just an age category. (I'll return to the questions this raises—about youth and the family, about leisure and pleasure—in Part Three.) The point I want to stress here is that from these different assumptions about the pop audience come different accounts of what popular music means.

American rock writers are mythologists: they comb music for symbolic significance, and their symbols are derived from a sweep through American culture in general. These rock critics write (and are read) as American culture critics. British rock writers, by contrast, are still pop fans, still isolated in a cult world. Their writing is a matter of documentation (the most loving archivists of American popular music are Britons) or solidarity—British writers have an acute sense of their young readers and their needs. And the issue here isn't just a critical strategy; there's also a problem of definition. The sociology of rock is, in the end, determined by its object of study. The ultimate question—one I've been avoiding—is: What is rock?

The implication of the argument I've been making is that rock (as an aspect of pop) can be defined in purely sociological terms, by reference simply to the process of its production and consumption: rock is music produced commercially for simultaneous consumption by a mass youth market. But rock can also be defined in musical terms, as a pop genre (the sound of the early seventies?). And rock is, further, an ideological suffix. To add "rock" to a musical description (folk-rock, country-rock, punk-rock) is to draw attention not just to a sound and a beat but also to an intention and an effect.

Rock, in contrast to pop, carries intimations of sincerity, authenticity, art—noncommercial concerns. These intimations have been muffled since rock became the record industry, but it is the possibilities, the promises, that matter. The trouble with a purely sociological definition of rock is that the object of the definition, the music itself, tends to disappear from view. This is a hazard I've always been aware of as a rock critic: I'm too easily drawn to other tasks—biography, history, commercial accounting, the iconography of youth—when the central task is to account for the pleasure of the musical texts themselves. The sociology of rock must be, in the end, the sociology of musical experiences, and these really can't be defined in terms of their commercial or youthful context. Rather than deducing the meaning of rock from the processes of its production and consumption, we have to try to make sense of rock's production and consumption on the basis of what is at stake in these processes—the meanings that are produced and consumed. Rock is a mass-produced music that carries a critique of its own means of production; it is a mass-consumed music that constructs its own "authentic" audience. The purpose of this book is to explain these contradictions.

A final note: rock is an American music, and much of what I'm going to say will draw on British experience and British examples. I'm not apologetic about this—my rock experience is a British experience, and it is this, ultimately, that I am trying to understand. And there are advantages in my position: rock is both a medium general to capitalist cultures and a specifically American form of music. How American music was generalized, how American sounds—pop and rock—are experienced (and produced) in other cultural contexts are important questions in themselves. The issue here is not just musical meaning, but also the slipperiness, the power, the idea of "America" itself.

# CHAPTER 2

# ROCK ROOTS

Rock is a form of music, and the obvious starting point in making sense of it is in terms of its musical qualities, its particular organization of sounds. But rock, despite the millions of words devoted to it, is seldom subjected to rigorous musical analysis. As Dave Marsh has commented: "Little rock criticism is concerned with music, because most rock critics are less concerned with sound than sociology." Writers are interested in the meaning of rock not as music but as a more vaguely defined "cultural phenomenon." Rock's critical terms are impressionistic. Sounds are described, but their effects and functions are treated in subjective terms. The most interesting questions—Why do these sounds have these effects, these meanings?—are the least frequently addressed. Musicians complain that rock writers lack interest in their musical purposes and problems. But even the musicians' musical analyses are limited. The little serious musical criticism of rock has come from outside rock culture and has had little influence on it. The gap between academic musicology and rock practice is well illustrated by these comments on the Animals' 1964 song "I'm Crying."

First, Richard Middleton, musicologist:

In "I'm Crying" ostinato and modal harmony are again used in a similar way, but they are organised within an overall 12-bar blues pattern (so that the ostinato is treated in fact as a riff). A refrain of modal vocal harmony is then added. The resulting cultural mixture is one typical of R&B. The cross relations in the ostinato (which is melodic and harmonic) are the equivalents of blue notes, arising from a similar conflict between melodic and tonal implications. The modal melodic movement of the ostinato, with its minor thirds, clashes with the tonal need for major triads imposed by the 12-bar blues structure. The cross relations are symptomatic of the harmonic complexity of the song, in which a modal/blue ostinato is placed in the overall context of a tonal, but stable and repetitive blues form, given a passionately blue vocal and followed by a refrain of triadic but modal "organum" (i.e. parallel triads). The resulting tension, similar in type and effect to that of city blues even though slightly different in cultural make-up, is only partly assuaged by the tribalising role of the ostinato and the universalising, depersonalising effect of the "organum."

Secondly, Alan Price:

Eric (Burdon) and I wrote "I'm Crying" together. We did it in the back of a van. I wrote the music and Eric did the words and we just threw it together in rehearsal in Blackpool on the North Pier on a Sunday afternoon. We just stuck it together and recorded it and by chance it was successful. We didn't set out to do anything much, we just had to do it, you know.[1]

One reason for the sharp difference in discourse is ignorance. Most rock musicians lack formal musical training, and so do almost all rock commentators. They lack the vocabulary and techniques of musical analysis, and even the descriptive words that critics and fans do use—harmony, melody, riff, beat—are only loosely understood and applied. I share this ignorance; this chapter will not contribute anything to the musicology of rock in terms such as Middleton's.

But rock must be understood, even from a sociological perspective, as a form of music. Its cultural effects have musical causes. One difficulty here is that rock is a song form—there is a temptation to analyze the words at the expense of the sounds. Words can be reproduced for comment with comparative ease, and rhymes are better understood than chords; sociologists of popular music have always fallen for the easy terms of lyrical analysis. Such a word-based approach is not helpful at getting at the meaning of rock. The fans know, in Greil Marcus's words, that "words are sounds we can feel before they are statements to understand." Most rock records make their impact musically rather than lyrically. The words, if they are noticed at all, are absorbed after the music has made its mark. The crucial variables are sound and rhythm.

There is a paradox here. Rock's cultural significance is as a form of music, while rock ideology is not articulated in musical terms. But behind this paradox lies the central musical fact of rock: it is a musical means, not a musical end. Rock is made *in order to* have emotional, social, physical, commercial results; it is not music made "for its own sake." As Lester Bangs puts his doubts about Blondie's avant-garde "serious" pretensions:

> If the main reason we listen to music in the first place is to hear passion expressed—as I've believed all my life—then what *good* is this music going to prove to be?[2]

Even when rock was first treated as an art form, in the late 1960s, its listeners were more interested in content than form, in what was revealed about experience and feeling, rather than in how it was revealed. The few serious avant-garde composers who learned from rock how to "suppress all rhythmic, harmonic, melodic and dynamic variation," and wrote music using rock devices (rhythmic repetition, feedback, studio-constructed electronic *musique concrète*) were rock technicians but not rock musicians; they were too detached emotionally from the social effects of performance.

Rock is, in a sense, primitive. It uses a primitive understanding of how sounds and rhythms—prelinguistic devices—have their emotional and physical effects. Its sound effects are those of daily life. The sound questions raised are nonmusical: Why do we respond the way we do to a baby's cry, a stranger's laugh, a loud, steady beat? Because so much of rock music depends on the social effects of the voice, the questions about how rock's effects are produced are vocal, not musicological. What makes a voice haunting? sexy? chilling?

Ignorance of *how* their music makes sense certainly puts no limit on a rock audience's appreciation; all that needs to be taken for granted is the common experience of desire, hope, fear. The response to the music is, to a large degree, physical. Interestingly, one of the effects of the music is the vicarious experience of producing it, as listeners mime the movements of the guitarist, the drummer, or the singer. But rock *pleasure* is a cultural as well as a physical matter, and the meaning of the music is not fixed. Rock is the result of an ever-changing combination of independently developed musical elements, each of which carries its own cultural message.

## BLACK MUSIC

"White folks got all the money
Colored folks got all the signs,
Signs won't buy you nothin'. . . ."[3]

Black musical forms and styles have been aspects of Western popular culture since at least the middle of the nineteenth century. Eileen Southern quotes a writer in the *Knickerbocker Magazine* in 1845:

Who are our true rulers? The Negro poets, to be sure. Do they not set the fashion, and give laws to the public taste? Let one of them, in the swamps of Carolina, compose a new song, and it no sooner reaches the ear of a white amateur, than it is written down, amended (that is, almost spoilt), printed, and then put upon a course of rapid dissemination, to cease only with the utmost bounds of Anglo-Saxondom, perhaps with the world. Meanwhile, the poor author digs away with his hoe, utterly ignorant of his greatness. [4]

Black music has always been central to pop; and rock 'n' roll, in using black musical ideas, used ideas that were already, in a diluted and distorted form, a part of the mainstream of mass culture.

The impact of rhythm and blues on youth music in the 1950s and 1960s was, in many respects, just another example of the continuing process through which white popular music has been invigorated by styles and values drawn from black culture—styles and values that lose their original force and meaning as they pass through the bland wringer of mass music but are rediscovered by each new generation of hip musicians and audiences.

A good starting point for an understanding of black musical ideas is Marshall Stearns's definition of jazz, the source of black music's impact on pop in the 1920s and 1930s. Jazz is

> a semi-improvisational American music distinguished by an immediacy of communication, an expressiveness characteristic of the free use of the human voice, and a complex flowing rhythm; it is the result of three-hundred-years' blending in the United States of the European and West African musical traditions; and its predominant components are European harmony, Euro-African melody, and African rhythm.[5]

I want to examine each of the elements of this definition, starting with *immediacy of communication*.

At the center of Afro-American music is the performance. Black music is performance music rather than composition music (even jazz composers, like Duke Ellington, wrote for specific performers). Black music is based on the immediate effects of melody and rhythm rather than on the linear development of theme and harmony, on "intentional" inflections rather than "extentional" development, to use Andrew Chester's terms. It is improvised—spontaneously composed—and it is the immediate exigencies of a performance (in African tradition the response of the audience, a fellow performer, even the weather) that determine the development of the music's beat, tune, texture, tempo, and effect. The value of black music derives not from its solutions to musical problems or from the performers' expertise in interpreting written pieces of music, but from its emotional impact, its account of the performers' own feeling. If, in Franklin Rosemont's words, "the spoken word, the chant, and dancing were the only vehicles of creative expression left to the slaves," then they developed with these elements an aesthetic of intense expression, which has remained the essence of black musical ideology ever since. Black music is immediate and democratic—a performance is unique and the listeners of that performance become part of it. They need no special training or knowledge to appreciate it—the qualities that are valued in spontaneous music making are emotional rather than technical; these musicians are judged for their directness, their passion.

The spontaneous basis of black music initially limited its pop possibilities. To make black music mass music its performances had to be brought to an audience far bigger than that which could actually be present. The solution to this problem was electrical reproduction, which meant that performances could be captured, preserved, and responded to long after their original circumstances had been forgotten. The "live" qualities of black music only became generally available, in other words, when they could be heard on a record.

The relationship works in both directions: if a performance-based music has been essential to the history of records as a medium, the development of that medium has had its own effects on the performances. The pop industry is organized around music as composition—American copyright laws protect composers rather than performers. It is songwriters who get royalties when records are sold or broadcast, not their performers, and the black singers who became popular in the 1920s and 1930s were systematically cheated of their due returns. Their music, however distinct, was in a legal sense "composerless," and it was white music publishers who rushed to copyright the resulting "spontaneous" compositions. Such exploitation of black musicians by publishers and record companies continued into the 1960s, and in fighting for their economic rights, these musicians learned that if they couldn't necessarily make money out of the recordings of specific performances, they could make money out of their *general* performing styles—they could become part of the star system. What a performer could sell, in other words, was his or her unique *approach* to songs. This brings me to the second element in Stearns's definition of jazz: *expressiveness characteristic of . . . the human voice.*

The essence of black music performance is the expression of the performers' feelings, and the possibilities of such expression depend on the music's vocal qualities. In Ian Hoare's words:

Even in instrumental jazz, the basic mode of expression lies in imitating the effects of the human larynx. Voices can express inchoate emotion directly by, say, laughing or screaming or moaning or grunting; or they can communicate reactions to the world in the form of description, analysis, evaluation—using the full potential of language, a potential not available to pure-ly instrumental music. [6]

This emphasis on the voice as the source of human expression has a number of musical consequences. Hoare contrasts blues vocal techniques such as melisma with the perfect pitch and enunciation of a classical singer; jazz critics describe players' unique "voices" on their instruments. It was the "vocal" qualities of the electric gui-tar developed by black musicians that inspired a generation of white rock stars in the 1960s, and in the 1970s bass players like Larry Graham were said to have "liberated" an instrument that was pre-viously "too electric." In Joachim-Ernst Berendt's words, "We were hearing from electric bassists sounds with human, expressive, emo-tional and even narrative qualities."

In gospel music, voices are used not just to express individual religious feeling but also, through vocal interplay, through the call and response of preacher and congregation, to express communal re-ligious emotion. Black singers used these vocal techniques to devel-op a song form that combined individual and collective expression. In traditional pop songs, by contrast, crooners appeared to direct their messages to individual listeners only—the white pop ideal was to make mass communication feel like a private conversation rather than a public event.

As black music became part of the pop business, its vocal qual-ities were subordinated to the star system. Record companies had to control expression, to package passion, to sell emotion. The per-formers' "soul" was marketed as a gimmick, a sound reproducible at will, so that every live performance could be as interchangeable as every record. Direct communication between artist and audience, in which the performance drew its meaning from the immediate ex-perience, became the rehearsed distance between the star and the consumer, and a tension developed between the artists' concerns, the audiences' demands for reassurance, and the industry's assess-ments of consumer tastes. This tension emerged most clearly with respect to the third element of black music—its *rhythm*.

Black music's most obvious influence on pop has been rhyth-mic. It was as dance music that black music first developed its cultural significance for whites, a significance determined by the meaning of dance itself. The most obvious feature of dancing as an activity is its sexuality—institutionalized dancing, a peculiarly constrained form of physical interaction, is redolent with sexual tensions and possibilities, as private desires get public display, as repressed needs are proudly shared; on the dance floor, gays, for instance, can pursue pleasure without harassment. One feature of the black musical use of rhythm, of which disco is the most recent example, is its clear expression of such tensions and needs. Whereas Western dance forms control body movements and sexuality itself with formal rhythms and innocuous tunes, black music expresses the body, hence sexuality, with a directly physical beat and an intense, emotional sound—the sound and beat are *felt* rather than interpreted via a set of conventions. Black musicians work, indeed, with a highly developed aesthetic of *public* sexuality. (History holds that sexuality was the only ideological issue on which slaves could musically comment, while white artists were confined by puritanism to more private expressions of eroticism—to literature and poetry.)

Black music makes obvious the potential chaos of sexual feeling, and rock's black-based dance forms have always been perceived by moralists as a threat to respectable codes of behavior. The media censors realized immediately that Elvis Presley's rock 'n' roll was a form of sexual display. Black music, in short, became a means for the public expression of normally private sensations for white teenagers in the 1950s, but the institutions in which black musicians played had always had an atmosphere of risk and excitement and promise; they offered to the young people drawn to them symbols of rebellion. In Britain, as in America, black music, from jazz to reggae, has been the background music of the hippest kids for at least four generations.

Black music's intimations of the real needs and forces in society, its hints of the truth behind mass culture's anodyne images, are not confined to its expressions of sexuality, but take their driving force from them. Paul Garon has argued that the blues are an "aggressive and uncompromising assertion of the omnipotence of desire and the imagination in the face of all resistances." Blues are poems of revolt against

> the degradation of language, the repressive forces of the church, the police, the family and the ruling class, against the

inhibition of sexuality and aggression, against the general repugnance of everyday life. [7]

Even "respectable" black music, the gospel sounds of family worship, involve an overt expression of spiritual desire, closer to the dance floor than to the white Protestant church. And if black music is essentially "body music," its arguments have also been poetic, taking a lyrical form. Even if, in Dave Harker's words, "the openness, explicitness and general honesty of the adult blues were left well alone" by the original rock 'n' rollers, rock fans subsequently did draw on what they heard as the social realism of black words. In the 1960s young white musicians found in the blues a more honest account of the world than in teenage pop, and it was, in particular, as a means of expressing *collective* experience, collective desires, that black music became a part of rock culture. Rock 'n' roll faith is faith in the music's black elements, in its sense of performance, its physical energy, its directness, its vocal and rhythmic techniques. These were the rock qualities that enabled 1960s musicians like Pete Townshend to retain a sense of rock communion even as they became superstars. And for the punks at the end of the 1970s, seeking to recreate rock as a communal music, the model was reggae, the music which expressed and organized the daily culture of the shantytown streets and rural byways of Jamaica. The aim of a group like The Clash was to make a music that fulfilled reggae functions for white youth, that combined musical intensity with explicit lyrics: "We wanna riot, riot of *our own*."

In the mid-sixties heyday of the white use of R&B, Motown, and soul, rock fans agonized over a difficult question: Can white men sing the blues? Much of the discussion of the quality of, say, Eric Clapton's "suffering" missed the point. White blues, like rock 'n' roll before it, was not being used to express individual angst but to articulate youth's collective feelings of frustration and aggression and rebellion and lust. Songs' individual lyrics were less important than their shared musical qualities—rock 'n' roll had developed its own forms of inchoate emotion, its own solidary beat, and these continued to be the source of rock's claims as a youth culture.

But if black music was the basis of rock's own language, it had been absorbed into the rock vocabulary via a paradoxical mediation. This became obvious in the late 1960s when rock fans, in claiming their music as art, began to *differentiate* white musicians' practices from those of black musicians. What had previously been considered the "liberating" possibilities of black music—its rhythmic emphasis, its physical expressiveness, its spontaneous account of emotion—were considered now to put limits on what could be said.

The assumption was that while black music was important as an expression of vitality and excitement—was, in other words, "good to dance to"—it lacked the reflective qualities needed for genuine *artistic* expression. (The crudest version of this argument appeared at the end of the 1970s as the back pages of *Rolling Stone* were filled with ads for "Disco Sucks!" T-shirts.)

This position assumes a straightforward distinction between mind and body. Black music, as "body music," is therefore "natural," "immediate," "spontaneous." Art, by contrast, is something deliberately created, self-consciously *thought,* and involves, by definition, complexity and development. In the late 1960s, rock musicians drew on artistic ideology to legitimize and make sense of their movement (following the Beatles) from live performance to the recording studio, from collective celebration to the individual lyric, from dancing teenage crowds to appreciative listening audiences. They moved, commercially, practically, and creatively, away from those places and activities from which rock 'n' roll and R&B had drawn their meanings. Rock music "progressed" and, in doing so, began to derive its cultural importance from the nonblack elements in its vocabulary. The only black musicians to be accepted as rock "artists" were those involved in similar trips of individual exploration—Jimi Hendrix and Stevie Wonder, and for a while Sly Stone.

It was precisely because R&B was, for rock fans, essentially a collective form that it was thought not to allow for genuine individual artistic expression. The new criteria of individuality, which had been brought to rock in the mid-1960s by folksinger/songwriters like Bob Dylan and Paul Simon, referred not to emotional effects but to literary ones. By the 1970s there was a general stress in rock on artfulness, on individualized skills, on "unnatural" (because personalized) accounts of experience; even blues groups were, following Cream, emphasizing technical rather than emotional expertise. Black music was, in this context, thought to be *too* direct; its very vocal qualities were what made it essentially incapable of artistic progression.

If the blues tradition was too natural to be art, black pop—soul—had become, by the end of the 1960s, too artificial. Record companies marketed soul as a package. They didn't expect their artists to change, simply to become more efficient at selling the sound they already had, and it was black musicians who came to symbolize show biz. Motown acts like the Supremes and the Four Tops, who in 1965 had brought a "natural" exhilaration to the charts, now dressed up in sequins and entertained in the glamorous ways no longer acceptable in rock. By the 1970s *Rolling Stone* was reviewing Motown records in these terms: "Tom travesties," "opportunistic commercial album making of the worst sort." "What happened to the days when black music was black," asked the *New Musical Express.* "and not this mush of vacuous Muzak and pretentious drivel?"

The issue here was the relationship between black performance and white pleasure, a relationship with a long, uneasy history that had been only temporarily concealed by soul's chart successes in the 1960s. The "slick" dance routines of the Motown acts, for example, crucial for both their show-biz success and their rock dismissal, were, in fact, the products of 1930s dance masters like Cholly Atkins, and their conventions could be traced back to the nineteenth century. The concept of entertainment itself (the concept of glamour and style and spectacle) has always been critical to the social relationship of blacks and whites; rock musicians, in using black musical forms, were drawing not only on particular conventions of emotional expression but also on an argument about leisure and freedom.

Whites have been entertained by blacks since the slave-ship owners compelled their captives to dance for warmth and exercise. The planters, in turn, claimed that their workers were "a large flock of cheerful and contented slaves, ever merry and ever working with a song." Eileen Southern quotes a slave's comments on this:

> We endeavour to keep ourselves up as well as we can. What can we do unless we keep a good heart? If we were to let it weaken, we should die. [8]

This matter of black life and death became a source of white relaxation. Slaves acted as the music makers for their owners' dances and balls, and thus, from the beginning of slavery, "entertainment" was established as the norm for black/white cultural relations. In 1851 a white traveler in the South wrote:

> The fiddler walks out, and strikes up a tune; and at it they go in a regular tear-down dance; for here they are at home. . . . I

never saw a slave in my life but would stop as if he were shot at the sound of a fiddle; and if he has a load of two hundred pounds on his head, he will begin to dance. One would think they had steam engines inside of them, to jerk them about with so much power; for they go through more motions in a minute than you could shake two sticks in a month; and of all comic actions, ludicrous sights, and laughable jokes, and truly comic songs, there is no match for them. It is useless to talk about Fellows' Minstrels, or any other band of merely artificial "Ethiopians," for they will bear no comparison with the plantation negroes. [9]

The irony in the contribution of black music to American popular culture is that the music of slaves is the most intense expression of human freedom and human desire. The slave-owners' response is pleasure tangled up with guilt. If the most exhilarating form of entertainment depends on the most intense human experience of degradation, then enjoyment of that entertainment must involve a furtive struggle with reality. Constance Rourke suggested that the Negro became a sympathetic symbol in nineteenth-century America "for a pioneer people who required resilience as a prime trait," but sympathy is an evasive emotion. The immediate aesthetic response to a performer is identity, and it is the difficulty of this relationship between black performer and white audience that lies at the heart of American popular culture—rock culture included; sympathy is a way of avoiding the issue. The power of black music is, after all, a form of black power—"Men and woman who dance like that have the strength for violence," commented a dance critic in 1929—and the attraction of black music for hip youth, whether the blues in the 1920s or Rastafarian music today, lies in its danger, in its very *exclusion* of white fans from its cultural messages.

# COUNTRY MUSIC

Country music has been called "white man's blues," and the histories of Southern, rural black and white musics can't easily be separated. In both of them there were parallel uses of harsh, raw voices and harmonies, instruments and instrumental techniques which gave even non-sung sounds individual vocal qualities. Black and white country audiences alike scorned the perfect pitch and enunciation of classical singers, the bland precision of Tin Pan Alley crooners (country fans remain suspicious of the trained country singer Vernon Dalhart, and of smooth pop stylists like Eddy Arnold or Jim Reeves). Black and white musicians alike were interested in the vocal qualities of their instruments so that, for example, the blues slide guitar and the country steel guitar were parallel developments from the Hawaiian guitar at the beginning of the century. In Southern churches, black and white gospel groups alike developed harmony styles which fused individual and collective fervor, while in the 1920s and 1930s in Southern recording studios black and white entertainers alike learned how to record spontaneity.

Another similarity between black and white country musics can be seen in the contents of their lyrics. Country lyricists used different techniques of naturalism than blues writers, drawing on deliberately mundane, flat narratives and tunes. But, as black singer Jerry Butler says, country and soul music

> stay around because they talk about everyday situations; they talk about true-to-life things. They don't get hung up in fantasyville and they don't get hung up on Broadway. They talk to people about things that happen to people. [10]

Black and white American rural music developed in the first half of this century to meet similar cultural needs. Both musics were sources of secular entertainment and spiritual uplift; both were musics for public celebration, for collective excitement, for religious expression and social commentary. Country musicians, like blues musicians, sang about the "shameful" aspects of Southern life—racism and sexuality (although their songs on these subjects have been muffled since the rise of Nashville and commercial country sounds). And when Elvis Presley and the other rockabilly singers put the two musics together to make rock 'n' roll in the 1950s, the shock was not musical (the "first rock 'n' roll record" has been claimed for both black and white dance bands in the 1940s) but ideological: it was the overt, assertive, *social* intermingling of black and white that was threatening. Musical intermingling had been a fact of Southern life for a hundred years.

But there are differences in the ways in which black and white musics have evolved. Country music, for all its realism or populism, is a conservative form carrying a conservative message. The emphasis of its lyrics is on people knowing their place, and the tensions which result, for women, for example, are treated as unfortunate, even tragic, but not soluble: "Been that way since the world began," as Loretta Lynn sings. From country music have emerged the powerful, dignified voices of the "silent majority"—women, the working class—but their dignity derives from their passivity. Country music tells it like it is—and argues that making it into something else depends on luck, individual hard work, blessings from God; wry stoicism is the country tone of voice. There is no country equivalent of the aggressive political music developed by blacks in the 1960s. The message of country populism remains "We're a loser!"

Similarly, if country music acknowledges and expresses sexual feelings, they are rarely celebrated; the dominant theme, in even the raunchiest country music, is shame. Country music, much more clearly than black music, is a form of family entertainment. The development of its mass popularity in the 1920s and 1930s was based on radio, a family medium. Even the honky-tonk music of bars and jukeboxes argued that casual sex and drink and fun were expressions of loneliness, the absence of family.

The conservatism of country music is a matter of form as well as content. Changes in instrumentation have been slow, each move—to drums, to electric amplification—hard-fought, and there is a much greater emphasis in country than in black music on songs (rather than sounds).

The original nineteenth-century rural musicians drew on a communal repertoire of British and Irish folk songs. In fact, the focus of country performance has always been less on improvised creation than on the virtuoso treatment of tried and tested standards. The professional task of the country musician has been to provide these standards, to write songs that other performers could sing, too. In the 1920s and 1930s, consequently, country musicians found it easier than black musicians to become a part of the mainstream of American show business—they had better access to radio as family entertainers whom Southern advertisers were happy to employ, and they were, as songwriters, better rewarded for their music, better able to exploit their commercial successes. There have been contradictions as country music has been commercialized (particularly since the 1950s), as homemade music became big business, as the boys and girls next door left their communities to become stars. But country glamour has rarely become bohemian, and, more than any other type of popular entertainer, the country performers continue to articulate the values of their audience, to cultivate a direct relationship with their fans.

In the ideological history of country music in the last twenty years (and in its rise to mass commercial popularity) its conservatism has been apparent. Contemporary country records symbolize the past, exude nostalgia, describe a way of life that city dwellers value more now that they don't have to live that way again. This is the central difference between the black and white elements of American populist music: the white form is, in its own self-description, country music; black music has developed from country blues to the sound of the city. Country music reacted to social change by reemphasizing rural values and patterns; it entered the mainstream of American mass music as a *sub*-urban means of expression.

Country was an important musical element of rock 'n' roll because of the rockabilly singers' own Southern rural origins. But for the young 1950s rebels like Elvis Presley and Jerry Lee Lewis, who added a black drive to hillbilly sounds, the obviously limiting feature of country music was its very country-ness, its conservatism. It provided no obvious space for rebellion or hedonism, no symbols for the social concerns and restlessness of the young; it described the problems of life as poor white trash but not the new, postwar possibilities. For country teenagers, black music was the source of musical sexuality, nonconformity, and fun, and the resulting black/white fusion wasn't confined to the moment of rock 'n' roll. The "kicker" culture of white Southern teenagers with their gun racks and pearl stud shirts continues to be expressed in an aggressive regional rock music, using country instruments and traditions but based, still, on the blues.

The formula rock 'n' roll = blues + country is deeply entrenched in rock history, but whatever its accuracy as a musical description, its cultural significance is not easily assessed. Greil Marcus (in *Mystery Train*) argues convincingly that the original rock 'n' rollers' country musical values bound them to the rural culture of the American South, and that rock 'n' roll was a contradictory form, blending its pride with shame, its celebration with guilt, its anger with acceptance. These contradictions gave a rock 'n' roll artist like Elvis Presley his sensitivity and power. From this perspective, rock's country elements—its use of fiddle and steel and rhythm guitar, its yearning vocals and rolling beat, its songs of self-pity and

self-sufficiency, its sense of age and change and history—reflect
general cultural needs. Country rock, in particular the music developed by Gram Parsons with The Byrds and commercialized most
successfully by the Eagles, is a deliberately nostalgic form, an attempt by musicians to draw on long-gone roots. If the teenage
rockabilly singers were smothered by country respectability, country-rock musicians draw on rural sounds to emphasize their "adult"
concerns.

This is the rock response to a general cultural phenomenon:
the tension between the country and the city. The country symbolizes the past, the family and the community, stability and a sense
of place. As city culture became commercial culture—centralized,
homogenized, mediated through the *mass* media—the country came,
too, to stand for "authenticity."

## FOLK MUSIC

The early days of the American folk "revival" (via which route folk
styles most clearly influenced rock) were bound up with rural romanticism, with a search for values and ways which could be opposed to urban corruption, to commerce, to mass music. The postwar
New York interest in blues and bluegrass echoed the turn-of-the-
century British interest in British rural music. But if Cecil Sharp
and his fellow British collectors were fearful of the urban proletariat
and its music, in America rural nostalgia became, in its folk form,
an integral part of political populism. In the radicals' version of folk
ideology folk music wasn't a source of regret (as "organic communities" of the past were compared to the class conflicts of the present), but a source of inspiration, a way of countering the debilitating
effects of the mass media and imbuing the working class with "folk
consciousness."

The American folk movement of the 1930s was based on a contradiction. The "spontaneous folk creations" it celebrated were the
result of musical judgments made by outsiders, by urban performers
(the British folk "tradition" had, similarly, been constructed in the
first place by bourgeois scholars). What was at issue was a definition
of "the people," and a crucial role in the development of this definition was played by the Communist Party.

American workers' organizations (the Wobblies, for example)

had always seen music as an important source of organization and inspiration and had written songs accordingly. But in the 1930s Communist Party policy changed from writing "a *new kind* of song, which will be so identified with the workers that nobody can take it from them," to using, in the words of party spokesman Mike Gold, the existing "native folk consciousness and tradition—a treasury of the people's art." The party thus adopted rural music as the most suitable expression for the urban worker; the party's intellectuals became "people's artists" by singing folk songs dressed in Oakie clothes. The political problem remained the same: how to use music to attract people into an organization, to develop their class consciousness. If the tactics changed—from developing a new form of workers' music to using an old form—the cultural position didn't: "correct" songs were still correct insofar as they developed a sense of class solidarity. The authenticity of music was, despite the folk language, still being judged by its effects rather than its sources. Even Woody Guthrie, the model performer in social terms for 1960s folk-rock, made his music for an urban, educated, politicized audience rather than for the rural workers about whom he sang. None of Guthrie's songs was found among the Oakies and Arkies who fled the dust bowl—their lives were already dominated by the commercial sounds of the radio and phonograph. Guthrie's achievement, in other words, was not to bring "correct" songs to the Oakies, but to articulate their experiences to the New York left.

The radical tradition of American folk music was primarily the 1930s creation of this group of metropolitan, left-wing bohemians. Their account of "the people" was as rooted in myth, in their own circumstances, and in the political use of nostalgia as that of their more respectable, bourgeois, folk predecessors. Nevertheless, it was within the folk movement that musicians kept alive a popular music that was defined, politically and musically, in opposition to commercial pop. American folk music may have become, by the 1960s, in Denisoff's sour words, simply "what was listened to at the informal gatherings and social affairs, at the hootenannies given by the radicals," but the conventions of these gatherings were to be drawn on later by rock musicians to justify their own claims of musical authenticity.

"Sing the truth as simply as you can," advised the Almanac Singers, "and repeat it as many times as it has to be repeated." The folk emphasis was on lyrics and their plain presentation. The central musical instrument was the voice and it was by reference to vocal conventions that sincerity could be judged. In people's music there were no stars or hits, no distinctions between performers and audiences, and this too was established by musical convention, by the norms of collective performance—the use of repetition and chorus and clichéd melody, the lack of vocal flourish, the restriction of instruments (guitars, pianos) to accompaniment. The folk community was the community created by the musical performance itself; folk consciousness was the effect of folksinging. By the end of the 1940s, with the decay of popular political radicalism, the use of folk music shrank accordingly, and such singing was almost entirely confined to college campuses. Even at these middle-class hootenannies, though, students could get, according to folk ideologists like Irwin Silber, "a sense of the real America." The songs may not have been sung by "authentic" working-class singers, but they still represented authentic working-class experiences.

In the 1960s, as young whites, particularly on college campuses, became politically active again, they found in folk music the only expressive form that could be made directly responsive to their political concerns, that could serve the same cultural purpose as black music did for its listeners; the two concerns and musics came together most obviously in the civil rights movement.

The resulting "protest music" was not confined to political events. The 1960s folk revival brought with it all manner of folk institutions—clubs, coffeehouses, festivals—and it was in these settings that the 1960s folk community was defined. It was an ideological community, bound by its attitude to music-making itself. In the folk clubs there was, in theory, no separation of performer and listener; anybody could get up and sing. The aesthetic emphasis was less on technique than on truth, and the musical "honesty" of performers was measured by what they didn't do. As singer Jean Ray remembers:

> Young people in the sixties who had any touch on the pulse of folk music couldn't be satisfied with going and doing all the external movements of selling a song like pop singers do, with hand movements and all. It became taboo to do that. You were just to stand up straight and deliver your message. No frills. No fancy phoney stuff. [11]

The folk movement was self-consciously opposed to the conventions of mass music-making and its values were developed in isolation from the usual practices of pop. These values became increasingly resonant as the power of rock 'n' roll was sapped by the banalities of *Bandstand*. Pete Seeger's great achievement had been to sustain an alternative way of music-making throughout the cultural repression of the 1950s, and this alternative was particularly important for musicians unwilling to commit themselves to a life of manipulation and exploitation by pop moguls. They found in folk

> the idea that songs could concern themselves with topics far wider than the conventional love themes, that musicians could approach their work as self-expression, rather than "giving people what they want." [12]

In the mid-1960s, as folk musicians, beginning with the Kingston Trio and Peter, Paul and Mary, were commercially successful, these ideas were introduced "into the heart of mainstream popular music," and the folk emphasis on songs and lyrics, on honesty and commitment, was slowly adapted by the performers and their record companies alike to the commercial needs of rock. The irony was that it was on the basis of its folk conventions that rock developed its claims as a "high" art form.

Part of rock 'n' roll's appeal as teenage music had been that anyone could do it—anyone could make such simple music, could write such straightforward songs. The 1960s folk performers developed a different argument: if anyone could play folk music—the guitar and harmonica techniques were easy to learn, the harsh and muttered vocals came naturally—not just anyone could play it with *originality*. Bob Dylan became the symbol of the new argument. He was valued for his individual genius, his personal insights, his unique voice and style. His songs, even as they began to use rock sounds, had dense poetic forms and rambling melodic structures that made audience participation impossible—the choruses came at irregular, long-delayed moments; nothing was explained.

If not everyone could make such music, then not everyone could appreciate it—"insight" was needed by the listener as well, a notion that suitably flattered the new, "intelligent" rock market. Excellence was increasingly measured in terms of musical, lyrical, and emotional complexity, in terms of artistic qualities that differentiated rock from the "banalities" of teenage pop. Rock 'n' roll rebellion had been against adults but not against adult record companies, not against the cultural practices of adult entertainment. Only now, post-folk, did a rock culture develop which explicitly opposed the ideology of mass music-making, but as folk became folk-rock its political position became increasingly, inevitably, compromised.

In 1965 Phil Ochs told a *Village Voice* interviewer:

> I'm writing to make money. I write about Cuba and Mississippi out of an inner need for expression, not to change the world. The roots of my songs are psychological, not political. [13]

Marc Eliot suggests that in the New York folk scene in the mid-1960s there was a movement from "the romance of politics to the politics of romance." This shift meant a new relationship between performer and audience, a new definition of "authenticity." In the early days of the postwar folk revival, songs were still propaganda; their aim was to invoke solidarity, to draw listeners into political organizations. By the mid-1960s folk songs had become rhetorical; they expressed only individual discontent with events. Conventions in lyrics became increasingly literary and the artistic distance between singer and audience was confirmed musically by the shift from accoustic to electrical instruments, from the stage to the studio.

In the original, political version of folk consciousness there had been a contradiction: on the one hand, folk music was an offensive weapon, a means for driving out bourgeois ideology from working-class culture; on the other hand, folk was the spontaneous expression of the people themselves—this was the political significance of the folk tradition. Folk "authenticity" was, in other words, judged in two ways: according to its political correctness and according to its popular origins. The radical trick was to equate these two measures. Folk performers *represented* the people, both instructing and learning from them. Popular interests were thus *mediated* through folk performers, who were expected to operate anonymously, impersonally, as a sort of musical instrument—played *by* their audiences.

In the 1960s folksingers like Ochs and Dylan rejected the idea that they *represented* their audiences, that they were subordinate to them, but their argument wasn't just a matter of politics—they still shared their audiences' political concerns. Their argument was

e relationship of music and experience. As Alan Lomax had
n *Sing Out!*, the "authentic" folksinger had to "*experience
the feelings that lie behind his art*," and it was this concept of authenticity—truth to self rather than truth to a movement or an audience—that the folkies retained as they became successful
singer/songwriters, as they made the move from communal to commercial ways of music-making.

## POP MUSIC

Record companies by nature don't much care what forms music
takes as long as they can be organized and controlled to ensure profit—musics and musicians can be packaged and sold, whatever their
styles. But the music business is not without prejudices. Music was
a commerical product long before rock 'n' roll, and the industry's
values and preferences derive from its own origins as a publishing
business at the beginning of the century. Tin Pan Alley practices
were developed to promote songs rather than performances, and
while it was transformed in the 1920s—from a system for selling
goods for musical creation (sheet music and pianos) to a system for
selling goods for musical consumption (records and record players
and radios)—the "bland universal well-made song" (Ian Whitcomb's description) remained its *essential* product.

From the 1920s to the early 1950s the music industry aimed
its products at the family audience. Records reached the public on
family radio and on the family phonograph—most homes had only
one of each. The development of the record business in this period
involved two processes (both of which systematically excluded black
musicians from pop success, despite the starring presence they had
won in vaudeville). First, to be popular a record had to transcend
the differences between listeners: it had to appeal to all ages and
classes and races and regions, to both sexes, to all moods and cultures and values. Second, musical pleasure had to be moved from
the dance hall and bar into the living room—popular music lost its
edge of risk, its emotional critique of social routine; pop records had
to be cheerful and uplifting, they had to fit into the domestic round.
Such "nice" music was determined, too, by the technological limits
of early radio and recording. Subtlety of tone and harmony and melody were impossible to reproduce; nothing too long or discordant or

intricate or noisy could survive the primitive recording techniques; songwriters were advised to stick to the notes in the middle range of the piano.

The musical values established in the early days of the record industry are still apparent in the concepts of "easy listening" and "middle of the road." They informed, too, the way the music business responded to rock 'n' roll in the 1950s: record companies sought to produce bland, well-crafted songs for the teenage market, to groom performers as teenage entertainers. The primary aim was to give singers the right image, to create teen idols who looked the part. The show-biz convention of the "sincere" performer was now articulated by the girl or boy next door, the teenage heartthrob. Rock 'n' roll stars were established in films and television programs, on touring package shows; they were sold in established show-business routines. By the late 1950s adult record producers dominated the creation of teenage music; records were organized as packages of sound, and the stars simply presented the music they were given, sold their "personality."

Charlie Gillett has documented the subsequent "decline in importance of dance rhythms; words and sounds became pre-eminent," and those words and sounds were created along the usual Tin Pan Alley lines. Teenage pop, like adult pop, described a romantic fiction; making pop songs youthful simply meant filling in teenage references—first meetings, hasty partings, finding love, losing friends. There was little, formally, to distinguish the teenage pop songs which emerged from the Brill Building from the similarly well-made love songs that had been pouring out of Tin Pan Alley for decades. David Riesman's 1950 description of the pop picture of adolescence in America—"a happy-go-lucky time of haphazard clothes and haphazard behavior, jitterbug parlance, coke-bar sprees, and 'blues' that are not really blue"—could have also been applied accurately to teenage music in 1960.

In the 1960s, however, the ideology of adolescence became an ideology of youth: "The Young Ones" became "My Generation." Adolescence had always been romanticized in song, the teenage world had always been idealized, but youth had previously been presented as a stage on the path to adulthood: the concept of courtship, for example, implied that emotional and sexual needs would be met in the *future*—the point of courting was marriage. The 1960s argument (and this was one sign of the difference between 1960s "rock" songs and 1950s "pop" songs) was that youth was preferable to age and that no one need ever grow old. What was at issue was not chronology but ideology. If youth was the most desirable social condition and to be young meant to be free from the narrow routines of maturity, to be sexually vigorous and emotionally unrestrained, then anyone who lived and thought right, regardless of age, could be "young." Teenage culture, the model of "irregular, spontaneous, unpredictable, exhibitionistic behavior," became the basis for a more general pursuit of pleasure as a way of life, and content analysis of hit parade lyrics revealed the increasing celebration of what J. T. Carey called "existential choice": romance was no longer presented as a once-and-for-all-affair, the selection of a partner for life. Boy/girl relationships were active creations, remained valuable even when they ended; the instability of adolescent sex was another measure of young people's honesty, truth-to-self, refusal to conform to social conventions.

Sociologists like Carey, analysts of the contents of lyrics, were limited in their explanations of pop meaning by their techniques. They asserted that songs reflected social mores but couldn't explain how such "reflection" worked. But their concern for words is worth pursuing, for pop's significance has always depended on its use of the song form.

In 1899 the British composer Sir Hubert Parry suggested:

> The modern popular song reminds one of the outer circumference of our terribly overgrown towns. . . . It is for people who live in those unhealthy regions, people who have the most false ideals, who are always scrambling for subsistence, who think that the commonest rowdyism is the highest expression of human emotion; for them, this popular music is made, and it is made, with a commercial object, of snippets of slang. [14]

Music-hall songs were made out of common speech, and like American popular songs in the 1930s, their tone was wry as well as sentimental. They were bittersweet love songs; the fantasies of courtship were set in the pragmatic context of working-class marriage. Such pop songs lacked the passion or "realism" of, say, the blues, but they did not lack cultural power.

One way in which rock differentiated itself from pop in the 1960s was in its lyrics—this was the symbolic importance of Bob Dylan's success. In rock, words mattered; in pop, it seemed, they did not. Rock verse was poetry; pop verse was mired in the limited language of sentiment, in the rhyming simplicities of moon and June. But the resulting distinctions were conventional: "poetic" lyrics (which developed out of the folk movement) were poetic because they used certain forms of language—archaisms, clumsy constructions, mystical/pastoral/historical references. National Lampoon parodied the result in their "Art Rock Suite":

A canyon filled with dream whipped cream, a castle in the
   air,
The footman knows your secret, as he meets you on the stair,
The jester gleams with emeralds, as he juggles in the
   hall. . . .
But the unicorn is weeping on the rug upon the wall.

Someone's dying, someone's born,
Purple fog is drifting over endless fields of corn.

The problem with the "poetry of rock" was its confusion of the use of words in music. In songs, words are the signs of a voice. A song is always a performance and song words are always spoken out—vehicles for the voice. The voice can also use nonverbal devices to make its points—accents, sighs, emphases, hesitations, changes of tone. Song words, in short, work as *speech*, as structures of sound that are *direct* signs of emotion and marks of character; songs are more like plays than poems. Songwriters, therefore, draw on our conversational knowledge of how voices work, which is why they use common phrases, snippets of slang.

Pop songs celebrate not the articulate but the inarticulate, and the evaluation of pop singers depends not on words but on sounds— on the noises around the words. In daily life, the most directly intense statements of feeling involve just such noises: people gasp, moan, laugh, cry, and so on. They measure the depth and the originality of their emotions by reference to their *inability* to find words for them—phrases like "I'm frightened" or "I love you" seem inadequate to the state of mind they are describing. This is why songs get sung in the first place, and in day-to-day terms, people distrust the silver-tongued, the seducers, politicians, salesmen, who've got the gift of gab. Inarticulateness, not poetry, is the popular songwriter's conventional sign of sincerity.

In black music, singers articulate awe and fervor through an apparently spontaneous struggle *against* words—soul refers to a quality of sincerity which can *only* be described in terms of sound, in terms not of what is sung but of how it is sung: the test of soul conviction is the singer's way with non-words. Pre–rock 'n' roll white popular music rested, by contrast, on the commercial possibilities of artifice and on the unique ability of the voice to communicate directly, which underpinned pop's dominant vocal convention, crooning intimacy: songs were written so that singers seemed to talk straight to their listeners. Rock performers put the two conventions together to speak to us in the words *and* sounds of our everyday language. Writers use different forms of conversation—from casual chat to intense heart-pouring; but words and music are being used to construct our sense of the singer, to transform our experience of a record into a live, immediate relationship—a relationship not only with the singer but also with other listeners.

Words in all pop genres work as recruiting symbols; their writers draw on a communal language to create a sense of community. This is both the folk norm (popular music expresses shared experiences and activities) and a commercial ploy (records sell on feelings of fashion; the pleasure of pop consumption is the pleasure of shared consumption). In general terms, the language of lyrics is used to construct pop genres: disco lyrics endlessly invoke us to dance, effectively connoting consumption; country lyricists use plain language, reported speech, and country singers come across as the detached observers of emotional plight; the message of punk lyrics comes simply from the odd words that stick out of the noisy chorus—the punk sound was a variation on a short, hard assertion: "won't/want."

Our response to songs is determined in part by our assumptions about their performers, and one function of lyrics is to meet these assumptions. Punk language was used to establish the fact that its users were punks—incoherent, vulgar, annoyed—just as literary language marked its users as poets. Singer/songwriters defined their "honesty" in the language of confession. And all pop performance rests on a series of frauds: show-biz stars fake sincerity, rock poets fake intimacy, everyone fakes an image and a voice. The gap between the appearance and the reality of a performance is the source of pop lyricists' central tool—irony—and of their central verbal device—banality. It is in this gap that skilled song interpreters work, bringing a personal intensity to all-purpose phrases; and it is here as well that listeners work, applying the words to their own situations. The most exhilarating pop writers can create for us unexpected twists out of the expected set of words.

This was the point missed in the poetry-of-rock discussions, which took for granted that poetic language (long words, archaic constructions) was more meaningful than the commonplaces of day-to-day pop. Bob Dylan himself reputedly called Smokey Robinson "America's greatest living poet," but few of his fans stopped to wonder why. Robinson's skill was to give new life to old saws. He used unexpected juxtapositions of image and phrase, self-conscious puns and metaphors: "What's so good about good-bye," "The hunter gets captured by the game," "The love I saw in you was just a mirage." He took dull, public words—"I second that emotion," "Shop Around"—and gave them romantic fervor. Nineteen-sixties black pop songwriters like Smokey Robinson obviously drew on the blues tradition. Black lyricists had always been adept at disguising their political and sexual messages. "He boiled first my cabbage/And he made it awful hot" began one of Bessie Smith's most erotic verses; "When he put in the bacon/It overflowed the pot!" But Robinson was equally concerned with using the rhythms of daily speech to make plain talk dance.

Compare this to the technique of a 1930s white pop lyricst like Ira Gershwin:

The only work that really brings enjoyment
Is the kind that is for girl and boy meant
Fall in love—you won't regret it,
That's the best work of all—if you can get it.
Holding hands at midnight, 'neath a starry sky . . .
Nice work if you can get it, and you can get it—if you try.

Pop lyricists work on the ordinariness of language. They make our most commonplace words and phrases suddenly seem full of sly jokes and references. With an array of verbal tricks and playful clichés, good lyricists, from Bob Dylan to Ira Gershwin, add to our sense of *common* language. Their songs are about words: they give us new ways to mouth the commonplaces of daily discourse.

The power of pop singers is, in other words, the power to make ordinary language intense and vital; the words then resonate—they bring a touch of fantasy into our mundane use of them. Pop songs work precisely insofar as they are *not* poems. When Pink Floyd sang "we don't want no education," they were not saying anything significant about the school system; they were providing school children with a funny, powerful, playground chant (which is why "The Wall" was banned in South Africa). The pop song banalities people pick up on are, in general, not illuminating but encouraging: they give emotional currency to the common phrases that are all most people have for expressing their daily cares. The language that hems us in suddenly seems open—if we can't speak in poetry, we can speak in pop songs. They give us a way to *refuse* the mundane.

## MUSIC AND MEANING

At the beginning of this chapter I argued that rock doesn't have a fixed musical meaning, but involves, rather, a play of meanings. Rock is eclectic: it uses rhythmic rules, expressive conventions, and song forms developed in a variety of American popular traditions; it draws from black music and country music, from folk songs and Tin Pan Alley pop. But in looking at how these source musics work, it became clear to me that musical meaning is not just a matter of sounds and words, but is also determined by culture and context— the meaning of *popular* music has to be related to wider issues of leisure and entertainment. The problematic issue that runs (if in different ways) through the history of all forms of popular music since the development of industrial capitalism is the relationship between music as a means of popular expression and music as a means of making money. The questions raised—who makes popular music? for whom? with what effects?—are important precisely because the meanings of music are not fixed by the sounds alone, but can be disputed. As I will try to show in this book, rock fun is never really "innocent"—there are always manipulative processes involved; but neither is rock consumption necessarily therefore "passive"—rock meanings aren't *determined* by their commercial means of production. It is to the suggestion that they are so determined that I will now turn.

# CHAPTER 3

# ROCK AND
# MASS CULTURE

In 1835 the British composer George Hogarth suggested:

> The tendency of music is to soften and purify the mind. The cultivation of musical taste furnishes to the rich a refined and intellectual pursuit, which excludes the indulgence of frivolous and vicious amusements, and to the poor, a *laborum dulce lenimen*, a relaxation from toil, more attractive than the haunts of intemperance.

Sir John Herschel, writing in 1839, was less sanguine:

> Music and dancing (the more's the pity) have become so closely associated with ideas of riot and debauchery among the less cultivated classes, that a taste for them, for their own sakes, can hardly be said to exist, and before they can be recommended as innocent or safe amusements, a very great change of ideas must take place. [1]

The power of music both to arouse—to war, to debauchery, to revolution, to religious ecstasy—and to comfort and pacify became, in the nineteenth century, an aspect of new class relationships, of new experiences of work and leisure. The "innocence" of popular music was, from the beginning, an issue for political dispute, as music became a nationalist device and a commodity in the marketplace, as the "audience" was articulated as "the people." By the end of the nineteenth century popular *participation* in music-making was in decline. In 1894 Robert Blatchford commented in the *Labour Prophet*:

A few centuries ago the English were a musical people. Part-singing was very popular. The majority of people could read music, and sing at sight; and the English glees and madrigals of the period are unsurpassed. But how many of our Lancashire workers can read music or sing it today? How many of them would prefer a correct rendering of "Since I First Saw Your Face" to a noisy howling of "The Man That Broke The Bank At Monte Carlo"? Amongst the many Lancashire operatives who have pianos in their houses, how many tasteful and correct players are there? Look at the music in their houses, and see how much of it is real music, and what proportion the quantity of real music bears to the quantity of Moody and Sankey, the tin-pot comic song, and sloppy ballad, and sew-saw waltz.

The rise of Tin Pan Alley and the emergence of the mass media involved an increasingly centralized and commercialized control of what could be heard: as fewer people made music for themselves, public taste was easier to control. The "innocence" of musical fun was now irrevocably tainted by the terms of commercial exploitation and manipulation. Popular music emerged from the processes of commodity production; its cultural effect was as one of the new forms of "mass consumption." Since the 1930s the crucial cultural arguments about popular music have concerned the meanings and the effects of "mass culture."

Most writing on mass culture is gloomy. The mass media are censured according to the values and practices of both "high" and "folk" art. Rock critics use the same contrasts: records and songs are valued for their artistic intensity, for their truth to experience; yet they are condemned for commercialism. The belief in a continuing struggle between music and commerce is the core of rock ideology. At certain moments artists and audiences break through the system, but most of the time business interests are in control. Thus, for example, Jon Landau writes:

> Rock, the music of the Sixties, was a music of spontaneity. It was a folk music—it was listened to and made by the same group of people. It did not come out of a New York office building where people sit and write what they think other people want to hear. It came from the life experiences of the artists and their interaction with an audience that was roughly the same age. As that spontaneity and creativity have become more stylized and analyzed and structured, it has become easier for businessmen and behind-the-scenes manipulators to structure their approach to merchandising music. The process of creating stars has become a routine and a formula as dry as an equation.[2]

This is the critical argument that underpins rock historians' correlations of competition and creativity; they suggest that rock progress comes from independent local labels and attribute rock's stagnation to the major music corporations. The assumption is that rock music is good music only when it is not mass culture, when it is an art form or a folk sound.

## MASS CULTURE

The critical analysis of mass culture is dominated by the (overlapping) approaches of Leavisite literary criticism and Marxist ideological criticism.

The Leavisite approach stems from the comparison of mass cultural objects—standardized, escapist, passively consumed—with works of art—unique, challenging, instructive. Mass culture is analyzed with the tools of literary criticism and condemned accordingly: mass music is worthless because there is, in Leavis's terms, "nothing essential in the music itself which belongs either to real emotion or to an inner unmistakable vitality."

This judgment involves not a comparison of the good taste of an educated elite with the bad taste of the uneducated masses, but looks instead at the processes by which different cultural objects are produced and consumed. Leavisites, indeed, celebrate the values of "popular" art; they argue that mass culture is a "corruption" of such art. The key critical concept is "authenticity": a culture created for commercial profit must lack "a certain authenticity" even if it "dramatizes authentic feelings." Mass teenage culture is, as Hall and Whannel put it, "a contradictory mixture of the authentic and manufactured—an area of self-expression for the young and lush grazing ground for the commercial providers."

For Leavisites, mass cultural production is production according to formulas which limit individual creativity, and the mass cultural audience is an audience of consumers making market choices which limit artistic response. The mass cultural account of the world is, therefore, trivial. Such a culture corrupts feeling; it makes no demands on its users but titillates them with its stars, its flattery of mediocrity, its myth of the mass consumer as the common man.

The commercial basis of mass culture explains both its existence and its quality. Mass art is produced for profit and the pursuit of profit determines its form and content. The problem is to explain cultural consumption, to account for the replacement in the last hundred years of popular art by mass art. Reference to the power of advertisement, to market manipulation, is not enough: mass cultural solutions may be "false," but the needs to which they are a response are real.

The reference to "needs" recurs in mass cultural criticism though it is, as we shall see, a problematic concept. The Leavisite critics in particular have to explain why people get pleasure from "false" art, and it is for this purpose that they use the concept of "need." David Holbrook, for example, hears pop explicitly as the *degradation* of art: the music draws on the power of real fears and emotions, but instead of dealing with them exploits them. Teenage pop plays with the psychological tensions of puberty and offers only a "manic moment of uplift." Holbrook argues that the exploitation of adolescent "needs" rests on the deliberate creation of a commercial youth "culture" designed to separate the young from their families and communities, and so make them more vulnerable as consumers. Rock, as a mass medium, is therefore a false art serving a false community.

This equation of corruption and commerce is consistent with

Leavis's own account of industrial capitalism, and Marxist commentators describe youth culture in similar terms. The British Communist Charles Parker, for example, modifies the Leavisite account of pop only by rooting rock culture in the political as well as the economic processes of capitalism: "Pop is, in fact, now cherished by a ruling class as a peerless form of social control."

Parker's argument is that youth culture was created for ideological as well as commercial purposes; what is powerful or radical in youth experience is channeled through rock into "the false community of the cosmopolitan teen-scene where the identity is submerged in a common, conditioned response of the viscera." Rock, "this Witches' Sabbath of meaningless orgiastic utterance," is deliberately used by the power elite to safeguard its political position, to control and divert popular expression. *but protest music defies the*

For Marxists the commodity form of mass culture is another as- *commodity* pect of the general process through which capital has transformed *fetish* social relations. The problem here is not conspiracy but ideology—Marx's own comment was that the ruling ideas in a society are always those of the ruling class.

The most sophisticated account of mass music from this perspective is that of the Frankfurt school. Adorno, in particular, argued that it is the production of music as a commodity, to be consumed, that determines its cultural quality—popular music has to be something which *can* be consumed, a means (to profit on the one hand, to well-being on the other) rather than an end. The consequent standardization of musical form is the source of its ideological effect—a soporific social consciousness—and the reduction of culture to commodity and ideology is made possible by the technology of mechanical reproduction, by the techniques of recording and broadcasting which make cultural consumption an individualized, alienating process. Mass music consumers have no real relationship with either the music's producers or their fellow consumers. Art has become entertainment, cultural response has become selection in the marketplace, popular creation has become the commercial attempt to attract the largest possible number of consumers.

Adorno used Freudian psychology to account for the effectiveness of mass music. This is his 1940s description of pop fans:

In general they are intoxicated by the fame of mass culture, a fame which the latter knows how to manipulate; they could just as well get together in clubs for worshipping film stars or for collecting autographs. What is important to them is the sense of belonging as such, identification, without paying particular attention to its content. As girls, they have trained themselves to faint upon hearing the voice of a "crooner." Their applause, cued in by a light-signal, is transmitted directly on the popular radio programs they are permitted to attend. They call themselves "jitter-bugs," bugs which carry out reflex movements, performers of their own ecstasy. Merely to be carried away by anything at all, to have something of their own, compensates for their impoverished and barren existence. The gesture of adolescence, which raves for this or that on one day with the ever-present possibility of damning it as idiocy on the next, is now socialized. [3]

*transcendence again*

For Adorno the aesthetic basis of art is its "practically useless, imaginative element," its utopian protest against reality. Art is the source of human hope, the inspiration to the struggle for social change. Mass culture, in contrast, settles with reality and so corrupts its imaginative base and renders its consumers impotent—Adorno hears "jazz," his term for all mass music, as a symbol of castration:

> Expression, the true bearer of aesthetic protest, is over-taken by the might against which it protests. Faced by this might it assumes a malicious and miserable tone which barely and momentarily disguises itself as harsh and provocative. The subject which expresses itself expresses precisely this: I am nothing, I am filth, no matter what they do to me it serves me right. . . . Art is permitted to survive only if it renounces the right to be different, and integrates itself into the omnipotent realm of profane. . . . Nothing may exist which is not like the world as it is. Jazz is the false liquidation of art—instead of utopia becoming reality it disappears from the picture. [4]

Adorno's is the most systematic and the most searing analysis of mass culture and the most challenging for anyone claiming even a scrap of value for the products that come churning out of the music industry. His argument (like that of later American Marxist economists) is that modern capital is burdened by the problem of overproduction. Markets can only be stimulated by *creating* needs

*the market did not create protest music, tho*

(that term again), needs which are the result of capital rather than human logic and therefore, inevitably, false. The culture industry is the central agency in contemporary capitalism for the production and satisfaction of false needs.

False needs can be thought of in two ways. Some theorists suggest that musical commodities work to construct "the subjectivity of the listener": the need satisfied by consumption is the need to consume. Popular music, from this perspective, calls forth direct emotional and physical responses from its listeners but associates those responses with the pleasure of possession. Consumption, in Fredric Jameson's words, has become "its own ideology"—the commodity form of music is its ideological content, and the "need" the music meets, the need to consume, is invested with such emotional force that *what* is consumed has little significance. Mass culture has realized the ultimate capitalist fantasy: *any* commodity produced is purchased—its use value *is* its exchange value.

Other analysts have argued that what is at stake is not the creation of a need from nowhere but the transformation of existing "real needs." Mass music conceals the conditions of its own production so that it can be consumed as a *pure* emotional effect. The real needs of its consumers—to make sense of their situation, to overcome their isolation—are dissolved in a transitory emotional moment. Mass cultural consumption excludes thought, excludes the possibility that social conditions could be understood and changed; mass cultural goods meet real needs, then, only by offering a momentary escape from them.

The problem with the arguments inspired by the Frankfurt School is their abstraction. The actual use of music by pop fans is scarcely examined—passivity is assumed. The supposed effects of pop are, rather, deduced from the nature of the music itself. Frankfurt musicology was in addition an abstraction from a European critical tradition. Adorno used a musicological discourse that actually made no sense at all of jazz, for example, that was performed with quite different principles and effects.

The unabashed arrogance with which Adorno dismissed a music he knew little about reflected the general attitude of 1930s European intellectuals (Marxists and Leavisites alike) to the mass media. Their *starting* point was that the media corrupted European culture; their evidence was always an assessment of mass culture *in terms of* European traditions. No attempt was made (none was needed) to account for the mass media in the terms of the conventions of the media themselves—Adorno himself seems to have been no more interested in American culture when he lived in New York in the 1940s than he had been in Germany. This was the reason he gave such an unconvincing account of the audience appeal of American cultural forms. He was evading a crucial aspect of their appeal—their very American-ness.

The "Americanization" of European popular culture was, indeed, remarkably rapid in the 1920s and 1930s. Hollywood provided the films people increasingly wanted to watch in the cinema; American jazz performers and pop singers made the music people increasingly wanted to hear on the radio. European popular newspapers adapted the American tabloid approach; American advertising agencies began to dictate European approaches to selling new consumer goods such as cosmetics and clothes. Adorno interpreted this American influence in terms of its form—the dominance of capital; but "America" was equally important in terms of its content. Songs and films and advertisements represented desirable ways of life, offered audiences images of abundance and vitality that were, by definition, American. The American Dream became an inextricable part of mass cultural fantasies. In German film director Wim Wenders's words, "The Americans colonized our subconscious." This is the point I made in Chapter 1: America, as experienced in films and music, has itself become the object of consumption, a symbol of pleasure.

This became obvious in the 1950s when the debate about mass culture became an explicit debate about American culture. American sociology came to mass culture's defense. The immediate concern was empirical evidence. Sociologists were interested in the "measurement" of cultural consumption, and their investigations focused on the social structures in which the use of mass media was embedded. Their aim was to show that the media/consumer relationship was a complex one in which the media were only several among many sources of meaning; their cold-war concern was to provide a positive account of America and its cultural capitalism. They challenged the very concept of "the mass audience," arguing that, as the media were used by different groups in different contexts, the sociological problem was not to establish a single significance for mass culture but to describe its many meanings. Mass culture meant democratic culture.

In the 1960s this argument was made theoretically more complex by the interjection of interactionist concepts. It was now argued that outside analysts couldn't make sense of cultural symbols even if they could describe the structure in which they were used—their meanings were as much the creation of their consumers as of their producers. It was therefore impossible to analyze the meanings of cultural texts without reference to the readers involved. The commodity form didn't *determine* cultural possibility; to decide whether a pop record was "inauthentic," a detailed investigation of its audience was necessary.

A similar argument was developed by Marxist theorists. Even in the 1930s Adorno's sour view of mass culture was complemented by Walter Benjamin's celebration of the positive possibilities of "the work of art in the age of mechanical reproduction." Benjamin argued that the technology of mass reproduction was a progressive force, the means by which the traditional authority and "aura" of art was broken. Mass artists were democratic artists; their work was shared with an audience in which everyone was an "expert." The technology of the mass media had changed the relationship of the masses to art and opened up new possibilities for cultural work. Creation had become a collective rather than an individual process; the development of socialized means of expression enabled the development of a socialist aesthetic.

In the 1950s the Marxist problem was to explain the lack of opposition to the capitalist social order and thus to account for the mass media's ideological effectiveness. In the context of the cultural conflicts of the 1960s, as the civil rights and anti-Vietnam War movements fed into a general critique of the capitalist establishment and bourgeois morality, these questions lost their force and Benjamin's points were rediscovered. They were particularly suggestive for analysts of popular music: the emergence of a radical youth movement meant that a new assessment had to be made of the ideological effects of rock. Dave Laing, for example, argued that capitalist cultural forms contained liberating as well as oppressive elements; rock was "squeezed out" of the conflict between commercial machinations and youthful aspirations. If the industry was seeking to exploit a new market, the youth audience was seeking a medium through which to express its experience, and musicians, who were at the center of this conflict, were able to develop their own creative space. Laing concluded that the mass media were the location not of cultural pluralism but of cultural struggle: if the capitalist organization of cultural production was not entirely determinant, then both artists and audiences could fight for the control of the meanings of cultural symbols. Benjamin's original point was remade: it was the technological and socialized basis of mass music production that made cultural struggle possible.

This sort of argument lay behind both the radical claims for rock that began to be made in the 1960s and punks' political claims in the late 1970s. It suggested that popular music could—in some circumstances—express something more than the culture of profit; that record buying could—under some cultural conditions—mean something more than passive consumption. The question was, in what circumstances? under what conditions? What was it that exempted rock as a form of pop music from the strictures of the mass culture critics?

## ROCK AS FOLK MUSIC

The distinction between mass and folk cultures has always been important for the mass media's critics, who contrast mass and community, fragmented consumption and collective creation, alienation and solidarity, passivity and activity. The ideology of the original folk music movement, at the end of the nineteenth century, rested on exactly such contrasts. Sir Hubert Parry, for example, praised folk music in these terms:

> It grew in the heart of the people before they devoted themselves so assiduously to the making of quick returns; and it grew there because it pleased them to make it, and what they made pleased them; and that is the only way good music is ever made. [5]

"Folk" culture is thus created directly and spontaneously out of communal experience. It is the culture of the working classes—it expresses the communal experience of work. There is no distance between folk artist and audience, no separation between folk production and consumption. As A. L. Lloyd puts it: "The main thing is that the songs are made and sung by men who are identical with their audience in standing, in occupation, in attitude to life, and in daily experience."

The folk argument is that this form of popular creativity—"real, raw, rank and file music," to use Dave Harker's terms—has been destroyed by the means and relations of artistic production under capitalism. Cultural products are now produced and sold for profit, and the accompanying processes of taste manipulation and artistic exploitation have been made possible by recording techniques—music can now be mass-produced and individually consumed. Folkies, by contrast, celebrate a tradition of live performance in which performers are not even distanced from their listeners by amplification—Bob Dylan was booed at the Newport Folk Festival simply for playing with electrified instruments.

Undaunted by these arguments, Jon Landau claims that rock and roll

> was unmistakably a folk-music form. Within the confines of the media, these musicians articulated attitudes, styles and feelings that were genuine reflections of their own experience and of the social situation which had helped to produce that experience. [6]

Greil Marcus suggests that rock 'n' roll was a "secret" that bound a generation and made it culturally independent of its elders; Robert Christgau argues that the music was a source of solidarity. For these writers, it was not rock 'n' roll lyrics (all those teenage topics) that made it a genuine form of youthful expression, but its beat: it was as dance music that rock and roll became a folk music, gave symbolic form to the energy of its users.

There was, the claim continues, no distance between rock 'n' roll musicians and fans. In Landau's words, "There existed a strong bond between performer and audience, a natural kinship, a sense that the stars weren't being imposed from above but had sprung up from out of our ranks. We could identify with them without hesitation." And it was the technology of rock 'n' roll, particularly radio, that enabled it to provide its disparate audience with an experience of community. As Marcus puts it:

> We fight our way through the massed and levelled collective taste of the Top 40, just looking for a little something we can

call our own. But when we find it and jam the radio to hear it again it isn't just ours—it is a link to thousands of others who are sharing it with us. As a matter of a single song this might mean very little; as culture, as a way of life, you can't beat it. [7]

Wilfred Mellers suggests that the long-playing record has "transplanted ritual from temple or theatre into any place where two or three may gather together." Rock culture is not confined to ceremonial occasions but enters people's lives without aura; the rock audience is not a passive mass, consuming records like cornflakes, but an active community, using its music as a symbol of solidarity. This audience isn't manipulated but makes real choices; the music doesn't impose an ideology but, in Marcus's phrase, "absorbs events," absorbs its listeners' concerns and values.

By the end of the 1960s the argument that rock music was the folk expression of a new youth movement had become cliché—it was the organizing assumption, for example, of Carl Belz's *The Story of Rock*, the first academic treatment of the music. The problem with this argument was its circularity: the music was folk music because its audience was a real community, but this community could only be recognized by its common use of the music—hence the vacuous concept of "the Woodstock Generation." The only way out of the circle was through an independent measure of the rock community, and here there were two rather different positions: rock was either heard as the culture of adolescence, the sound of the community of teenagers, or as counterculture, the sound of specific vanguard youth groups.

The first argument was, in terms of folk, limited. The meaning of rock was derived from vaguely defined teenage needs and values—the problems of puberty, family, school; the music was taken to express teenage fun, excitement, anxiety, and sexiness. But the problem was not to establish rock's overall relevance for young people, but to establish the expressive authenticity of particular records; to this end, teenage folk claims were not convincing. Youth is an ideological rather than a material community. It describes a shared state of mind but not a cooperative way of life. Rock celebrates leisure rather than work: its performers are stars, distanced from their audiences in status and power and situation; it is used by teenagers as entertainment. Rock's relevance for the young, its meaning as a mass teenage medium, is not as folk culture but as popular culture. I will come back to this point in Part Three.

The second argument was more convincing. In 1950 David Riesman had identified a minority group among American adolescents that rejected the image of youth the mass media presented. Riesman suggested that "such a 'youth movement' differs from the youth movements of other countries in having no awareness of itself, as such, no direct political consciousness, and, on the whole, no specialised media of communication." But in the 1960s this assessment had to be revised—rebel youth became both self-conscious and politically assertive; it developed its own media and forms of expression. The hippies were the source of the new folk claim that rock was a counterculture. This account of rock rested on an analysis of the way the music was produced as well as consumed, and it was important for the counterculture's position that rock musicians remained part of the community for which they made their music, that their art remained an explicit expression of communal values—the music was a folk form not despite commercialism but in conscious opposition to it, and musicians' claims to "represent" their communities were thought to be compromised by involvement with the capitalist organization of the record industry.

The argument is that countercultural music represents the interests of the particular youth groups to which the musicians belong—punk musicians made the same communal claims for themselves in the 1970s that hippie musicians had made in the 1960s; the problems arise when such "authentic" musicians achieve commercial success and are charged with "selling out." The technology of rock has contradictory implications: amplification and recording, the basic means of rock expression, enable the businessman to take control. As local live performers, musicians remain a part of their community, subject to its values and needs, but as recording artists they experience the pressures of the market; they automatically become "rock 'n' roll imperialists," pursuing national and international sales. The recording musician's "community," in short, is defined by purchasing patterns.

The implication of this argument is that rock operates as counterculture only at moments. There are creative breakthroughs, when the music does express the needs of real communities, but it never takes the industry long to control and corrupt the results. Indeed, the record companies' task has been made easier by the confusion of countercultural ideology with the ideology of youth. As Michael Lydon argued at the end of the sixties:

> In fact, rock, rather than being an example of how freedom can be achieved within the capitalist structure, is an example of how capitalism can, almost without a conscious effort, deceive those whom it oppresses. . . . So effective has the rock industry been in encouraging the spirit of optimistic youth take-over that rock's truly hard political edge, its constant exploration of the varieties of youthful frustration, has been ignored and softened. [8]

It was explicitly to explore the hard edges of youthful frustration that punk emerged a decade later, but its commercial development, too, seemed to confirm the argument that rock can express the values of specific communities only briefly. Rock, in other words, is rarely a folk music; its cultural work is done according to different rules.

## ROCK AS ART

In the 1970s, as the countercultural argument lost its force and became a selling technique, the special status of rock's best music was increasingly explained in terms not of community but of art.

The distinction between art and mass culture is based on distinctions between individual sensibility and mass taste, between "enrichment" and "escape." Wilfred Mellers, for example, suggests that entertainment is merely a simulation of experience, a substitute for it; pop music titillates its audience but lacks "commitment or threat." Rock art, by contrast, involves complex symbolic structures that relate directly to the musicians' own experiences and are a genuine challenge to the listeners.

Analyzing rock as art raises two problems. First, rock music, like other works of art in an age of mechanical reproduction, is not made by individual creators communicating directly to an audience—record-making depends on a complex structure of people and machines. Rock critics have had to establish their own version of *auteur* theory. Jon Landau, for example, claims that "the criterion of art in rock is the capacity of the musician to create a personal, almost private, universe and to express it fully."

The rock *auteur* (who may be writer, singer, instrumentalist, band, record producer, or even engineer) creates the music; everyone else engaged in record-making is simply part of the means of communication. For many fans it was this sense of individual creation that first distinguished rock from other forms of mass music—the fact that the Beatles wrote their own songs freed them from Tin Pan Alley ideologically as well as economically, and by the 1970s it had become routine to equate art with personal confession. Self-consciousness became the measure of a record's artistic status; frankness, musical wit, the use of irony and paradox were musicians' artistic insignia—it was such self-commentary that revealed the *auteur* within the machine. The skilled listener was the one who could recognize the artist despite the commercial trappings; this became the professional job of record reviewers.

The second problem for rock's claims as art is its continuing function as entertainment. Entertainers neither "improve" nor "instruct" their audiences; their music comes easily, while true art makes people work. One solution to this problem was to make the rock audience work, too, by complicating the structure of songs, by aping classical music or jazz, by changing emphasis from performance to composition, by moving the audience from dance floor to concert hall. Listeners began to deny that their immediate response to the music exhausted its meaning: rock could no longer just be enjoyed, it had to be addressed like any other form of art; its tensions and contradictions had to be absorbed and interpreted. Bob Dylan was a rock artist, according to Dave Harker, because "you had, literally, to make over the significance of his songs in terms of your own experience." Dylan couldn't be consumed because "you had to produce these songs *for yourself.*"

The trouble with such descriptions of records as the hard work of rock *auteurs* is that they are rarely illuminating, and the image of the individual creator is quickly absorbed into the star-making machinery (this is the easiest aspect of rock ideology to exploit). All musical texts are, in fact, social products, and rock musicians, like any other mass artists, are under constant pressure to confirm their status, to provide their audience with more of the music that gave them that status in the first place. There is a permanent contradiction between being an "artist"—responsible only to one's own creative impulses—and being a star—responsible to one's market.

The problem for rock-as-art fans became one of explaining how their chosen musician-artists could sustain their individual impulses in the face of these market pressures. The conclusion was that, for the most part, they couldn't: the story of folk's creative break-through and commerical incorporation has a parallel artistic version. Rock's claims as art are based not on the cultural form itself but on the achievements of a handful of disparate individuals—artists *despite* their means of cultural production. Most rock musicians aren't, in fact, different from any other group of entertainers: their objec-tive is to give a particular market what they think it wants, and if that market wants artists then that's what it gets. In Robert Levin's words:

> Rock's superiority over previous popular musical forms is sim-ply the result of its existence in a period of expanded and heightened social, political, and psychological awareness, a pe-riod which makes possible and necessary a hip and relevant popular music. [9]

We're back to rock as popular culture again, only this time as the popular culture not of teenagers but of sophisticated, individual-istic, suburban and campus youth. Such young people may sneer at disco and the "mindless pop" of teenage culture, may have ex-changed their pinups for LP sleeves and their dancing shoes for headphones, but their music arrives on the turntable as the result of the same commercial processes.

I began this discussion by asking why rock was thought of as a liberating form of pop music; why it, unlike previous pop, seemed to realize the positive aspects of mass culture. It turns out that, for many of rock's proponents, the answer is that rock isn't a form of mass music at all—it is interpreted as a folk form or as an art. These arguments are unconvincing. Rock is a commercially made mass music and this must be the starting point for its celebration as well as for its dismissal. The question at issue is, in fact, a simple one: What makes a work of mass culture good or bad? The problem is to decide the criteria of judgment.

High art critics often write as if their terms of evaluation were purely aesthetic, but mass culture critics can't escape the fact that the bases for cultural evaluation are always social: what is at issue is the *effect* of a cultural product. Is it repressive or liberating? Corrupting or uplifting? Escapist or instructive? The aesthetic question—how does the text achieve its effects?—is secondary. The evaluation of rock performers and records (the daily practice of all the music's users) means placing them according to a general theory of what rock is thought to be capable of. The point I've been making in this chapter is that positive claims for rock as folk culture or art are claims about what musicians can do *despite* their implication in a mass medium. The inference is that most pop products are culturally worthless; the more sure rock fans are of the special worth of their artists, the more contemptuous they are of the pleasures taken by the rest of pop's consumers. But the popular cultural value of rock is, after all, that its messages are *not* confined to specific folk communities or artistic coteries. Therefore, we still have to answer the most important question: What possibilities of expression are *opened* to musicians, or musical communities, by rock's status as a mass medium?

# THE IDEOLOGY OF ROCK

The question common to all studies of mass media concerns ideology. How do different media work ideologically? What are their ideological effects and how are they achieved? The issue here is the concept of signification: How do different media organize the *meanings* with which and on which they work?

"Realist" theories assume that the media operate with some degree of transparency: media images represent reality as if through a window or in a mirror; they are ideological to the degree that they are false, and this can be measured against non-ideological representations, against experience. The political question is why media distort reality, and the answer is found not in media forms (which are examined only to see how distortion works) but in their controllers. There are different degrees of control—from straight censorship to the vague "feel" of media professionals—but all have the same ideological effect: the reproduction of a false account of how the world works. The way to change this media message is to seize the technical means of message production, the machines themselves. Ideology is a problem of content and control; the media simply communicate the messages that are fed into them.

"Formalist" theories concentrate, in contrast, on the formal means of signification. Their assumption is that media images don't reflect or copy reality but construct it. Media forms are structures of meaning which bind us to an ideological account of the world; the very notion that we can judge such accounts against experience is "an ideological effect of the realist discourse." The form has the same ideological effect, no matter who owns it, and the political problem thus becomes not how to control a neutral process of production but how to read a structure of signification; it is a question not of access, but of meaning. The ideological effect rests on the relationship between media texts and their readers, rather than on that between media images and reality.

The recurring problem for culture theorists is to relate general accounts of ideology to the structures of particular media. There are obvious difficulties in describing music in semiological terms, for example. Most theories of cultural representation have come from literary critics and aren't immediately available to music critics unless we reduce music to songs and songs to words. And, precisely because the content of music is not obvious, the question of its control is more confused than in, say, the politics of television. The state does seek to regulate musical communication—in Britain, for example, records are banned from radio, groups are banned from town halls—but this is a limited form of control ("Anarchy in the UK" was still a best-seller); and, anyway, offense is almost always taken at the verbal or visual images involved—there are no obvious ways to pin down the subversiveness of groups' *music*.

It is difficult, then, to say how musical texts mean or represent something, and it is difficult to isolate structures of musical creation or control. (Who owns the means of music-making—the musicians? their record companies? broadcasters?) Radical music critics usually analyze rock not in terms of form and content but in terms of production and consumption: the argument is either that the ideological meaning of music lies in the way it is commercially produced, in its commodity form, or that consumers create their own meanings out of the commodities offered.

Production and consumption were, as we have seen, the focus

of the mass culture debate. The Frankfurt argument was that the production of music as a commodity determined its cultural quality, that standardizing music produced its ideological effect. The subjection of creativity to "capital discipline" was made possible, according to Adorno, by the technology of mass production; and popularity of mass music could be explained in psychological terms: the pleasure of mass culture was the pleasure of a particular kind of consumption—a passive, endlessly repeated confirmation of the world as it is. Mass texts did their ideological work through their construction of an *illusion* of reality. Consumers "experienced" mass art as if they were grasping something for themselves; but there was, in fact, no individual way of constructing meaning: subjectivity, in this context, meant nothing more than market choice.

The weakness of this argument lay in its account of consumption, for the argument reduced a complex social process to a simple psychological effect. Walter Benjamin's contrasting celebration of mechanical reproduction rested on the argument that because the artistic authority of cultural goods had been broken, their significance had become a matter of dispute: the ideological meaning of mass culture was decided in the process of consumption, and the grasping of particular works by particular audiences was a political rather than a psychological event. (How such works got to the market was of less significance—Benjamin himself tended to treat the means of mass communication, in technological terms, as neutral factors.)

Critical accounts of popular music still depend on the Adorno/Benjamin positions. Out of Adorno have come analyses of the economics of entertainment in which the ideological effects of commercial music-making—the transformation of a creative people into a passive mass—are taken for granted (as in Chapple and Garofalo's study of the American music business, for example). From Benjamin have come subcultural theories, descriptions of the struggle for the sign: youth subcultures are said to make their own meanings, to *create* cultures in their acts of consumption. The problem, then, is to determine the relationship between rock's commercial function and its cultural use.

# TWO

## ROCK
## PRODUCTION

# CHAPTER 4

# MAKING MUSIC

The British rock musician Manfred Mann once commented that "the more people buy a record, the more successful it is—not only commercially but artistically." The ideological power of popular music comes from its popularity. Music becomes a mass culture by entering a mass consciousness, by being heard simultaneously on people's radios and record players, on bar and café jukeboxes, at discos and dances. Mass music is recorded music and—whatever their particular artistic claims, their authenticity and interest as music—records which don't sell, which don't become popular, don't enter mass consciousness. Because rock is a mass medium, attempts to claim its products, records, as folk music or works of art, as we have seen, miss the point: a record's ideological influence is determined by what happens to it in the marketplace.

The mass cultural critics claim that he who controls the market controls the meaning, and they argue that the mass audience plays no part in cultural creation because even its market choices are manipulated. But this does not make much sense with regard to rock. The vast bulk of the music that is aimed at the mass market never reaches it. The music business is organized around the realities of overproduction—its daily practices reflect not the problems of creating needs but of responding to them. Few labels have the capital or the courage to risk stirring up new demands, and the record industry has always made its money by picking up on needs independently expressed: punk rock, for example, was developed as a musical style by musicians and audiences operating outside the usual record business relationships; it was taken over and exploited by record companies only when its market potential seemed assured. In general, the rock business was built on two great market discoveries: the discovery of working-class teenagers in the 1950s and middle-class youth in the 1960s. The industry had to *learn* about these audiences and their demands, and the musical results followed rather than led youthful tastes and choices.

For its critics all pop music has the same psychological function, and the choices made within it are, therefore, insignificant—they reflect merely the competitive calculations of the producers and the random irrationality of the consumers. But if the power of popular music lies in its popularity, then the particular choices that the people make are significant. This is the source of the distinction between mass culture, whose ideology is completely explicable in terms of producer stimulus/audience response, and popular culture, whose ideology results from genuinely popular attitudes and values. Rock is a capitalist industry and not a folk form, but its most successful products do, somehow, express and reflect its audience's concerns.

In *Mystery Train,* the most sustained and subtle attempt to treat rock as popular culture, Greil Marcus argues that rock, like all mass culture, functions to provide a sense of community to an audience fragmented by the experience of competitive capitalism. Most mass culture plays this role safe—American-ness or British-ness is presented as the bland and conventional acceptance of a lie, that the way things are is just dandy. For Marcus, mass culture can only become art if it can convey unconventional visions that are so powerful they can't be evaded even by mass consumption. The central worry for popular artists is that "if you get what you have to say across to a mass audience, that means what you have to say is not deep enough, or strong enough, to really matter."

This is also the worry of the cultural critics, but Marcus goes on to suggest that the mass media can communicate disturbing truths and be the vehicle for a popular art, if they draw on and respond to ideas that are already disturbing and powerful in popular thought. Rock is popular art insofar as it expresses and deals symbolically with contradictions, and Marcus's particular concern is with American rock's treatment of the ideology of equality, an ideology particularly fraught with difficulty: not only is the ideal of equality contradicted by daily experience, but there are contradictions within the ideal itself—it opposes ambition and the sense of private worth to community, to the collective prejudices that support the unequal in their individual failure. It is this contradiction that Marcus finds expressed in the most powerful rock music: on one hand, ambition and risk-taking, a sense of style and adventure, a refusal to be satisfied; on the other hand, a feeling for roots and history, a dependence on community and tradition, the acceptance of one's lot. The central image of American popular culture is Elvis Presley, demanding good times, getting them, and finding them all too easy. As rock 'n' roll became rock and forced its way into the culture of a much wider community of white youth, its tense combination of dissatisfaction and guilt took on meaning as a vaguer contradiction between utopianism—California as the promised land—and cynicism—California as the final resting place of dead souls.

Marcus takes it as a given that cultural meaning can be made out of commodities, but a question remains: How free can such creation be? What are the limits of rock songs not as commodities but as texts, signification structures with rules and restrictions of their own? This takes us back to the questions raised in chapter 2—questions about music, about form and content. Musical texts are volatile. This accounts partly for the deadlock in the debate about rock as commodity: meanings change so fast that both sides seem always to be right. Thus, the effect of Elvis Presley, the Rolling Stones, the Sex Pistols moved rapidly from shock to nostalgia; different listeners use the same music for quite different ends; the same record can be consumed socially (as dance music) and individually (as a market purchase). The meaning of popular music is the result of a process in which the significance of the text itself, the particular organization of sounds (and by "text" I mean the aural combination of music *and* words), is neither static nor determinant but involves a number of con-textual questions, questions about entertainment and musical pleasure.

## MUSICIANS

Rock musicians themselves have always argued that although their music is made for a mass market, its meaning is not simply commercial. Record companies' pursuit of profit does not, according to the musicians involved, *determine* rock's cultural significance. The relationship between making music and making money remains, though, the musicians' central problem. They experience tensions in their dealings not only with the industry that packages their music but also with the audiences that consume it.

In the 1950s rock 'n' roll singers were assumed to be working-class teenagers. The media archetype was Elvis Presley, the poor Southern boy who escaped a life of truck-driving by remaking American music; his subsequent career was a matter of luck as much as talent, manipulation as much as art, image as much as music. For years rock musicians were presented as the boys-next-door, street kids or rural hicks, making music for a working-class audience that identified with them, that shared their background, culture, and values. Rock 'n' roll fit into the long show-biz tradition of middle-class songwriters and producers *fronted* by working-class performers. In Britain, where such class distinctions are culturally sharper, there was also an element of sexual fantasy: the sharp, college-educated music pushers were, unusually often, homosexuals; stars there were given a surly, sensual, leather-boy appeal. The assumption that rock stars were, by definition, dumb prole puppets was so common that, during the beat boom of the mid-1960s, Paul McCartney's high school exam successes and Mick Jagger's time at the London School of Economics provoked repeated news comment.

By the late 1960s such backgrounds for rock musicians had become commonplace. The folk-rock input came from the campus and the new stars had degrees, suburban homes, and made knowing references to literature and art—it became hard to pin down any obvious relationship between class and musical style. The 1950s images of rebellion without a cause merged with the 1960s images of rebellion with a cause; the 1950s show-biz sincerity became the 1960s artistic sincerity; the sharpest distinctions between rock musicians involved not background or ideology but success and situation. By the 1970s, "being a rock musician" covered a huge range of experience: from that of a superstar—moving leisurely, luxuriously, excessively between studio and stadium, cocooned (and cocained) by an entourage of servants and sycophants—to that of a local bar band—moving desperately and sporadically between welfare and squalid gig, sustained only by dreams.

It is not easy, then, to generalize about rock musicians, and the task is made harder by the thousands of words that are turned out in the music papers' weekly diet of interviews: the more we find out about individuals' tastes and hopes, the less easy it is to uncover shared beliefs or values. Music press and show-biz myth have themselves fed musicians with the clichés they feed the public.

The show-biz myth equates pop success with genius (will-out-despite - being - hidden - in - rags / oppressed - by - philistines / raddled-with-drugs) or luck (he-just-happened-to-be-standing-on-the-pier-when-the-producer-drove-by), but "creative input" isn't really plucked from the sky. Skill and invention are the result of training and practice, and show-biz success has always been based, in fact, on the Protestant ethic of hard work and dedication—the select earn their star status with years of good work; the show-biz hero is really the professional. Being a musician is not just a matter of self-expression, but requires the right attitudes and values, the right approach to the audience. Grace Slick replaced Signe Anderson in Jefferson Airplane because, "You've got to be able to move and do more than just sing the notes to rock and roll. You just can't stand there and pat your thigh and expect people to get off on it." Even hippies had to follow the advice of the handbooks to show-biz success:

> Whether you're a performer or writer, you're the designer, manufacturer and salesman of your own product. Just like a company producing a new line in household goods, you must put time and effort into the initial development. Furthermore you will have to invest money in the promotion and presentation of your product.[1]

Rock stars changed the terms of this advice but not its underlying argument: the years of "dues paying," the time of starvation are now rewarded with the years of "making it," the time of stardom; but now as always "everybody gets what they deserve!"

# MUSICIANS AND THE BUSINESS

Popular musicians make their living by selling their services to record companies and promoters. To understand their lives we have to begin with these economic relationships. Two sorts of service are involved. First, there are musicians who are just that: their craft is their music, and they sell only their musical skills. Thus, session musicians offer their services to anyone who is making a musical product: producers and record companies, radio and television, film score makers and advertisers. Until the mid-1960s ambitious teenagers thought a rock 'n' roll career still meant this kind of work. Al Kooper, for example, was, from his early teens, involved in numerous music-biz activities—writing songs, producing and arranging records, playing with various musical lineups for various functions—and his job was always to make precisely the song, the sound, the commodity his employer asked for.

Second, there are musicians who are also entertainers: they sell their music to the public directly. In the pop business there is, in fact, no sharp division between music and other forms of entertainment. In clubs and cabarets, on TV shows, performers move from song to comedy to sentiment—the musical values involved are derived from general notions of what it means to entertain a crowd.

The basic rule of the pop business is that the purchaser of a musical service determines its content: on one hand, the record producer or jingle maker asks for an A flat or a boogie rhythm; on the other hand, entertainers prove their professionalism by giving the people "what they want." Most popular musicians are involved in both processes at once: they sell their services to an agent who is seeking to satisfy a public demand *and* have some flexibility in interpreting the expectations of their employers. It was in this context that musicians' craft organizations developed: the American Federation of Musicians and the British Musicians' Union took shape around the interests of the musicians employed by dance bands and orchestras in the 1920s and 1930s.

The musicians' unions seek to control the conditions in which their members sell their services. They negotiate the minimum rates of pay for recording sessions, for work in clubs and cabarets, in orchestras and theaters, on radio and television. Over the years the unions have fought to maintain employment opportunities and, like all craft unions, they have been especially concerned to establish closed shops. The AFM, for example, has always resisted new forms of popular music-making, interpreted them as threats to the demand for their members' established skills. In 1901 the union ordered its members to stop playing ragtime—"the musicians know what is good, and if the people don't we will have to teach them"; with the rise of jazz, the AFM's closed-shop policies became explicitly racist, excluding black musicians from union locals, hence keeping them out of radio and recording work. Since the war the unions' main fight has been to stop bars, dance halls, and radio stations from replacing live musicians with jukeboxes, discos, and deejays. Their efforts have not been very successful.

Union policies rest on two assumptions. The first is that the majority of its members are "standard" musicians selling "standard" services. All artistic unions have the problem of providing a collective organization for sellers of individual and individually priced talents, and their chief concern has to be for their routine workers rather than for the successful stars. But in the musicians' case this policy has led to anomalies, anomalies that are well illustrated by the British Musicians' Union's attitude to foreign musicians. The union's principle is that no foreign musician should be employed to do what a British musician could do equally well; the difficulty is to define the musical skills that are so reproducible. The union does have a category of "concert musician" whose skills are accepted as unique, but this description has always been more readily applied to classical than to popular musicians. For the latter the union's policy has been that it "is ridiculous to say that there was only one man in the world who could do what you wanted. We would say you would have to find a British musician who could do want you want." This policy has had ridiculous consequences, particularly for black music—since the 1930s jazz has been heard as an easily acquired *technique* (even in the 1960s Ornette Coleman had to play classical venues to get "concert musician" status).

The second union assumption is that their members are primarily live performers. The unions have always seen the development of recording as a threat to musicians' employment, and treat it as exceptional work rather than as the core of popular musical success. They have been slow, for example, to develop mechanisms to protect musicians from exploitation by record companies in the ways that they are protected from exploitation by their "live" employers—the

promoters and agents. When the unions do deal with record producers they usually do so on behalf of the session musicians (negotiat-
ing "standard" recording fees, for example) rather than the
contracted artists.

Because of their concern for standard musicians and live performers, the unions have seldom expressed the particular needs of
their rock members. Many successful musicians, indeed, are not
even members of a union—the AFM, unlike the Actors' Guild, cannot operate a closed shop: there are too many jobs available, the distinctions are too loose between amateurs and professional musicians,
for union organizers to exercise much work control, especially in
rock. Rock musicians do, though, live by selling musical services,
and their ideology still has to be related to their lives as professionals, even if there are great varieties in the concept of "professionalism" involved.

Some rock musicians are, quite straightforwardly, all-purpose
players, for whom rock is just another job. In his study of Hollywood session musicians in the 1960s, Robert Faulkner shows the
extent to which they were used to make rock records and how much
they despised the job: "You feel like a prostitute doing these types
of dates." Al Kooper, similarly, describes his pre–Bob Dylan New
York music-biz days as "whoring." Session musicians remain central to rock record-making, and, indeed, their abilities to make
sounds "to order" have become even more important as studio costs
have risen and as producers and bands have become more ambitious
in their use of studio technology. Today's session men are not as
contemptuous of their rock work as their predecessors were (these
days it is, at least, more challenging than jingle-making), but they
still lack responsibility for the results of their sessions, resent the
easy exploitation of their skills, and despise the "creative" clumsi-
ness of their employers.

Howard Becker describes the ideology of 1940s and 1950s
dance musicians as a result of the contradiction between their self-
image as artists (their music being a means of self-expression) and
their situation as service sellers (their music being subject to the va-
garies of consumer demand):

> The musician thus sees himself as a creative artist who should
> be free from outside control, a person different from and better
> than those outsiders he calls squares who understand neither

his music nor his way of life and yet because of whom he must perform in a manner contrary to his professional ideals.[2]

Becker describes how the musicians segregated themselves from their audiences, developed a language and life-style that brought out their differences from the common listener (the "punter" in British rock terminology). At the same time, though, professional musicians have to compromise with commercial reality, and, in the long run, have to justify their compromises. Commercial work can be seen to offer its own challenges and satisfactions: professionals take pride in their ability, as craftsmen, to solve musical problems, to do difficult jobs well. Musical pleasure doesn't only come from unfettered self-expression.

## MUSICIANS AND THE ROCK BUSINESS

Rock musicians experience similar tensions between their artistic ideals and commercial pressures, but in some respects their solutions have been different from those of their fellow professionals. One reason for this is the special status of rock as youth music: rock musicians are less clearly contemptuous of their audiences because part of their self-image lies in the belief that they express the values of youth in general (and not just of themselves in particular). I will return to this point in the next section. But another source of rock ideology lies in the history of rock musicians as professionals. In Becker's argument the musicians' problem lies in the adjustment to commerical status by players who started their careers as self-perceived artists. In rock the process has gone the other way: rock musicians developed their artistic claims from commercial origins; then, paradoxically, artistic integrity became, in itself, the basis for commercial success.

The traditional source of talent in show biz is not artistic self-expression but the ability to entertain. There is not, as for Becker's musicians, a conflict between skill and public demand; rather, skill is defined as the ability to meet public demand. It is possible that, in private, show-biz stars gather to laugh at the low tastes of their audiences, but I doubt it; basic to the entertainer's self-image is a belief in the people—it is, after all, their tastes that alone justify his or her activities. Entertainers, unlike jazz musicians, don't have independent criteria for their worth.

The early values of rock 'n' roll were forged in the context of entertainment, whether in local dance halls or on national TV shows. There was a new public—teenagers; and a new taste—rock 'n' roll. But the justification for the new musicians (many of whom were, indeed, old musicians) still rested on their ability to meet a demand. This was particularly obvious in Britain. In Tommy Steele's words:

> Someone was looking for someone to be the exponent of rock and roll, and I was there. Show business is really 90 per cent luck and 10 per cent being able to handle it when it gets offered to you. The teenagers around at that time suddenly found that they had control of a certain part of the leisure market. Now, no-one knows better than the leisure people; there were kids with pocket money, with their first years' wages, and they suddenly found, all of a sudden, that they could dictate policy. Just like that. They could dictate something. And they dictated music. And they turned round and said: "This is going to be what we want, and what we want is our own age-group, singing our songs, in our way. In order to show you that's what we want, if you can present us with it we'll buy it if we like it." And so I was an experiment.[3]

Tommy Steele and Cliff Richard and Britain's other original rock stars experienced no tensions between their music and their success; art and commerce were integrated. Popularity was the measure of their talent as entertainers; and if there were elements of rebellion in rock 'n' roll, they were directed not against the structure in which the musicians worked but against the adult generation, to whom the music was not intended to appeal anyway. The situation was little different for the Beatles and the Stones and the other British beat groups in the early 1960s. The issue was not art versus commerce but young taste versus old taste. The Rolling Stones, claimed their 1964 biography,

> have been Rebels With A Cause. . . . the Cause of rhythm 'n' blues music. They have drifted into the position of being shot

at by half the population. They have been derided by politicans in Parliament, laughed at by road-sweepers, jeered at by mothers, despised by fathers. . . . They were determined to express themselves freely, through their music. And they decided unanimously that they were going to make no concessions to the demands of commercialism that they, frankly, openly, despised.

But, on the other hand, as this routine show-biz bio goes on to point out, they were

> loved by the teenagers. For the teenagers have realised the courage of the Stones. The courage to kick hard against the solid, staid conventions and live life the way they feel it—and without causing harm or trouble to anybody else.
> They've gone out to produce sheer excitement for the fans and they've succeeded despite the criticisms.[4]

All that was involved in the Stones' "rebellion" was the substitution of one measure of commercial success by another. Even when these mid-1960s musicians began to write their own material, they didn't seem to experience any contradictions between art and commerce. Pete Townshend of the Who remembers going to the recording studio to cut the group's second single:

> They said: "We think you are a great R&B band, but the Beatles have set a trend of groups writing their own material. All the Liverpudlian groups write their own material, the Stones write their own material. You just really got to do it." So away we walked, and everybody looked round and said "Who's going to write?" And me being at art school, being able to say long words like "perspicacity," which I heard on a Spike Milligan album, I was elected to do the job. About eight to ten weeks later, the song I had written, "Can't Explain," was number 8 in the charts. So it all seemed automatic and easy to me.[5]

The notion of rock star as artist was slow to develop. A straw in the British wind was Eric Clapton leaving the Yardbirds in 1965 because "they are going too commercial." In the words of Paul Samwell-Smith:

> I don't know if Eric wanted success then, certainly not that kind of success where it meant standing on stage repeating the same old hit songs—pop top twenty songs—note for note every time, that you hadn't written, that you didn't like.[6]

But more important for the transformation of rock 'n' roll ideology than such blues purism (Eric Clapton was, in many ways, living a life more like that of one of Becker's jazz musicians than that of the average rock star) were the American folk arguments that gained force with the commercial success of Bob Dylan. Folk musicians, overwhelmingly middle-class and well educated, equated their activities with those of other bourgeois artists—poets, novelists, painters. Music was thus defined as self-expression and social commentary, as a matter of truth rather than popularity, and folk performers retained the traditional, radical rejection of the conventions of mass music-making.

Such folk purism was challenged by the Beatles' revelations of the continuing possibilities of commercial rock 'n' roll, but it was the folk rockers' uses of these possibilities that mattered. John Lennon remembered writing songs for the *Help* album in 1965:

> I started thinking about my own emotions—I don't know when exactly it started, like "I'm a Loser" or "Hide Your Love Away" or those kind of things—instead of projecting myself into a situation I would just try to express what I felt about myself which I'd done in me books. I think it was Dylan helped me realise that—not by any discussion or anything but just by hearing his work—I had a sort of professional songwriter's attitude to writing pop songs; we would turn out a certain style of song for a single and we would do a certain style of thing for this and the other thing. I was already a stylised songwriter on the first album. But to express myself I would write *Spaniard in The Works* or *In His Own Write*, the personal stories which were expressive of my personal emotions. I'd have a separate song-writing John Lennon who wrote songs for the sort of meat market and I didn't consider them—the lyrics or any-

thing—to have any depth at all. They were just a joke. Then I started being me about the songs, not writing them objectively, but subjectively.[7]

By the late 1960s musicians on both sides of the Atlantic were distinguishing rock as art from rock as entertainment: rock was a complex musical form; it could not be constrained by the pop tradition of singles, package tours, and reproduced hits. Pop meant groups put together, like the Monkees, to satisfy a fad, anonymous players bought—their personalities and all—to meet a need. In pop, even when the musicians were themselves responsible for how they pleased their public, they had to take account of that public's demand, and the youth market was as constraining as any other. Rock, by contrast, was a means of self-expression; it could not be subordinated to any market. This ideology of rock was explicitly anti-commercial, even if commercialism meant pleasing an audience of youth; and, for the first time, rock musicians began to experience a contradiction between their own artistic impulses and the consumer demand for commodities—like jazz musicians before them, they began to separate themselves, ideologically, from the circumstances in which their music was made.

Such a separation was made possible by the increasing importance, from 1967 on, of recording. Previously, the studio had been the creative focus only for businessmen, making teenage commodities. For most performers, music was made live—records were simply a means of reproducing the sound on a mass scale. The creative power and integrity of beat groups like the Beatles and the Stones derived from their origins as club musicians; they developed a rock 'n' roll form that was determined not by show-biz conventions but by the immediate demands of dancers. And, as Al Kooper, then of the Blues Project, remembers:

It was always rush time when we were supposed to record. In those days ('66) the artists did not have nearly (or any of) the control they do today. They had no say in what studio was used, had no concept of the stereo mixing processes, and were seldom consulted regarding the cover art. Sometimes (as with the Byrds on "Mr. Tambourine Man") they didn't even play on their own records. They just played and prayed, and that's the way it was with us as well.[8]

But as recording studios and devices got more sophisticated, as musicians got more time and money to indulge themselves, as the industry began to care about albums as a medium, musicians got a chance to experiment with their music away from the immediate relationship with an audience, away from the constant beat of dancing feet. Such constraints were now felt only indirectly, via record company assessments of the market; and as long as musicians could prove the record companies wrong—by cutting records that sold—they could simultaneously indulge their own interests and disdain crude commercial concerns.

Problems arose only when the market didn't respond to rock-as-art. But soon a second development in rock became relevant—the musicians' artistic pretensions were supported by a new audience that shared their ideology, that wanted to "appreciate" art rather than to consume pop, that had the same contempt for show-biz values, for rock-as-entertainment, for singles, package tours, and the rest. But the end of the 1960s the musicians' ideology of artistic freedom and self-expression had been integrated into the general youth ideology of freedom and self-expression—"doing your own thing" became the operative phrase. The professional rock musician had achieved a unique (and temporary) situation in which art and commerce were complementary not contradictory.

From the record companies' point of view, rock-as-art was not difficult to sell. Teenage stars had always been expected to come across as sincere, to appear to identify with their material, even when that material had been the product of a songwriting assembly line; and so the folk notions of honesty and sincerity were easily adopted by the music business—hence the singer/songwriter genre, the rock values of self-consciousness and truth.

Record companies were equally happy to accept the concept of rock "progress." The term tied in with their attempts to differentiate their stars from the mass of pop performers, to service the student market: increasing promotional emphasis was placed on musicians' technical skills, on their instrumental artistry, their willingness to experiment, their unwillingness to be bound by formulas or conventions. This sales strategy was a response both to an audience relectant to choose its idols on the basis of commercial manipulation and to musicians reluctant to be so manipulated. The new institutions of rock 'n' roll (LPs, stereo, concerts) and the new and affluent middle-class market supported "intelligent" musical values—improvisation, virtuosity, stamina, originality.

By the end of the sixties the rise of rock had changed musicians' attitudes to both their music and their audience in all pop genres. In country music, for example, a group of singer/writers took from rock the image of the musician as an idiosyncrat and challenged country assumptions about Nashville hacks, the Opry package, family entertainment. The "outlaws" used established country forms to explore rock themes—freedom, sexuality, nonconformity; they countered the stifling conventions of country pop with rock arguments about self-expression and restless youth (in many respects, indeed, rock's original hippie ideology was more sincerely, less cynically, developed by country musicians than by rock performers).

## MUSICIANS AND THE AUDIENCE

Rock is often analyzed as a contemporary folk music—a music made for young people, by young people, and thus an organic part of young people's culture. This argument is applied to rock in general and to particular styles—the Who's relationship with the Mods, the Sex Pistols' with the Punks. The suggestion is that the music originates as music made by and for friends and neighbors, and that the relationship changes only at the moment of recording, when the music ceases to be bound by a set of personal ties. Rock musicians, in other words, begin their careers by expressing the interests of a real community, and the problem of their authenticity only emerges later, when they are recording stars. But do rock performers really have such folk origins?

I have already suggested that it is difficult to pin rock musicians down to a specific class origin, and I now want to take the argument further: to be a rock musician is, indeed, to be detached from a class background—if rock is a way out of the working class, a path to riches, it is also a way out of the middle class, a path to bohemian freedoms. The move from neighborhood performance to mass production is not an ideological break. To succeed, rock musicians must be ambitious to begin with—they must want to make a musical living, to cut records, to reach unknown audiences.

The most recurrent sociological characteristic of British rock musicians, particularly those who emerged in the classic 1960s period, is an art school background. A remarkable number of British musicians left school at sixteen or seventeen to study art rather than staying on to prepare for college; among them were John Lennon, Keith Richards, Ray Davies, Pete Townshend, Eric Clapton, Jimmy Page, David Bowie. This list of the most famous only hints at the extent to which art school is a normal part of the British rock career. In the British education system art schools allow for a particular sort of mobility. They are places where working-class teenagers who reject a working-class future can go if they don't have the ability or desire to tread the meritocratic path (this was more true in the 1960s, when art schools had less clear academic entry requirements than now), and they are places where middle-class teenagers who reject a middle-class future can go without seeing themselves as failures. Or, in Keith Richards's words, "I mean in England, if you're lucky you get into art school. It's somewhere they put you if they can't put you anywhere else."

Art was the basis for such kids' luck, even if music replaced painting as the art involved, and the importance of the art school in the rock career suggests two general points about musicians as a class. The first is that just as the art school route to fulfillment is an individualistic one, so is the pursuit of fame and fortune in rock. Paying dues may be a collective affair; making it is not: even the most well-paid session musicians, long adjusted to their lack of individual status, define their situation as failure, in that they are not making music as unique artists but as replaceable craftsmen. To have a career as a rock musician you need a quality of self-obsession, an intensity of ambition that can survive whatever crassness the businessmen put it through.

The second point is that just as art schools offer a career that is "different" from the routines of both proletarian and bourgeois work, so musicians make a "different" living, practice a "different" profession than their listeners. As Cliff Richard explained to his young British fans in 1960:

> You see we live at the wrong hours of the day. Seldom do we get home before half past eleven and you tell me a hotel that's going to give you a hot meal at that hour of night. Not many.
>      After we've eaten we're too wide awake to think of bed, and the boys and I sit up till all hours talking away about all sorts of things. . . . You see all of us live, breathe and eat beat-music. We love it. Believe me, although the life is strenuous we never get tired of performing. It's not a way of earning money alone—it's our way of life.[9]

Cliff is describing the experience (usually rather less innocuous) of all popular entertainers. Their work is everyone else's leisure, their way of life is everyone else's way of escape. To be a popular entertainer is to be associated and involved, willy-nilly, with vice and indulgence. Rock musicians play in pubs and clubs and dance halls; they are surrounded by means of relaxation—alcohol, drugs, sexual partners. Indeed, musicians are themselves the symbols of leisure and escape; their jobs, even as neighborhood entertainers, are as much about spectacle as expression, about putting on a *show;* their style supports the audience's use of them as fantasy and briefly held dreams. What for them is routine, one night like another, is for their fans a special event, bedecked with the trappings of stardom. In Pete Townshend's words:

> Pop audiences and pop musicians are geared to different time structures, they lead different lives entirely. They say it's very difficult to go and see a group and feel totally in with what they're doing because they're on a different time trip. They are doing one gig out of a hundred gigs, whereas to the fan this is a very important occasion, like this is the only chance he's gonna get to see, say, The Cream and never again in his life.[10]

This relationship of musician and fan is not just a matter of success and glamour. Simply by being at work when other people are at play, all professional musicians, whatever their origins and however close their ties to a particular audience, are distanced from their listeners' lives. Even at the most small-time level, music-making means working in the world of all those people who don't have to get up in the morning for a nine-to-five business. Bohemianism is musicians' natural ideology: the values of leisure—hedonism and style—are elevated above the conventions and routines of "normal" society; and rock performers subscribe plainly to the traditional romantic opposition of creativity and production—on one hand, the artistic world of heroic, sensual introspection; on the other hand, the everyday world of work, discipline, materialism, reason.

Discussing this point with respect to the black jazz musician, Francis Newton argues that even if the musician was separated from the daily life of his community, his mode of behavior was, nonetheless, determined by his origins and role in the black community:

> If he was often bohemian in his ways, it was not on the pattern of the standard bohemia of the nineteenth-century arts, which

is at bottom the scale of the values of the lower-middle class turned inside out, but on the pattern of the unskilled labourer magnified. . . . For the star was what every slum child and drudge might become: the king or queen of the poor, because the poor person writ large.[11]

Newton distinguishes prewar jazz bohemians from nineteenth-century literary bohemians in three respects: first, jazzmen were not frightened of manual work and, indeed, often had to do it; second, the values and way of life of the jazzmen came less from a deliberate reversal of the respectable values of clerks and shopkeepers than from an exaggeration of the values of casual workers, their thrift-lessness and swank and indulgence; third, jazzmen were not con-temptuous of their audiences but felt themselves to be part of them. Peter Guralnick has described the relationship between traditional country stars and their white, rural, working-class fans in a similar way. Country glamour represents the fantasies of rural unskilled and domestic laborers writ large in wigs and sequins and Cadillacs and Nashville mansions (around which the tourist buses still solemnly drive). Country stars celebrate and confirm their fans' routines; they neither mock nor challenge them.

Rock stars are more like literary bohemians than they are like these ethnic representatives. The rock profession is based on a high-ly individualistic, competitive approach to music, an approach root-ed in ambition and free enterprise. Rock, no less than any other branch of show business, is a willing repository of petit bourgeois values. "Here," suggests the blurb on Cliff Richard's 1960 auto-biography, "is a fascinating story of what could happen to anyone with talent and determination in this wonderful age of opportunity." Al Kooper's 1969 ambition was "a million bucks and the ability to retire when I'm thirty." "You can get money if you want it," sug-gested Johnny Rotten of the Sex Pistols in 1977. "You can get what-ever you want. It's called effort. It doesn't take much, just a lot of guts—which the majority of the general public seem to be lacking."

When rock musicians began, in the mid-sixties, to distinguish themselves ideologically from the "hacks" of show biz, they added to their economic ambitions a hip contempt for clerks and shop-keepers (including those employed by their own record companies); but they sneered equally at manual work and its decencies (distanc-ing themselves, unlike the fifties rock 'n' rollers, from the "normal-ity" of their audiences), and the ideology of rock, in its uneasy combination of professionalism and nonconformity, remains essentially petit bourgeois. Royalty payments confirm the link between individual effort and reward, and it is not much of a move from hipster to tax exile, from maverick to "old fart." Rock star "politics" are derived from an aesthetic reaction to the social conditions of capitalism, from a resentment of *any* sort of social control of experience; they have little to do with collective consciousness.

There is, in short, a contradiction between rock musicians' communal claims and their private life-styles. On the letters pages of the music press this contradiction is usually blamed on success, and "selling out" is seen as the sacrifice of community—whether the community of street kids left behind by tax exiles or hippies betrayed by rock star capitalists—rather than art. But this misinterprets the problem. Success confirms the musicians' distance from their audience but it doesn't cause the separation. Keith Richards comments on the peculiarities of life on the road as a superstar:

> When you're canned up—half the time it's impossible to go out, it's a real hassle to go out—it was to go through a whole sort of football match. One just didn't. You got all you needed from room service, you sent out for it. Limousines sent tearing across cities to pick up a little bag of this or that. You're getting really cut off.[12]

But long before the Stones reached this status, Keith Richards was part of the isolated community of musicians. John Lennon remembered life when the Beatles first came to London:

> That was a great period. We were like kings of the jungle then, and we were very close to the Stones. I don't know how close the others were but I spent a lot of time with Brian and Mick. I admire them, you know. I dug them the first time I saw them in whatever that place is they come from, Richmond. I spent a lot of time with them, and it was great. We all used to just go around London in cars and meet each other and talk about music with the Animals and Eric and all that. It was really a good time, that was the best period fame-wise. We didn't get mobbed so much. It was like a men's smoking club, just a very good scene.[13]

At the time, then, when the Beatles and Stones most clearly articulated a youth culture they were already living in the privileged confines of "a men's smoking club." Where did their identification with "ordinary" youth come from? Their answer was their music. Central to these musicians' ideology was the argument that if they played youth music then they must represent youth culture—representation was a matter of art not politics. British rock has always used a peculiarly ironic performing style, a vocal approach in which the singers seem to watch and comment on their own acts. The classic British rock performers, from the Stones and the Who to Elvis Costello and Johnny Rotten, present themselves as performers, acknowledge the fan's viewpoint *musically*.

Such aesthetic claims to community can be both cynical and circular. "Teenage" songs and styles, "teenage" lyrics and rhythms are routinely turned out to meet (and manipulate) demand—the youthfulness of the results is simply a marketing phenomenon. But many rock musicians do believe that their music gives them a special intimacy with the youth audience. In the words of Pete Townshend:

> We all share the simultaneous experience of forgetting who we are at a rock concert, losing ourselves completely. When the music gets so good, and the audience are so relaxed and free and happy, the music isn't just good music it's also *dance* music—it makes you want to dance. Everybody for a second forgets completely who they are and where they are, and they don't care. They just know they are happy, and that now is now and life is great. And what does it matter if you're a big star— you just know that you are one of a crowd of people. If you have experienced that enough times, it starts to become something that you strive for, because it is so sweet.[14]

Problems remain. Pete Townshend's membership in a rock community depends on his experience of performance. It is live rock which binds audience to musician, creating the ties symbolized by rock festivals. The difficulty is to relate this experience to the reality of the rock business, whose basis is in records. The tensions in the role of rock in the 1970s were less those between the freedom of art and the demands of commerce than those between lonely strivings in the studio and collective energy on the stage.

Most rock performers begin their career on the assumption that their live shows prove their understanding of the youth audience (such proof supports them in their struggles with record companies for control of the means of record production); recording is simply a technical device for bringing their music to the greatest possible number of potential fans. Many bands, indeed, continue to make music on this basis long after their commercial success has become dependent solely on record sales. The claims to rock greatness of the Stones, the Who, Led Zeppelin and all the other bands who still ply America's huge rock stadiums are rooted in these live shows rather than in their platinum albums, which, at best, simply provide hints and reminders of the *ultimate* Stone or Who or Zeppelin experience—their performance.

For these musicians every post-album tour (which for their record companies is a matter of routine promotion) is a crucial musical test—songs created in studio isolation are now given their chance to draw meaning from the *real* rock relation. But this is an ideal. In practice, bands, especially successful ones, face pressure to recreate the same show forever. There is a contradiction between their own need to change and the crowd's demand for the confirmation of past joys. Bands are faced with a choice: to act out a fixed rock role for the length of their careers, or to retreat into the studio to make music with reference only to their own artistic or commercial concerns. The choice made depends, to a large extent, on the sort of music involved. Rock musicians tend toward a stylistic conservatism—their musical values are rooted in their *past* experience as listeners (they are remarkably uninterested in the music of their peers); in the end their ideological commitments are to *forms* of music.

Howard Becker's dance musicians experienced a conflict between their own criteria of musical excellence and those of their audiences; they resolved this through the creation of a suspicious but supportive musicians' community. Rock performers' references are wider, both socially and musically, and once they move out of a local scene it is not easy for them to give each other effective, exclusive, ideological support. By the 1970s, indeed, the successful musicians' community had become, *de facto*, a community of non-musicians. Fellow rock workers turned out to be business advisers and bodyguards; life on stage became more real, more valuable, more reassuring than life off it. In John Lennon's words:

All that business was awful, it was a fuckin' humiliation. One has to completely humiliate oneself to be what the Beatles were, and that's what I resent. I didn't know, I didn't forsee.

It happened bit by bit, gradually, until this complete craziness is surrounding you, and you're doing exactly what you don't want to do with people you can't stand—the people you hated when you were ten.[15]

All professional entertainers live an unreal life; "the road" is always sealed against the daily cares and concerns of the towns through which it passes. Peter Guralnick describes it this way:

Being on the road today remains a succession of petty annoyances. There are the fans, and there is the myriad of details, from checking out the club's sound system to buying a bus. There are promotions to do for the local PR man, TV shows and interviews and radio appearances. There are sessions sandwiched in between gigs, and old acquaintanceships to be renewed at four in the morning after the show. And then there are the pitfalls of the road, motor accidents, problems in the band, the clubs that combine the selling of drugs and women with their more official dispensation of music and alcohol. Most of all it is a world in which there are no real friendships, where you measure your closeness to fellow entertainers by how long you've both been out there. For the itinerant singer there is only the fraternity of the road; the fact that you embrace a fellow star who stops by the club to see you does not mean anything except that you share a similar background and experience.

But, as Guralnick comments about Bobby Bland,

there is no question that whatever the hazards of the road, they are nothing like the hazards of the real world. Where else could you get people to open doors for you, run errands, take care of your wants? Under what other circumstances could Robert Calvin Bland, black, uneducated, untrained, unskilled, stay in a $40-a-day hotel room, sport fancy diamonds and a big roll, command a small organization of individuals no different in background than himself, who are entirely dependent upon him and his fortunes? It is a sobering thought to consider the alternatives, and one that is not without its effects.[16]

The "effects" in Bobby Bland's case are suspicion and wariness—how long will this last? who can I trust? The effect for the country singers Peter Guralnick describes is a sense of guilt: the values they publicly celebrate are precisely those they don't, privately, live by. The effect for rock singers is a sense of nostalgia, as they end every gig with a rock 'n' roll medley. Rock is music made to celebrate being young and the musicians are always aware, even when their audiences are not, that they are growing older, gig by gig, that these moments are the only ones left that still justify their obsessions.

These days rock stars are rich professionals, in the privileged position of making money while pursuing their own artistic interests. There is, in fact, less conflict between art and commerce in rock than in any other mass medium—the biggest acts have contracts that let them do much as they musically like. (Jimi Hendrix was probably the last superstar to suffer from systematic commercial harassment; he remained sure that jazz, not rock, was the only source of "serious, creative music.") Even in 1974 it was estimated that at least a hundred British rock stars were earning in excess of £100,000 a year: the Moody Blues got around £450,000 for every album they produced, £100,000 from additional publishing royalties, and £1 million from touring. The group's total yearly income was £2 million; Emerson, Lake and Palmer, meanwhile, earned $5 million. Such earnings depended on the mass size of the groups' market; such incomes (and they covered a variety of necessary expenses) were based on the sale of 2 million albums, on concerts grossing at least $30,000 nightly. By the end of the decade the best-selling albums were reaching 10 million consumers and the stars were renegotiating their contracts accordingly. Paul McCartney was reportedly offered $8 million by CBS for American and Canadian rights to three LPs and some Beatles back numbers—the deal assumed 2 million sales as the starting point (he was, simultaneously, being offered £4 million by EMI for rights in the rest of the world). The royalty offer was 22 percent—compare the Beatles original deal with EMI—less than 2 percent for the four of them. (The average in the 1970s was 12 to 15 percent, although as late as 1975 the Jackson Five were reported as being on a 2.7 percent deal at Motown.) Paul Simon was, meanwhile, being offered a $13 million guarantee by WEA, the Who $12 million for American rights alone.

Superstar income is the result of a large number of relatively small purchases (records, concert tickets), and the income of the rock musicians who didn't make it—the majority—was throughout the 1970s extremely small: they were getting the returns from a small number of the same small purchases, and their fixed costs, if nothing like as high as those of the superstars, couldn't fall below the minimum necessary expenditure on equipment and studio time. Indeed, this minimum rose as the public became used to the higher sound standards set by groups which could afford the best facilities, as rock became more capital intensive.

The music industry markets far more products than it sells, and poor musicians are as necessary to the system as rich ones. But if the record companies can more than cover their losses from their wins, the unsuccessful acts involved cannot. It was no comfort to the members of an Unknown Band—struggling along on $50 a week, having to *pay* to get on decent bills as a support—that the members of Fleetwood Mac earned a couple of million dollars a year each (even if their record company was, meanwhile, writing off the un-recouped advance to the Unknown Band against another Fleetwood Mac 10 million seller). Even rock musicians who get recording contracts have to use their advances to pay off debts and many never sell enough records to go beyond that. It is not successful musicians who are "exploited" in this situation, but unsuccessful ones; and at the end of the 1970s there came, with punk (to which I will return), an unsuccessful musicians' revolt.

Commerce is then a serious constraint only at this lower level, for musicians getting into the business, being "broken" by their record companies; and even for these musicians the problem is to build their own audience rather than to preserve their own "creativity." For the traditional rock and boogie bands, successful or not, music, money, and audience are fused in a genial expression of male good fellowship and loyalty and energetic grace—the *status quo* is a way of life as well as a way of music. It took British punk bands, sent around America to sell their records at the end of the 1970s, to reveal the extent to which a commercial rock tour now meant an endless round of radio stations, ignorant deejays, company salesmen to be sweet-talked. Were *these* the people rock music was being made for? Punk songs were about the world (rock songs had been, for years, about rock) and punk musicians now asked the artistic question about the "rock 'n' roll community" that rock stars had been avoiding: What was the *risk* of this music?

# THE MUSICIANS' COMMUNITY

The musicians' world I have been discussing—whether John Lennon's smoking club, Keith Richards's hotel room with "dumb chicks," or Pete Townshend's rock 'n' roll brotherhood—is a man's world. Even a superficial survey of rock reveals the lack of women involved in creative roles: there are few female musicians and virtually no back-room girls—producers, arrangers, engineers (women's only chance here has been as writers). Women did have a place in 1970s rock, but almost always as singers, fronting a performance or record, their musical abilities confused with their visual images and style. Rock ideologues were keen to differentiate their values from those of show business, but their attitudes to women were not much different. The assumption was that women weren't musical.

The male-ness of the world of rock is reflected in its lyrics, with their assertions of male supremacy, narcissism, and self-pity; but, for musicians, what is most significant is women's exclusion from the heart of their lives: exclusion from their friendships and work together as comrade craftsmen in the studio, on the road, in performance. Women's job in rock is still to service their creative men:

> It is 5 A.M. Phil Ochs and David Cohen (Blue) stumble up to the Bleecker apartment, drunk. Alice (Ochs) in the bedroom, sleeping. They sit around, their heads thrown back. There is a knock on the door, Phil gets up to open it. Dylan rushes in, hot and fresh. In the living room he asks Phil to play something. Phil reaches for his guitar and does "The Power and the Glory." David Cohen does a song. Then Dylan plays, for the first time anywhere, "Mr. Tambourine Man." It slaps Phil sober. He sits up and tells Dylan, solemnly, it is without question the greatest song he's ever heard. Alice, awakened by the music, is standing in the hallway, smiling. Breakfast will be ready in a few minutes.[17]

Rock musicians derive their self-esteem from their skills as writers, instrumentalists, performers. Rock intimacy means friendship rather than sexuality and women are excluded from friendship—even their place in the rock audience is played down. The

Great Live Rock Experience is presented as an exclusively male affair, female fans reduced to teeny-boppers, potential groupies. Women musicians obviously have made it—there are a number of female rock stars—but most of them have done it by working within a man-made notion of how women should sound, by becoming "one of the boys."

Why have women been so systematically excluded from rock production? Are the ideological limits set by the musical form itself (the punk question) or by a more diffuse assumption about what music is for, what musicians represent?

The original role of the popular musician was one of a traveler, an observer, moving from place to place to give pleasure, but also to give perspective, to hint at the possibilities beyond the county boundaries. "The road" was central to popular musicians' lives long before their work was marketed as a mass commodity (to blues musicians in the American South, to pub entertainers in nineteenth-century Britain). It carried the mythical force on which Woody Guthrie drew, for political effect, in the 1930s; it is the dominant American metaphor for technological possibility, for political change, for social mobility (just as the car is the most celebrated tool of American leisure).

The resulting sense of abundance, space, and freedom has a B-side—"no roots, no home, no family, loneliness"; and in the 1960s this mythology was fused with that of the great American artist, the literary bohemian, rootless, detached. The result was obvious in the literary-musical cultures of New York and San Francisco. The rock artist took on the role of the beatnik poet—introspective, eccentric, elitist. Bruce Cook describes the beats' love of jazz in these terms:

> It was the illegitimate atmosphere of the jazz milieu, with its overtones of criminality, sex, drugs and violence, that brought them back night after night to spots like Birdland, the Five Spot. . . . There they could dig the soloist, one man against the world, a model for every poet, every artist.[18]

Cook suggests that, in fact, the beats had no sense of jazz as music, little success with their attempts at jazz poetry. But out of the beats came the hippies, and out of jazz came rock—"ur-jazz," accessible, with a heavy beat, easy melodies, simple to perform and appreciate. It was rock that was really beat music. Poetry was once more sung; the old coffeehouse chants were amplified and given mass power; mind and body were fused in volume; all would-be American literary artists were encouraged to choose rock as their means of expression.

Beatnik ideology equated creativity and unconventionality, and understood convention in terms of "roots, home and family." It thus developed a sexual ideology which excluded women from its institutions. The ideology not only detached sexuality itself from the usual terms of commitment, but also dealt with women as the *embodiment* of convention. It was mothers and wives who were taken to personally represent routine living, who sapped their men's creative energy, sought to tie them down, asked the dull questions about food and children and money. Women—this is obvious in many rock lyrics—were a threat, a threat to male independence, a threat to male art. They were physically necessary—"a woman's job is to stay home, cook, clean and look pretty for her man," in Phil Ochs's words—but psychologically, socially, artistically dangerous. (Ochs also believed that the women's movement was a CIA plot designed to undermine the radical left.)

These problems of men and women reflect a wider issue: How do you construct a social life out of an antisocial ideal? And the problem here is the relationship between literary bohemia—aggressively detached from "normal" people's daily routines—and popular music, significant precisely as part of those routines. Traveling musicians had used their detachment from local concerns to comment on them: their music was about their audiences' experiences; it explained communities to themselves through a form of poetic realism. The musicians' social detachment enabled them to judge their listeners' lives, but not to ignore or despise them. Their art was rooted in their audiences' needs, in their music's place in a rhythm of work and leisure. Literary bohemians, by contrast, aimed for separation from the masses. Their art was not made for popular consumption; popular tastes were both ignored and despised. Bohemian art was *essentially* elitist; the bohemian community was confined to the enlightened, to other artists.

Rock ideology since the 1960s has been an uneasy mixture of literary bohemianism and popular music-making, and the unease has focused on the concept of community: Do these musicians represent youth culture in general or a leisure vanguard?

Rock is mass music, the sound of the city, the radio, the recording studio. "The road" is, for rock performers, more often than not the street. Rock means commercial city leisure, the clubs and bars where bohemians mingle with the *lumpenproletariat*, where the bourgeoisie is robbed rather than shocked, where inner city fun is systematically detached from suburban respectability. Music here is not a comment on life but an escape from it, an alternative existence which only the leisure bohemians are reckless enough (or rich enough) to live fully. The old musical relationship has been reversed: it is now the audience that travels, the performers' way of life that is observed.

This is the setting in which artistic exclusiveness has such resonance (the setting for Becker's musicians' hip/square distinctions). Music-making and leisure take on a sense of risk, a demand for commitment, and a separation develops between those who take the risks and stay the course, and those who don't, who take the freeway home before it gets too late. Music is no longer commenting on a community but creating it, offering a sense of inclusion not just to the musicians, bohemian style, but also to the audiences, to all those people hip enough to make the necessary commitment to the music, to assert that it *matters*. The rock community is fragile, an ideological rather than a material structure.

This explains, I think, rock musicians' continued fascination with black music, from gospel and R&B to reggae: black musicians are thought to have a secure way of leisure; the romantic version of racism still has a purchase—blacks as pre-social, at ease with play. In practice, of course, there's been little basis for such naive fancies. One of the most obvious features of the rock community, after twenty-five years of rock 'n' roll and street life, is how poorly racially integrated it is, how much it still reflects the problems of white leisure and white youth, problems to which I will return in chapters 8 and 9.

# CHAPTER 5

# MAKING RECORDS

Historians of American popular music argue that musical innovation has always come from outside the major record companies. "Independent" companies have been the outlet for the expression of new ideas and interests, and only when such ideas have been shown to be popular have the major companies used their financial advantages to take them over, to turn them into new, "safe" products. Innovation, in such an oligopolistic industry, is only possible because technological changes open gaps in existing market control, and if, in the long run, competition means creativity (the more sources of capital, the more chance of musical progress), in the short run, the music business is intensely conservative, more concerned with avoiding loss than risking profit, confirming tastes than disrupting them. Records are made according to what the public is known to want already.

According to this argument, the only people who notice or encourage changing musical demands are entrepreneurs operating outside the existing music business structure. Such "independents" can only make money by creating or servicing new markets and they are, therefore, by necessity, the only real risk-takers, the only real cultural entrepreneurs. As their risks pay off, they are joined by other petty entrepreneurs who are able to compete in this small-scale scene; and there is, for a moment, a burst of musical creativity, industrial innovation. Eventually, though, returns are sufficient to attract the majors and the new practices are routinized, the independents bought out, absorbed, driven out by unfair competition.

Hence the rise and fall of rock 'n' roll in the 1950s, the rise and fall of rock in the 1960s, the rise and fall of British punk at the end of the 1970s. Rudi Blesh and Harriet Janis apply the analysis to ragtime: what began as "folk song," with "a robust, healthy, rural quality," was ruined by "the commerical tunesmiths of Tin Pan Alley"; and this musical development was a direct consequence of the economic moves by which song publishers were centralized in New York and took control of the music market. Large companies used their capital to squeeze out small ones; they increased the required costs of promotion and plugging, they dominated sales by discounting, they made exclusive deals with distributors, tied themselves in with new chain stores.

This is the American version of the European critique of mass culture. It is no longer music as commodity that matters, but music as oligopolistic commodity. The ideal music world is one in which musicians' and consumers' needs are met through the pure expression of supply and demand, by the hidden hand of perfect competition. Creativity is sapped not by profit seeking, but by big profit seeking, by the concentration into too few hands of the means of musical expression. The problem is not art versus commerce but big business versus small business; and the heroes of this version of musical history are not the musicians but the entrepreneurs, from ragtime publisher John Stork to Ahmet Ertegun to Sam Phillips to Tom Donahue and Bill Graham to Malcolm McLaren and Tony Wilson. These men may have exploited their musicians (their black musicians, in particular), but they exploited them with more charm and love than the corporate bureaucrats who took them over; and they were, at least, on music's side.

The most systematic analysis of rock from this perspective is Steve Chapple and Reebee Garofalo's *Rock 'n' Roll Is Here to Pay*. Their concern is "the co-optation of rock." They argue that rock's development as a "cultural commodity within a consumer economy

weakened any of the explicit anti-materialist content of the music."
Rock 'n' roll was, to begin with, created independently of the industry, which sold it as a commodity, but as sales rose this distinction
broke down: "the process of selling records inherently coopted both
music and musicians by commoditizing them." The suggestion is
that musicians can be placed in two groups—"those who want to
make it more than anything else, and those who care more about
their music than they do for money and adulation"—and that by the
mid-1970s the former had taken rock over from the latter.

I don't believe that pitting art versus business like this actually
helps us in analyzing a mass culture like rock. It is precisely because
music, money, and adulation *can't* be separated—by musicians or
audiences—that rock is so important. Rock fans and rock performers alike want their music to be powerful, to work as music *and* commodity. To reduce pop history to the struggles of musician (or small
businessmen) heroes and corporate clowns is to ignore the critical
issue: the music industry's strategies of market control (which certainly have their consequences for popular music) have been developed precisely because the market is one they can't control. The
usual suggestion is that this problem is solved cyclically: record
companies occasionally respond to the market demands revealed by
the independents' activities, but normally they manipulate the market, limit the choices available. What this doesn't account for is popular taste: on one hand, it seems, the public is always responsive to
innovations; on the other hand, however, it is also always hood-
winked by hacks. The resulting picture is of an industry sitting massively on top of public taste until unsatisfied needs have built up
such a pressure that they burst out, to be mopped up by independent entrepreneurs until they are capped, once more, by the corporations. But the questions are: Where do such new demands come
from? Why is market control mostly effective, sometimes not? Does
the public get what it wants? Always? Sometimes? Ever? The point
I want to argue in this chapter is that the commercial process
through which rock is produced is essentially *contradictory*.

The classical music publisher Ernst Roth once suggested that
what distinguished pop publishers from himself was not the pursuit
of profit as such but rather the problems involved in that pursuit:
whereas his task was "to make the public like what his composers
produce," the pop publisher's task was to make his composers produce what the public likes. In the words of Eddie Rogers: "My job

is to sell entertainment to the public. . . . I am no different to the man who sells soap or insurance. I don't tell the public what to like, I gave them what they want."

"Giving the public what it wants," the classic huckster's phrase, describes, in fact, a complicated relationship between "supply" and "demand." The music industry can be described (as it has been by Paul Hirsch) as a production cycle in which a large number of inputs (musicians, songs, records) pass through a "filtering process" that exludes all but a small number of outputs (successful musicians, songs, records) from ever even reaching the public. What the public gets, then, depends on the decisions of a series of "gatekeepers." A&R men at record companies decide which musicians to record, which records to issue and promote; agents and concert promoters decide which performers to present live; music journalists decide which acts to report; radio station program directors and disc jockeys decide which records to broadcast; record store owners decide which products to stock. In this process the emphasis on "public choice" seems spurious. The gatekeepers make the decisions that matter and the public's own options are limited by these decisions—all people can "want" is what they can get.

Public demand is, nonetheless, the organizing *idea* for the record industry. The gatekeepers themselves make their decisions on the basis of what they think the public will want, and they continue to argue that in the pop business music is made to meet demand: what the public consumes determines what gets produced. From this perspective the most significant "gatekeeper" is the consumer. In the words of record company boss Dick Leahy:

> The first essential factor, of course, is selection of product. I hope we know what records to reject. We don't go picking up products just for the sake of it—we always ask first "who is going to buy it?" If we can't answer that question we don't release the record.[1]

Record company wisdom is that "the only certain factor in marketing records is the uncertainty," and it has always been the object of record companies to defy the uncertainties of mass taste, to produce certain hits. The issue here is not market manipulation but market control. I argued in chapter 3 that mass culture can't be understood in terms of "passive consumption" and I'll return to this problem later. My point here is that the defining characteristic of the record industry is not the pursuit of profit as such but the problems of profit-making given the particularly "active" qualities of music and (as I suggested in chapter 4) musicians. Rock isn't just any commodity. It is music aimed at a youth market; and in analyzing how it makes money, this is where we must begin.

## MANAGING THE MARKET

The youth market wasn't specifically important for the music business until the 1950s, long after it had learned to cope with the reorganization of pop that had begun with the gramophone in 1899. The most significant technological development for the record business after the war made its effect negatively: television took over from radio as the basic form of home entertainment, leaving radio to specialize in its appeal. One of the most important "special" markets turned out to be teenagers and, with the simultaneous development of LPs, adults ceased to buy singles, the raw material of music radio shows. The day-to-day attentions of record companies became almost entirely focused on the young.

The old pop musicians were not slow to express their concern with the results. In Britain, singer Harry Roy complained that "when *we* sang a song we really meant it. We learned the business. It took me years, when I was in my brother's band, just to learn how to walk to the stand and take a bow. The kids of today couldn't care less about people who are artists." Frank Sinatra, more succinctly, called rock 'n' roll "the most brutal, ugly, desperate, vicious form of expression it has been my misfortune to hear." Alec Wilder just complained that rock had destroyed the "mature sensibilities" of American songwriters.

The music business was founded in the nineteenth century as a writing and publishing business, and the traumatic effects on it of broadcasting and recording were realized, for the most part, by the 1930s. Tin Pan Alley had ended up benefiting from radio. Its writers provided material for the bands and singers who were reaching an unprecedented mass audience, and the publishers' copyright organization, ASCAP, could even exercise control over *how* its members' material should sound—the emphasis in any arrangement had to be on the melody. But the coincidence of interests between song publishers and radio stations didn't survive the 1930s, and in response to an ASCAP demand for higher performance fees the radio stations created their own publishers' organization, BMI, which began work in 1940. The ASCAP/BMI division drew attention to the increasing divergence between Tin Pan Alley's material and the sorts of songs (country songs, blues) that more and more radio programmers wanted. The switch of radio and record company attention to youth reinforced this division: rock 'n' roll was, by definition, BMI music (and it is now clear that the payola investigations of the late 1950s were an attack on rock 'n' roll radio that was inspired by ASCAP interests).

In Britain the publishing establishment was similarly worried. Rock 'n' roll was heard as a new and dangerous expression of an old trend: the "Americanization" of British pop. The Song Writers' Guild sourly noted that "of course, if you plug American music there is bound to be a demand for it," and demanded a quota on foreign songs and records played on the radio: "only so will it be possible to arrest the persistent foreign infiltrations which have for some years strongly and undesirably influenced every department of popular music in this country." The secretary of the Guild argued that Elvis Presley's records were only bought because teenagers sought to follow fashion, not because they really liked them: "If the BBC started plugging quality songs for a change I'm sure the kids would go for them." As it was, deejays had too much power: "If we have to have a high proportion of American hits in our popular music diet, then it would be refreshing if British artists were allowed to make their own individual interpretations of these imported tunes." Such arguments were in vain. The teenage market already existed and record companies, British and American alike, were more interested in meeting its needs than those of aging songwriters.

The economic importance of teenage taste had first struck the independent record companies that serviced the black music market in the early 1950s. Jerry Wexler, for example, remembers that white youth first started buying Atlantic records in the Carolinas and along the eastern seaboard. The company referred to these surprise sellers as "beach records"—white teenagers were picking up on black sounds as they gathered on beaches to party and tuned their radios in to the best dance music; and at the local level, particularly in the South, entrepreneurs noticed that it was black records that teenagers were buying and requesting, black music that they were watching and imitating for themselves. The risk taken by responsive deejays and retailers (and the record companies that began to service them) was to *focus* on this market, to discard their non-youth, non-rock 'n' roll interests; but it was only such exclusive concentration that revealed the market's extent, and as the market grew, so did the number of rock 'n' roll entrepreneurs, until it became difficult to separate cause and effect. Denisoff quotes Mitch Miller's complaint about what was happening to radio (Miller was then head of A&R for CBS):

> You carefully built yourselves into the monarchs of radio then you went and abdicated your programming to the 8 to 14 year olds, to the preshave crowd that makes up 12 percent of the country's population and zero percent of its buying power— once you eliminated ponytail ribbons, popsicles and peanut brittle. Youth must be served—but how about some music for the rest of us?
>
> Does the demand for the record come because you play it first, or do the kids demand it because they heard it first on Top 40? If Top 40 is an election, will somebody please blow a whistle for the Honest Ballot Association. . . .[2]

Miller's sarcasm was pointed, but his target was wrong. Teenagers' buying power may have been limited, but it was limited precisely to teenage goods like records, and radio stations that focused on youth got better ratings and more advertisers than they had had when trying to compete with television for the adult market. Miller was complaining about a situation that was reflected by radio, not caused by it. The problem was the postwar transformation of American leisure habits, and the postwar baby boom: the U.S. birthrate rose 65 percent between 1945 and 1947, and the population of thirteen-to-thirty-year-olds increased every year until the end of the 1970s, producing a bulge of young citizen-consumers working their way into the marketplace.

Miller's unstated concern was his company's record sales. The majors' share of the bestselling singles halved between 1955 and 1958 (the independents' share remained high until the mid-1960s); and in the end CBS, like everyone else, did have to respond to teenage taste, did have to add a rock 'n' roll star or two to the company roster, did have to learn how this new market worked and how it could be reached and influenced. By 1958 there was a new network of sales devices—top forty radio stations, teen-aimed record racks, teen-beat magazines, teenage television programs and films (the cinema, like radio, had to specialize in the face of television, and had also gone for the youth market: "Rock Around the Clock" made its national impact via *Blackboard Jungle*—Elvis was promoted via Hollywood almost from the beginning of his RCA career).

"It was during this time," writes Dick Clark about the late 1950s, when he was the youthful host of the TV program *American Bandstand*, "that I decided to go into the record business. I got into talent management, music publishing, record pressing, label making, distribution, domestic and foreign rights, motion pictures, show promotion and teenage merchandise."

The rise of teenage music involved, then, a variety of new money-making opportunities, but it did not affect the underlying structure of the music business: by the end of the 1950s, the exploitation of the youth market meant simply an old form—the standard pop song—with a new content—teenage angst. This was particularly obvious in Britain, which had no black music market and little youth radio. There had been some shift in market demand, a move to American records (to ensure a continuing flow of American product, EMI bought the American company Capitol in 1955), but the dominant British companies, EMI and Decca, remained dominant, marketing their own rock 'n' rollers (Cliff Richard, Tommy Steele) and continuing to share at least three-quarters of the hits.

It was because of rock 'n' roll's lack of real impact on the record business that skiffle, the British version of American folk-blues, was so important for the development of a British youth market. It was skiffle, an acoustic music played on cheap and homemade instruments, that gave young British musicians the chance to develop their own ideas (which soon reverted to rock 'n' roll or R&B) outside the framework of the industry; skiffle gave them the folk confidence to play without polish, without show business, without advice, without capital. The most immediately noticeable thing about the Beatles, when they eventually arrived in the hit parade (and Lennon and McCartney had begun their musical lives in skiffle groups) was their detachment from Tin Pan Alley—they wrote their own songs.

And they signed with EMI. All the British groups in the "beat

boom" were signed to major companies—in 1963–1964 Decca and
EMI produced nearly 80 percent of Britain's best sellers. In industry terms not much seemed new (except in the radio response, with
the first broadcast in 1964 from the pirate station Radio Caroline).
And *Retail Business*'s special issue on records that year made two
firm predictions: the volatility of the teenage market would continue—"even the Beatles' expectation of life 'at the top of the pops'
should be measured in months not years"; and stereo records, then
commanding about 12 percent of the British market, would not increase their sales—"the future of stereo would seem to be limited
by the fact that its technical advantages can only be fully realised
in the case of classical music. . . . There are important marketing
considerations which make it unsuitable for the pops market."

Two years later *Retail Business* recorded the arrival in the market of a cheap stereo pickup and the continued rise of LP sales—
"this may be the most profitable section of the market"; in 1968,
for the first time, as many LPs were sold as 45s; by 1969 all records
were manufactured in stereo. In each of these developments Britain
was following the market lead of the USA, where, by 1969, stereo
LPs accounted for 80 percent of the value of record sales.

In Britain, cheap stereo was the technological development and
pirate radio (open, via payola, to small record companies) the promotional development that made it possible for "independents"
(small, single-label record companies) to compete with the "majors,"
Decca and EMI, Pye and Philips—by 1970 they accounted for 20
percent of the year's top ten hits. But direct competition was also
coming now from the Americans. In 1964 CBS took over Oriole and
its distribution network. RCA was already operating on its own and,
at the end of the decade, these two companies were joined by WEA.
Britain, having begun the rock revolution, was beginning to suffer
its consequences.

The most important effect of the Beatles' success was to spread
rock appeal from its working-class teenage base. In Britain the general popularity of the Beatles and the Stones, the development of
cheap stereo, the opening of pirate radio, and a new college- and
club-performing circuit meant the emergence of a youth market that
the established record companies did not immediately understand.
These young people generated their own enterprises, their own
clubs and venues, their own music. By 1968 the commercial viabil-
ity of "progressive" rock was obvious. There emerged, too, a new

breed of independent record producers and management companies, concert promoters and salesmen (many of them had begun as "entertainment officers" at college—this became the new starting point for a record business career). In 1968 EMI launched its own "progressive" label, Harvest, which was followed in the next couple of years by Philips's Vertigo, Pye's Dawn, Decca's Nova and RCA's Neon. These labels worked distribution deals with the new independent producers and none of them was particularly profitable; only Vertigo and Harvest still survive.

A parallel development was the creation by successful musicians of their own labels. Apple was formed by the Beatles in 1968 "to open the way to artistic fulfillment for writers, musicians, singers and painters who have hitherto been unable to find acceptance in the commercial world." The Moody Blues followed a year later with the similarly idealist Threshold. Neither of these labels lasted, however, as much more than outlets for the stars themselves, and the independent British companies that were successfully established in the late 1960s—Island, Chrysalis, Charisma—were extensions of management and production companies, their independence based on financial rather than ideological considerations, their success based on their response to a new market rather than a new music. As David Betteridge, then managing director of Island, puts it:

> There was a new intelligent rock—I don't mean that in any cynical way—there was a college circuit being built and a new audience was emerging. And we were running in tandem, supplying their needs. We were the vehicle for them so it all just clicked together. [3]

Or, in the words of Rohan O'Rahilly, boss of Radio Caroline, "Youth was busting out all over. There was a lot of money to be made."

The new labels reached the new market through new promotional and distributional forms—concentrating on LPs rather than singles, putting lyrics on the sleeves and selling sound quality, using college theaters rather than dance halls, plugging the rock rather than pop programs on radio (the pirate ships were silenced in 1967 and the BBC started Radio 1, its own version of a Top 40 station), and using mail-order sellers like Virgin Records. These moves came at the end of the record-making process; they related directly to the audience. Every town and province had its hip promoters and pubs, its festivals and head shops. In London there was a flowering of hip studios and record sellers, "underground" clubs and magazines. "Progressive" rock was institutionalized, and *Rolling Stone* proclaimed a "new community."

Britain's hippie moves were conscious imitations of what was happening in America, but the shake-up of the U.S. music business also began with the Beatles, who, like Elvis, arrived in the charts as "outsiders" and revealed a new sort of music market. The late 1950s consolidation of rock 'n' roll into teenage pop had limited its audience in both age and class—record sales declined, indeed—and the Beatles were originally sold to America as a teenage pop band— they were broken by Ed Sullivan and the Top 40 airwaves. But, as in Britain, the Beatles also appealed, in ways the record companies failed to predict, to a non-teenage market, to a suburban, student audience, to people who thought they had grown out of rock 'n' roll, who had escaped from *Bandstand* banalities to folk clubs and concert halls—and who now remembered how much they liked to dance.

It was, again, at the local level that the implications of the new rock 'n' roll taste were worked out. The 1960s youth culture was a leisure culture, first expressed in new patterns of consumption, and radio programmers were first to pick up on the commercial possibilities of youth's new habits (their exclusive focus on this market was made possible by the AM/FM split). They were quickly joined by a variety of other musical entrepreneurs—shopkeepers, club owners, festival organizers, concert promoters—all using the new "underground" institutions, its radio programs and newspapers, as the means of new promotional techniques. And if the Monterey Festival symbolized the entrance of the major companies into this scene (the Festival stars were hastily signed up), its aftermath revealed its novelty: rock musicians were not absorbed into traditional ways of star-making but became new sorts of idols. Their music was marketed as an artistic commodity; their dealings with their record companies were kid-gloved (mediated through the "company freak"); their audiences couldn't be pushed around the stage set of *Bandstand* but had to be controlled through the musicians themselves. The shift of record company attitudes was most obvious in the treatment of the Beach Boys, the most important American rock group of the 1960s. Their pre-Beatles approach to music-making prefigured much that was to come: the Beach Boys didn't only write their own songs, they also produced their own records, used their own studios. But for most of their time on Capitol they were treated, packaged, and sold as a teenage party band; they only became "artists" when they moved to Warner Brothers, after the rock revolution was won.

This "revolution" was explicitly about creativity and competition. Rock ideology rested on the concept of choice—artist choice, consumer choice—and choice was, supposedly, guaranteed by the fact that there were more people, younger people, involved in the record business than ever before. This opening up of the record industry did not, though, have the expected effects. By the end of the 1960s record companies had discovered that there was far more money to be made out of rock music than out of other forms of pop. The Woodstock Festival of 1969 was, indeed, a symbol of the vast size not just of the rock "community" but also of the rock market. The stars involved made four- and five-figure demands for appearance fees that far exceeded anything they had earned previously but now became the rock concert norm, and the major record companies began to use their superior capital resources to sign, record, promote, and control all successful rock acts. American companies invaded Britain, for example, using it less as a market than as a source of talent; and the success of Cream and Jimi Hendrix in the huge, unsophisticated American teenage market confirmed that rock was a less problematic commodity than its original ideologues had claimed. A new sort of relationship was forged between the established record companies and the "independent" rock entrepreneurs. By the end of the 1970s record production involved buying and selling a series of specific services (services offered by "independent" managers and lawyers, radio and concert consultants, promoters and publicists, security firms and limo drivers, studio and stage equipment designers, etc.). The "co-optation of rock" had involved not "commoditization" but professionalization, as all these rock specialists demanded precise efficiency from each other.

For many rock fans the rise of the rock professionals has been grating. The disillusion is well captured by Stephen Holden's novel *Triple Platinum,* an insider's account of the unpleasantness of record business personnel, their sin being not so much greed as torpidity.

Colin MacInnes once argued that

> ever since the days of ancient Egypt and beyond, popular arts have always been sponsored, initially at any rate, by loud-

mouthed hucksters with artful patter and a big drum: in other
words by impresarios obsessed by the whole enterprise of promotion, themselves emotionally involved in the adventure
whatever their other motives may have been. [4]

The trouble now is that the hucksters have become bureaucrats;
they're involved in rock not as an adventure but as a career. This
development reflects the contradictions of rock-as-commodity, contradictions that revolve around the couplet innovation/control, or,
in economic terms, maximum profit/minimum loss. If the huckster
represented the cultural capitalist as risk-taker, the bureaucrat represents the cultural capitalist as risk-avoider. The paradox is that
while most record business practices are designed to avoid loss by
simply and efficiently servicing established markets ("giving the
public what the public already wants"), the biggest profits come precisely at the moments and from those acts which defy normal market
wisdom. If the successful hucksters, in consolidating their gambles,
have to become bureaucrats, so the dullest bureacrats yearn, for all
sorts of reasons, to hustle.

Music can never be *just* a product (an exchange value), even in
its rawest commodity form; the artistic value of records has an un-
avoidable complicating effect on their production. The use value of
cultural goods (the reason why people buy them) depends on aesthetic preferences; the demand for them is much less manageable
than for more straightforwardly ultilitarian goods—the culture industry has to make available a far greater number of goods than are
eventually sold. Of the four to five thousand LPs that are issued every year, for example, only about 10 percent make money, and only
another 10 percent cover their own costs (there are similar statistics
in book publishing, an analogous culture industry). Because record
companies don't sell most of the titles they release, they must, instead, maximize the profits on the records that do sell, minimize the
losses on those that don't—hence the critical status of the rock
"risk."

The music business capital investment per item is actually comparatively small (compared with the costs of moviemaking, for example). Record company costs relate, rather, to the maintenance of
an "infrastructure"—pressing plants, recording studios, A&R departments, and so on. The outlays on these have to be covered continuously (whatever the cost of making any particular record) and

record companies try, indeed, to exploit their fixed capital to the fullest—to operate their pressing plants without slack, to use studios twenty-four hours a day, to keep their sales teams permanently busy. Most of this energy is expended on records that don't pay for themselves, but the records that do well cover their own costs many times over *and so* cover all these general costs, too. The record company risk is not that any particular record won't sell but that *none* of their releases will hit; the record company problem is that the sales needed depend on competitive marketing mechanisms that the record makers don't, themselves, completely control. It is this marketing problem that sets up the "filtering process" designed to ensure that companies *respond* efficiently to the market demands they can't manipulate directly.

There is, again, an obvious comparison here with book publishers: both record and book publishing companies depend for the income that covers their long-term costs on the sales of a small number of best-sellers whose moment of popularity is usually brief; both industries have developed strategies to maximize these sales, have learned how to strike when a product is "hot," how to cut the losses when it is cold. The record industry's filters are, in other words, a way of handling built-in problems of overproduction—record companies always have too many products on hand, always need ways of focusing their attention on the potential hits. It is in this context that we have to examine the work of the music industry's gatekeepers. The three crucial decisions are who records, what is recorded, and which records reach the public.

## DECIDING WHO RECORDS

A&R stands for "artist and repertoire." An A&R man (there are still very few A&R women) is responsible for what music goes out on a company's label—for signing artists to the label, for keeping them there (or dismissing them), and for the records that are issued in their names. It is the A&R men who, like football managers, have to carry the can for failure; and their job, like football management, requires diverse skills.

A large part of an A&R man's time (and that of his field staff) is taken up with watching and listening to unknown acts, assessing their potential—"a groupie with a checkbook" is one self-description. But this is only one form of talent-spotting. Another is poaching—picking up an act when its contract with a rival company runs out. There are various reasons for doing this. Sometimes the hope is to revitalize a fading career; sometimes the move involves a complete change of musical direction; sometimes the new company simply offers an act greater freedom to carry on doing what it's doing, in the belief that it has yet to reach its maximum market—in these deals an A&R department is offering sympathy as well as money. At a more cynical level a company might simply outbid its rivals for a known successful act; the decision is based on a straight cash calculation: What is the act's earning power? What can we afford to offer? These signings are the equivalent of trades in professional sports—even with the biggest stars, judgments have to be made continually about future playing potential. And A&R men are, equally, in the business of selling their acts: "It's a good business," in Jerry Wexler's words, "selling artists that are finished—before the other companies find out they're finished." Musicians are treated as property, each with a price, a measurable value that can be exploited, increased, realized in the marketplace. Experienced artists know just how such evaluation works. Dick Clark remembers that Tony Bennett "would call me to tell me his contract was coming up for renewal and that he needed a booking on *Bandstand* to boost his record sales."

A&R men don't just judge acts, they've also got to be able to spot records. There are foreign catalogues to go through—is a British record, for which a licensing deal is available, likely to be an American success? There are the possibilities of an astute rerelease from the back catalogue—there's less money lost if an oldie flops and the profits on a successful rerelease are greater; going through back-numbers is part of A&R routine. Most importantly, there are tape and record deals offered by "independent" producers—are they worth it?

Even in 1970 Paul Hirsch estimated that there were as many independent producers as A&R men in America—they acted as a safety net for the business. By independent producers he meant non-company employees who found artists and recorded them themselves and sold or leased the resulting tapes to the record companies; independent tape deals became even more important in the 1970s as more and more record companies realized that tapes could reduce the costs and risks of their own A&R departments. Under leasing agreements (which are now the usual deal) a producer gives his tape to a record company to manufacture and distribute in exchange for a percentage of the returns from any resulting record sales. If such leased records are successful the record company has to pay a higher royalty on each copy sold than if it had signed and recorded the act directly (there's the additional cut now to the independent producer), but if the record flops it is a cheap deal—the company is spared the production costs. This is a particularly attractive way of avoiding risks in an uncertain market or with types of music a company is not used to organizing or selling (like disco and punk in their initial forms). And it is, simultaneously, a way back into the rock adventure for A&R men bored with company security—most successful company men are, eventually, tempted to go it alone (often financed initially by their ex-company in return for the first licensing option—the notion of "independence" in these circumstances is not as straightforward as it sounds).

All A&R decisions are basically financial and the calculations have to be precisely made. Companies don't just sign a group and leave them to get on with it; they weigh the necessary investment against the possible returns. There are obvious questions to be asked: How ready is the act to record? How much rehearsal time does it need? What advance should it get for equipment? What recording costs are necessary? How much help should the company give with organizing gigs and tours and publicity? How big should its advertising budget be?

The answers depend on one simple consideration: How much is the act going to earn? And this is where the problems start. Not only may companies calculate this incorrectly, but they can't avoid splitting their acts into potential earning divisions—just as in book publishing, a potential best-seller (a judgment made in advance) gets more investment that an artist with supposed "specialist" or "minor league" appeal. The aim is a successful career, and what is being judged is the possible longevity of musicians' appeal—"is the group a redwood or a Dutch elm?" as a CBS boss put it. Minor league musicians inevitably feel neglected and this becomes one of the major causes of transfer deals—a minor league act with one company hopes to be treated as major league with another (thus Gladys Knight and the Pips went from Motown to Buddah). In this context competition between record companies is obviously unequal—some have much more capital to risk than others, some can take a much longer-term view of career-building, some can even deliberately take on "uncommercial" acts to give their label "a well-rounded image" (a WEA ploy). Small companies, by contrast, have to pursue returns from every record they release, and their strategy is to develop a specific identity and only sign acts that match it. Motown did this as a soul label in the 1960s. Partly inspired by its example, Island followed suit as a progressive rock label—the company's aim was to build up an audience that trusted the logo and would listen sympathetically to *any* act associated with it. This was also the approach of progressive punk labels like Factory and Rough Trade at the end of the 1970s.

An artist is bound to a record company by a contract that demands so much "product" per year. The A&R department has to ensure that the terms of the contract are met, and the A&R man's task at all record companies is to translate the talent he's signed into a saleable product. "Clive Davis," says Janis Ian of her days at CBS, "didn't believe in an album that was a personal statement unless it had a single on it"—unless, in other words, it had a track on it that had some chance of getting radio and jukebox play. Mary Martin, at WEA, comments similarly:

> I really believe that the artist's responsibility to the record company is delivering the best possible product, and by *best* I mean *accessible* to the air waves for the media within the talent's perspective. Not all this self-indulgent bullshit that's being written to mesmerise little teenagers' minds. That's a lot of bull. Commerciality should be truly borne in mind.[5]

But there's no way to force a musician to make music, and certainly no way to force a musician to make good (or commerical) music (or to perform well, although live albums are the usual solution to lack of inspiration). Enforcing a contract means keeping everyone happy: keeping the costs down and the spirits up; preventing freakouts and piss-abouts; papering over group cracks; having the musicians on the road when they should be on the road, in the studio when they should be in the studio; putting them through the "artist development" department; turning them into good pros. Most A&R departments now assume that this job is impossible unless the group has its own efficient management.

The manager's primary task is to win his client the highest possible income, and if the job varies as the client's career develops—from the early stages of getting an act known to the final stage of protecting a star from exploitation—the basic concern is always to organize finances, to negotiate the best deals. The relative power of the two sides in the record company/musician relationship depends on the popularity of the act and on the state of its contract; when the time comes for contract renewal, for example, a successful act can use the competition for its services to improve both its financial returns and its musical control. The role of mediator works both ways, though. A&M dropped the Sex Pistols, despite the advance they'd just been paid, because the A&R department realized that it wouldn't be able to work with manager Malcolm McLaren. The manager, in other words, is not just the representative of the musicians' own interests, but also guarantees that they will be, in record company terms, "reasonable."

The earliest involvement of a manager with an act is often, in fact, as a banker, a source of the capital that enables a group's members to buy their equipment, to support themselves while they rehearse. The usual financial arrangement is that the manager gets a percentage (20 to 25 percent most commonly) of all his clients' earnings; and a group can then be as much an investment for the manager as for the record company. Tony Stratton-Smith, manager of Lindisfarne, Genesis, Bell 'n' Arc, and Van Der Graaf Generator in the early 1970s, comments:

> All our bands are on a wage or a retainer, whatever you want to call it. The reason for this is that in the early days their earnings are very uneven and sometimes they'll have a good week, sometimes they'll have a bad week, and I feel that a minimum amount of security anyway is necessary for a band to . . . remain really objective about the important things, the important things being their performance and their writing, and as long as they can pay the rent and live and all this sort of thing every week they're more likely to work well. It's the old thing about contented cows giving the best milk. Therefore you've got to be prepared, on our method anyway, to run a band on a deficit for quite a long time.[6]

Most managers are also involved in the creation of the "product" itself. They see their role as showmen: their task is to ensure the overall impact of their clients, to organize the image that will best sell them. This is agent Frank Barsalona's account of Dee Anthony, the most successful rock manager of the mid-1970s (with Humble Pie, and Peter Frampton):

> The main reason that Dee is so good is that he does what a lot of the young managers don't do. In the old days, when an act played clubs, you helped them put together an act with a strong opening and hills and valleys. You constructed an act for visual effectiveness, for emotional appeal and all of those things. The young managers today have never been involved in those things. They don't know about putting together an act. So, it's by trial and error. And it's during the trial and error period that a lot of acts get lost. Dee works with his acts and moulds their shows. Humble Pie, for instance. The first night they played in America, we went out to see them in Detroit; the show was all wrong. We had a meeting the next morning with Humble Pie and we changed the whole show around. That night, they barely got any applause. The next night they got two encores. Dee can instill incredible confidence in his acts. He will huddle with the group before the show like Knute Rockne. It seems funny, but it works. His acts really believe they're stars before they really are. And Dee believes it too.[7]

The implications of this description are that rock acts and their managers work as a team, with a mutual interest in success, but in practice the manager/client relationship can be the focus of many of the contradictions of rock-as-commodity. Musicians may decide that their managers are not good enough at getting business (this happens to managers who begin as bands' non-playing friends or local acquaintances and then can't cope with increasing national success). A manager may decide, alternatively, that the musicians don't fit into his business plans; arguments begin not just about money but also about music and image. This is most likely to happen when an experienced show-biz manager takes on a new, inexperienced band. There is often bitter argument, for example, over who made a successful band what it is.

In 1974 Clifford Davis, by then the ex-manager of Fleetwood Mac, disputed the musicians' right to the band's name and began promoting a quite new version of the group. "I want to get this out of the public's mind, as far as the band being Mick Fleetwood's

band. This band is my band. This band has always been my band."
Davis soon lost his "ownership" of the Fleetwood Mac name, but
in the 1970s many successful manager/producers did put groups together to realize their own rock visions and did legally succeed in
preventing their musicians from making any independent moves.

The combination of management and record producing roles is
always a source of potential conflict and the most bitter record com-
pany/musician disputes (at Motown in the 1970s, for example) oc-
cur when the record company also acts as management. The Motown
arguments arose precisely because when Berry Gordy signed up his
relatively unknown acts in the early 1960s, he also signed them to
elaborate management deals. Motown's paternalistic responsibility
for its acts' songs, sounds, appearances, clothes, dance routines, and
work schedules was certainly effective, but when Motown musicians
became successful (and compared their arrangements with those of
other stars) they realized that their contracts were extraordinarily restrictive in terms of both money and artistic control. Motown musicians didn't have independent managers to help them dispute
these terms—and a significant number of acts departed from the label as a result.

In rock, such record company/management tie-ups are less
common, but similar problems have arisen in the widespread man-
agement/production schemes (when the manager is, simultaneously,
his clients' independent producer, recording their music himself and
leasing the tapes to a record company directly). The most obvious
example of such problems in the 1970s was the lengthy dispute between Bruce Springsteen and manager Mike Appel. Such wrangling
is not welcomed by record companies—because of Springsteen's
fight with his manager, CBS was deprived of new Springsteen products just at the moment when he had become "hot."

Partly because of such problems, partly because of the rise of
the rock superstar, there has developed now a form of "professional" rock management which fits neither the amateur nor the show-
biz pattern. Record companies during the 1970s came to believe
that the most efficient form of artist exploitation meant not the best
financial deal they could put over some innocent, badly advised,
poorly represented musician, but involved, rather, high royalties
and a considerable measure of artist control in return for guaranteed
delivery and promotion of product. Record companies wanted acts
that would behave responsibly in the studio, cooperate on the road,

sweet-talk local deejays and shopkeepers, and do all this according to the record companies' master sales plans. Such cooperation depends on a "professional" manager, someone without delusions of his own grandeur, someone whose services can be precisely defined—the typical 1970s rock manager was a lawyer, not a showman. If, in the 1950s, it was obvious that Elvis Presley worked *for* Colonel Tom Parker, his manager, by the end of the 1970s rock's superstars were, equally obviously, employing managers (or management companies) to work *for* them.

The change reflected the increasing power that rock musicians had in their dealings with the record companies. The show-biz recipe for rock success is "sufficient talent, efficient management, and an enterprising record company," and the central ingredient in this recipe is indeed the company. The company makes its equipment available to musicians to turn their music into saleable mass commodities, and the resulting arrangement can be described simply. "The artist signs directly with the record company for the purpose of making records. The record company pays all the recording costs and pays the artist an appropriate royalty on the records sold."

But the record company does not just act as the record publisher. The standard recording contract makes it clear that record companies, who are the legal owners of the finished product, the physical recording, expect to exercise the rights of their ownership, controlling what music is issued, how it is produced, when it is released. Companies may decide what songs will be on a record, in what order, with what packaging; they are at liberty "to determine arrangements, accompaniments, etc."; they can organize an act's performing schedule, as an aspect of record promotion. Companies have the final power to decide whether a song or sound is of sufficient quality to meet the artists' contractual obligations—they are thus able to prevent them from recording elsewhere.

The standard contract begins: "We hereby employ you to render personal services for us or in our behalf for the purpose of recording and making phonograph records." But if recording artists are providing a service, they are not (like session musicians or the people who pack the discs) paid for it by the hour. The recording artists have a stake in the finished product; their payment derives from a proportion of the profit made on every record sold. On signing with a record company, musicians get a lump sum advance against their future royalties, and this advance and the costs of their records' production have to be met before further royalty payments are due. The risk for the record company is that a record may not sell well enough to cover its initial investment. The reality for many musicians is that the value of their contract is deceptive: many of the costs of record-making—the studio charges, for instance—are deducted exclusively from artists' royalties, even though it was the record company that organized the session, put the money down.

On paper, then, the record companies hold the power (a power which they obviously exercised in their treatment of, say, rock 'n' roll in the 1950s). In the 1970s, though, these companies' intensive competition for the services of rock superstars (the apparently *guaranteed* best-sellers) gave these stars unprecedented power to write their own contracts—power that reflected both the ideology of rock (the demand for artistic control) and its mass sales.

There was a parallel development in book publishing, where the promotion of potential best-sellers on television—as in the case of Jacqueline Susann—both intensified the competition for book rights and vastly increased the influence of the authors' representatives, their agents (whose role resembled that of musicians' managers). Again, the emphasis was on professionalism: publishers began to expect their authors to go on the road, to do the rounds of the TV talkshows and the in-shop book signings. In both book and record publishing it became increasingly difficult to decide where "creativity" stopped and marketing began. The rock culture assumption that the relationship between record-company-as-capitalist and musician-as-artist is essentially *exploitative* became more and more difficult to maintain.

# DECIDING WHAT IS RECORDED

Music becomes commodity in the recording studio, and it is here that we can see most clearly that rock is not a matter of art *versus* business. All mass music reflects a combination of artistic and commercial impulses; no rock musician can make a simple choice between true expression and false sales, and the varieties of musics now available as "rock" reflect the varieties of ways in which commercial and artistic impulses can interact and coexist.

Record producers, who are responsible for what happens in the studio, play, in consequence, the crucial rock role: they act as the link, the mediator, between musicians as artists and their music as commercial product. The producers' first role is as organizers and coordinators. They have to get the artists into the studio, make sure the necessary session musicians and engineers are on hand, the right recording equipment set up. This means musical as well as administrative decisions: in planning a recording session the producer is determining how the potential material will be arranged and embellished. As John Anthony put it: "There's one right way to do an album and four hundred wrong ones. That's the point of having a producer."

Producers are, therefore, liable to clash with the musicians they are recording (the musicians' managers usually keep out of the way at this stage), and they have to be able to handle the tensions themselves, to keep their teams happy in what can be an extremely tedious process. In the words of Bob Johnston, "The whole thing of record producing to me is psychiatry really"; for Gus Dudgeon "the whole job of the producer is to make the artist as comfortable as possible"; Jimmy Ienner uses "wrath"—he challenges musicians' egotism by harping on their technical insecurities until "the group isn't thinking anymore" and trusts his production decisions without argument.

In these organizational and administrative respects a record producer's job is like that of a film producer, and he has a similar production team: an arranger, equivalent to the screenplay writer; an engineer, equivalent to the cameraman; numbers of technicians, from tape operators (this is the normal starting point for a career in record production) to highly skilled and experienced session musicians. This world, the hub of the rock business, is almost exclusively male.

In other respects, the record producer's job is more like that of a film director, more creative: it is the record producer who is responsible for getting the sound that is the essence of a record. To some extent he is dependent on technology for this; the possibilities of sound recording lie in the technical equipment available in a studio. In the 1930s the record producer simply had to get the musicians into the studio, open the mike, and record what happened as cleanly as possible. Even when George Martin began recording the Beatles, his only concern was to come out of the studio with a "concise, commercial statement." His musical judgment was confined to approving the group's material; once the recording started all he had to do was to ensure that the performance was the right length, the musicians were in the right key, the sound was "tidy." It was only when multi-track recording began that a producer could deliberate, change his mind, and, in Martin's words, "stamp his own unique impression on the recording." Martin claims that after the recording of "Yesterday," the Beatles' style "was partly of my making."

As recording got even more complex in the 1970s the record producer became more dependent on the skills of the studio engineer. The latter's job may have been simply to "get on tape what's going on in the studio," but his individual ear is important, even in this electronic process. As engineer Glyn Johns points out:

> If one of the engineers in there and myself, if we both did a session with identically the same set-up, even, and the same musicians, the same piece of music, it'd sound totally different. It's the way that the engineer hears the piece of music. He injects a tremendous amount into the atmosphere, that's the other thing. Any record, to my way of thinking, has to have, has to give you a mental picture when you hear it. I think the engineer's job is to present a mental picture in sound that he thinks suits the number and the artist.[8]

The engineer's "mental picture," like the producer's "sculpture in music," is a form of creativity. This is most obvious at the mixing stage (equivalent to the editing stage in filmmaking): the results of recording sessions are mixed to bring up certain sounds and obliterate others, to alter tones, to overdub harmonies, wipe off mistakes; sessions are cut and edited without any consultation with the musicians involved. The record that results may be as much an expression of the technical skills of the producer and his engineer as of the musical skills of the credited artists (who may never have even been in the studio together); even in live rock performance the sound mixer is nowadays a crucial musical member of a rock group.

Edward Kealey has analyzed the rise to prominence of "sound mixers" in terms of the transformation of the job from craft to art. In the late 1940s recording studios were still organized in terms of craft unionism. Studio engineers were employees of big companies, their skill was technical correctness, concert hall realism, and there were clear divisions of labor in the record-making process. In the 1950s and 1960s there was a move towards the entrepreneurial mode. Technological change, the reduction of studio costs, and the opening of radio to independently made records encouraged the rise of small studios, often owned by their own technicians. The divisions of labor in record-making became blurred, union control of the studio declined, and the services sold by an engineer or record producer became more diffuse. In the 1970s, as rock musicians began to produce their own records and operate their own studios, producers and engineers began, simultaneously, to see themselves as artists, making individual contributions they thought deserved rewarding in the "artistic" way—with royalty payments.

This shift, from craft to art, was also related to the increasing commercial importance of the record producer as record companies looked to him as a source of sales success, the possible owner of some magic "hit ingredient." In this context we can distinguish two approaches to the hit-making job.

The success of some producers rests on their ability to translate an artist's music into a recorded sound, on their ability to realize on record musical ideas that are fundamentally those of the musicians concerned. Production, from this point of view, is not just "doing the best you can for the artists to get their music out," but guaranteeing the best. "The true *profession* of being a record producer," to use George Martin's emphasis, is "where the element of chance is not part of the game"; and the producer's primary professional obligation is to the record company that is employing him (rather than to the musicians who will, in fact, eventually foot his bill)—the object of recording is to realize music in a commercially successful form. Arif Mardin: "I still always look for a single when I'm doing an album. Sometimes in the course of sessions, inspirations may be great and solos may tend to be longer than they should, so it's up to me to shorten them so that we could have a single from it."

This emphasis on the single makes clear what's at stake in the studio—a sound that can be fitted into the appropriate radio selling-slots. It is the producer, not the musician, who is expected to be the expert on commercial sounds. In the early days of Motown, for example, Berry Gordy systematically translated his acts' music into records that would sound good on cheap transistor and car radios (even, apparently, mixing the records through appropriately tiny and tinny speakers). Nineteen-seventies rock producers, by contrast, were concerned with what sounded good on FM stereo radio and expensive hi-fis, but they could get just as irritated with the musicians who were, supposedly, employing them. In Mickie Most's words: "The trouble is, most artists have a private view of themselves and most of the time it's wrong."

Partly as a consequence of this difficulty, a second approach to production has developed—the producer not as realizer of a given sound but as its creator. In this case it is the musicians who express the producer's ideas and not vice versa. The results of this approach can be heard clearly in teen-beat singles, like the Monkees' records in the 1960s or the Bay City Rollers' in the 1970s, a genre in which the producer's traditional task has been to perfect—and reproduce endlessly—a bestselling *sound* (to which every other aspect of a record—melody, lyric, performance—is made subordinate). In disco, similarly, the concentration on function and effect puts all the creative power in the hands of the producer, the organizer of the music. The pop paradox is that the most commercial use of the studio is, simultaneously, its most creative use. It is these commercial producers, from Phil Spector in the late 1950s to Giorgio Moroder (Donna Summer's producer) in the late 1970s (and including Jamaica's "hack" reggae engineers) who have most clearly used recording as an artistic, experimental medium in its own right—not just a means of elaborating music, *Sgt. Pepper* style, but a way of transforming our aural expectations.

# DECIDING WHAT REACHES THE PUBLIC

Record producers know that their clients' music won't reach its audience directly but will be mediated through a further set of gatekeepers—disc jockeys, concert promoters and so forth. A "commercial" sound is not just a matter of public approval—to be commercial it first has to reach that public; hence, the studio emphasis on the single, a track aimed explicitly at radio station playlists. Decisions about how a record should sound can't be separated from a further set of decisions about how that sound will reach its most likely listeners, how it will be promoted and sold.

This music paper story describes the typical promotion process:

Things started to move for Queen about a year ago when they recorded their first album for Trident, who have a distribution deal with EMI. An advance was paid to them to help with the immediate costs of putting them on the road. Review copies of the album—about 400 of them—were sent out to everyone who might conceivably have any influence on the record buying public, from discos to the national press. Copies were personally distributed to radio and TV producers and extensive advertising space was bought up in the trade papers.

"They're all good-looking guys and I did a round of the teeny papers and all the girls in the office swooned over them. Brian, the lead guitarist, had made his own guitar and a couple of the nationals picked up on that. It was good, gossipy stuff." [John Bagnall, EMI promotions man]

Queen's publicity machine was working from all angles because they were also getting extra promotion from Tony Brainsby's promotion office. . . . The intensity of it all paid off when they were invited to do a spot on the Old Grey Whistle Test. Radio Luxembourg latched upon the single "Keep Yourself Alive" and played it regularly.

Their first local tour, supporting Mott the Hoople, got the full works. Local press was saturated with releases about this new band which was shortly coming to their town, elaborate displays were arranged at the front of the house on the night of the concert, local disc-jockeys were informed, and window displays made in about 200 local record shops.

"Trident and EMI committed themselves right from the start to this band, to make sure they had a PA which was better than other bands had and to make sure they had the right clothes. Some of their outfits cost £150 each," said Bagnall.[9]

As it turned out, neither Queen's initial album or single made the charts but their subsequent success justified the original campaign which cost between £5,000 and £10,000; in America a big promotional campaign in 1970 cost about $50,000 and the price rose rapidly during the decade—CBS spent $250,000 promoting Bruce Springsteen's *Born to Run* LP in 1975, and by the end of the decade the average price of producing, promoting, and supporting a new album was between $350,000 and $500,000 (promotion accounted for about three-quarters of these costs).

Each record company has its own publicity office whose task is to get coverage for the company's acts and releases. Its focus is mainly the press. Press officers are, essentially, salesmen advertising a product, but in practice they try to control *all* the information about their acts that reaches the public. Record companies' public faces are often, interestingly, female: the press office is one of the few areas in the music business in which women can have a career; "feminine" qualities are seen as valuable aids in the job of charming favors from the sources of publicity.

The work of the company staff is complemented by that of independent publicists, employed directly by artists or their managers. Their approach can be more intense—they can concentrate on their client and don't have to cope with a new product every week—but their object is, equally, "free" publicity, publicity not directly paid for (like the companies' advertisements) even though it may be paid for indirectly in the costly distribution of free records and drinks and parties and promotional trips. "You can also," points out Arista promo man Mike Klenfer, "use artists in other creative and social ways. We took the Bay City Rollers up to a children's hospital. People don't usually think of promotion in terms of things like that. But it generates publicity and good will."

Publicity is the obvious job for a musical huckster (Colonel Parker used to sell his Elvis photos personally), but even it has been professionalized. As long as the record business was expanding, selling could be seen as a simple matter of shouting in the marketplace, but as the acceleration of sales has slowed, record companies have become more cautious—and sophisticated. In the 1970s they began to research their markets, to pay attention to the occasional record buyer as well as to the fan. TV advertising (pioneered by a "demonstrator," K-tel, rather than by the record companies themselves) revealed the sales possibilities of the occasional market, but as far more money had to be invested in such promotion, so it had to be invested more rationally. Advertising agencies were brought in to coordinate campaigns—designing and writing not just the advertisements but also the sleeve and sleeve notes, the press releases, the video spots. Videotapes themselves became an expensive but effective promotional device: they can be slotted into a variety of pop programs across the world (this was one of the factors in Abba's international success); they can be used in stores to affect consumers and in company meetings to encourage salesmen; they help sell acts to foreign licensees. By 1978, Jon Roseman Productions, the largest of the independent video-promo companies, was doing $1 million worth of business a year in Ameria alone. I have already stressed that the process of music making and selling can't be separated (record producers always have one ear for the music, the other for the market), and the rise of video promotion makes it clear that the relationship has always worked in reverse too—record sellers are also concerned with production. They produce the images (styles, personalities, visual appeal) to match the sounds.

# RADIO

Most record companies agree, however, that the most effective form of promotion is airplay. Telling people to listen to a record isn't the same as making them hear it, and one spin on the radio is worth any number of full-page ads or good reviews in the music press. To sell a record, companies must, in the end, get a *sound* to the public and to do this they have to go through a disc jockey, the most significant rock "gatekeeper." This is the critical problem for rock as a merchandising industry: the most effective form of record-selling is not under record company control. The deejay, whether on radio or in a disco, is independent not just legally (payola, record companies' attempt to control airplay by direct or indirect payment, is illegal in the USA and banned by BBC and IBA regulations in Britain), but also because of the nature of the job—to please the public. Deejays can't just service the record industry. If they don't play what pleases their audience, their ratings will drop and they will be out of work themselves. No amount of airplay, in Dick Clark's classic phrase, "can turn a stiff into a hit," and deejays don't like to be associated with stiffs. This is not to deny deejay's commercial importance. Like it or not, they control what the public hears, and a disc jockey who never moved anyone to buy anything would be a failure even by his own standards. Deejays hope that the records they play will sell, not because that directly benefits them financially, but because if their taste is thus confirmed then their audiences will continue to tune in to their shows, come to their clubs.

Even when payola is possible it has its limits. There have been radio stations on the British music scene, for example, on which companies could buy plays direct: this was one source of income for the pirate radio ships, and from 1946 until 1968 it was possible for companies to buy quarter-hour segments on Radio Luxembourg's

English language programs which were, in effect, record company commercials. In 1968, however, the station started using live deejays (rather than prerecorded slots) and insisted that bought plays be spread through the schedule; and in 1970 program control was made even tighter: plays could still be bought but they were now programmed according to the needs of the radio station itself. It had become clear that the two goals that were involved—to sell records on one hand, to attract listeners on the other—were not identical; when the two clashed too obviously, not even direct payment was sufficient to ensure that the station would organize airplay according to the industry's needs. The history of Radio Luxembourg in the last decade has been the history of a radio station reasserting its control of its programs, and all British radio is now, like American AM radio, organized around the playlist.

Playlist broadcasting originated in the States in the 1950s when television took over as the basic medium of home entertainment. Radio stations, in order to attract the disappearing advertisers, began to research their audiences in detail and to aim their programs at the specific markets they discovered. It was soon found that teenagers were less TV-bound than their parents, and, especially with the spread of portable and car radios, far more regular, if casual, radio listeners. In the mid-fifties a style of broadcasting evolved that was aimed exclusively at the teenage audience. Daylong shows, based on a limited number of records played extensively for a brief period (four to six weeks—the model derived from jukebox programming) were split into four-hour segments by teams of deejays who developed their own individual quirks and styles. Deejays' importance for record promotion had been recognized by the industry since the 1940s, but their power now increased rapidly; there were fewer and fewer syndicated or networked items and programming relied more and more on simple permutations of locally produced record shows. Radio stations and record companies were aiming at exactly the same narrow market—teenagers—and airplay took on a greater significance for record sales than ever before. Radio hit parades were used to calculate ASCAP and BMI copyright returns; radio playlists determined record shops' stocks, record companies' promotional campaigns.

This new radio power was largely in the hands of the deejays. A 1941 FCC regulation designed to increase competition had resulted in a large number of small stations that were heavily dependent on records for cheap programs (record companies had begun to distribute records to radio stations free) and on their deejays for putting these programs together. Radio deejays became influential local musical figures (promoting live performances too—concerts in the gym, appearances in shops and car parks). This was the setting for payola, which was not just the most effective form of promotion (it guaranteed airplay), but also the cheapest (thus giving the independent rock 'n' roll labels the opportunity to compete with the majors):

> Payola is the greatest thing in the world because it means that you don't have to spend time with some schmuck you don't like, eat dinner and all that, you pay him off and tell him to fuck himself. Instead of having an army of promotion men spending your money, fucking your broads, living off your expense account, you give it all to one guy and save yourself a million dollars.[10]

Payola was outlawed by a Federal Bribery Act in 1960 after an extensive, muckraking Senate investigation (that was at least partly designed to show that rock 'n' roll was corrupting youth), and the result for radio was a tightening up and standardization of the music format. Program directors were put in to supervise the deejays, who became increasingly anonymous; playlists were drawn up by these directors and the deejays could only play records which appeared on their stations' lists; direct payments were replaced by the elaborate conventions of plugging as record companies began to employ even more intensely their professional radio salesmen, the pluggers, to persuade program directors to playlist their wares, to gamble on their success. The big companies regained their promotional advantage and Top 40 radio emerged: tight programming according to a fixed formula—hit/station jingle/hit/news/oldie/hit/station jingle/hit—all punctuated by recurrent commercials. In 1965 KHJ of Los Angeles refined the formula even further to make "Boss Radio": a weighted playlist from the Top 30 (the higher the chart place the more often the play) plus three "hit bounds," a pile of oldies and virtually no chat. Even the musical content was regulated—one ballad an hour, one soul record, one singer/songwriter, and so on. The subsequent development of American Top 40 radio was merely an "improvement" on this KHJ formula—some stations reduced their playlists to as few as eighteen titles.

The basis of the playlist is popularity (indicated by the sales figures, playlists elsewhere and popularity charts published weekly by national trade papers like *Billboard,* by the tip-sheet suggestions of professional radio consultants, and by local listener requests), and there is obviously a circular argument involved: a record on the playlist has a good chance of being popular; a record not on it has hardly a hope—hence the recurring temptations of payola. The current record company strategy in America is to link the volume of advertising bought on a radio station to its "favorable" treatment of the company's product, advertised or not; in Britain, companies "fiddle" the charts—the BBC is dependent for its playlist on shop returns, and so companies can get their releases into the charts artificially by buying the necessary copies themselves, in the hope that the subsequent playlist exposure will translate into real sales.

Radio molds as well as responds to public taste, and record companies respond to as well as mold the playlist. Field promoters may not be able to persuade program directors to use airplay deliberately to benefit their company, but they can persuade them that their company is producing the sort of records that are a means to the program director's own ends. The plugger's task is to convince a radio station that a record is right for its shows, fits its ideology of entertainment, meets the needs of its audience; and even if record companies have no direct control of the "gatekeepers" of the airwaves, their guesses at the passwords are, nonetheless, well informed and routinely accurate.

Commercial radio stations' advertising rates and revenues depend on *comparative* listening figures. Behind the development of the tight playlist lay the research finding that teenagers switched stations the moment they heard a record they didn't like. In their attempts to reduce the risk of playing an unpopular record, Top 40 stations have made their programming policies dependent on records that have either proved their popularity already—by local and countrywide sales and airplay—or have shown strong evidence of potential popularity—in the playlists of "barometer" stations or professional tip-sheets.

The logic of Top 40 radio is that a station can attract listeners by playing the records that, on the evidence of sales, the listeners currently most like. These records are then played over and over again; programmers believe Top 40 listeners are irregular, always switching off or over, impatient to hear their favorite tunes. If they

keep a station on for a longer period, it's only as background music—the listeners' attention is assumed to wander even when they're
not pushing buttons. The success of Top 40 radio rests on one of
the central paradoxes of the record industry: radio programming
policy is determined by record popularity as measured by sales—
i.e., the number of people buying a record so that they can, presum-
ably, play it at their own convenience. Why, then, do they also want
to hear it so often on the radio?

Teenage pop listeners have always used their radio stations just
as they use their records, as an ever-present background to their leisure activities—"their sound" is a way of distinguishing their places
from those of adults. Record companies have never really understood this feature of record use, and the result has, on occasion,
been an ambiguous attitude towards radio. In the 1960s, for example, British record companies were convinced that the declining sale
of singles was the result of their "overexposure" on the pirate radio
stations. But there is little evidence for such fears, and the basic
principle of Top 40 radio continues to be that the greatest number
of listeners can be attracted by playing the currently bestselling records as often as possible.

Another aspect of the rationalization of American music-radio
in the 1960s was the increasingly sophisticated use of "demographics" by broadcasters and their advertisers. Researchers broke down
stations' markets according to the day of the week and the time of
the day, according to the most precisely measurable buying habits.
The process by which radio had become a mass medium was reversed: using this data, stations that had, in the 1930s, sought to
put together huge heterogeneous audiences now concentrated on exploring the differences between small homogeneous ones or servicing precisely the musical (and consumer) tastes of specific age,
ethnic, or local groups. One market gap became increasingly evident
to the market researchers who were surveying listeners' tastes for
the radio industry: if Top 40 radio stations catered to nine to eighteen year olds, and if MOR (middle-of-the-road pop) radio stations
catered to thirty-five to forty-nine year olds, who was tapping the
consumer potential of eighteen to thirty-four year olds? This age
group was still tuning in to the Top 40 stations on which it had
grown up (rather than to MOR pop or classical music), and advertisers could still reach it that way more efficiently than any other
way (via television, for example); but this age group's listening hab-

its were becoming increasingly desultory—Top 40 programs contained less and less of the music it wanted to hear; the LP boom and the development of stereo seemed to be passing music-radio by.

It was in this context that "underground" FM radio emerged, with its programs of album tracks, laid-back deejays, and long stretches of uninterrupted music. These FM stations were, initially, the consequence less of a systematic pursuit of the new rock market than of a new federal radio policy. In 1964 the Federal Communications Commission, in pursuit of greater choice and competition in local radio, ruled that where a broadcasting company controlled both AM and FM wavelengths, it must program them differently (previously the same shows had simply been carried on both outlets). This freed the FM bands from the AM formulas, and, with their possibility of high sound quality, the new FM stations (the regulation came into effect in 1967) were ideal for broadcasting rock music. In terms of initial licensing costs, FM radio was, in addition, cheaper than AM; it could run on fewer commercial breaks.

FM radio, however "underground" in its initial exploration of the demands of the eighteen-to-thirty-four-year-old audience, was very quickly standardized and soon became as vital a form of record promotion as Top 40 radio—the rise of Warner Brothers as a rock label is commonly seen as having been dependent on the simultaneous rise of FM radio stations. In its brief underground days (1966–68) FM radio had been drawing on rock and hippy tastes that were not yet commercially organized—deejays, themselves hippies and rock fans, simply presented selections of music they liked themselves and measured their "anti-commerciality" by reference to AM conventions. FM deejays were "real," unbound by the glib insincerities and sales patter of their AM jock colleagues. But FM deejays, stations, and advertisers were, inevitably, also engaged in the construction of a new *market*. FM radio, by its very nature, defined the rock community as a community of consumers—consumers with measurable, predictable, serviceable tastes. Nowadays, indeed, FM stations take as many pains as AM stations to keep the ears of their specific demographic profile, to avoid the risks of unpopularity. In the words of the historian of American broadcasting:

> Radio, which had been at the start of the broadcasting empire, had gone back to its beginnings, relying mainly on gramophone records. But most stations now aimed at unity of mood, to hold

specific audience groups. . . . The specialised, fragmented nature of radio programming made it easy for the average listener to get push-button confirmation of his tastes and prejudices. Once he had "his" station, he was in "his" world.[11]

The point of commercial radio is profit and the source of profit is the difference between program costs and advertising revenue. Record-based music-radio developed in America because it contributed to the profit formula on both sides—it was cheap and it could attract an audience large enough to interest advertisers at good rates. The audience itself is not the end for commercial radio; it is the means to the end of advertising revenue. American music stations, whether Top 40 or FM rock, must attract the audiences that their potential advertisers want to reach—which means not necessarily the biggest possible audiences, but the biggest possible percentages of particular audiences: Top 40 radio is aimed at teenagers, FM radio at eighteen to thirty-four year olds; advertisers buy airtime accordingly. Commercial broadcasters have no obligations to their non-listeners, the people outside their demographic profile.

The problem for an American radio station, given the competition, is to ensure that its audience, once attracted, stays with it; and once a station is down to its minimum of legally and commercially necessary talk, only particular records can turn listeners off—on comes a bad record and punch goes the button. This was the reason for the ever-narrowing chart-based playlist—people are less likely to dislike one of the Top 40 than they are one of the Top 100. This was the reason for the rapid standardization of FM radio—people are less likely to dislike a rock superstar than a rock risk-taker.

Commercial music-radio is, then, inherently conservative, but it was, nonetheless, a crucial factor in the major changes in popular taste in the last thirty years—into rock 'n' roll in the 1950s, into rock in the 1960s. I grew up in Britain, where radio broadcasting was dominated by the noncommercial BBC, and the resulting differences in the relationships between popular radio and popular music were apparent. 1950s rock 'n' roll tastes were serviced not by the BBC but by the few programs of American records transmitted by Radio Luxembourg, a commercial station based in Luxembourg but broadcasting in English in the evenings. The British beat boom of the mid-1960s rested, in radio terms, not on the BBC but on the pirate radio stations which operated from 1964–67, evading British radio law by transmitting from ships just outside British waters. British pop fans experienced these commercial stations as an aspect of the cultural freedom that marked the emergence of British rock. In most respects, in fact, the "free" pirates simply represented American commerical interests—ideologically (their program ideas and styles) and materially (their sources of capital and advertising).

Commercial radio seemed radical rather than conservative in Britain because it offered, for the first time, daily competition to the BBC, pop rivalry to Radio Luxembourg. The direct result was that in 1967, as the pirates were legislated off the air, the BBC started its own version of Top 40 radio, Radio 1. The BBC compiled its chart-based playlists according to different principles than those of commercial broadcasters: if American stations use sales as a guide to what to exclude from their programs, the BBC uses them as a guide to what to include. Using the sales charts compiled by the British Market Research Bureau from retail returns as the only available measure of popular taste, the BBC aims to ensure that *everyone* in the mass market hears a record they do like, that every taste represented in the hit parade is represented on radio—the BBC is still concerned about building a heterogeneous audience. Radio 1 has, as a result, an oddly eclectic sound—anything in the charts may be played, from punk to MOR. It is partly for this reason that BBC deejays are so important.

The art of commercial radio programming is to integrate records and commercial breaks in such a way that the words slide in and out of the music—smoothly enough to keep the listeners cool but firmly enough for the product name to stick. The advertisements are the focus of commercial radio, not the deejays, who, in America, are anonymous these days (despite the obvious exceptions)—at the end of a Top 40 day it's not the deejays' names you should remember but the names of the products they've plugged. For Radio 1, with its audience as the end in itself, the deejays are not just equal to the music as a source of entertainment but, in many ways, more important—they give the programs their personality, carry the listeners through the records they don't like, counter the effects of chart eclecticism. Radio 1 does not confine its records to any particular genre, but it does tend to select from within each genre the easiest-to-listen-to sounds: it broadcasts easy listening punk, easy listening disco, easy listening rock.

The BBC constantly reminds the record industry that it is not in the business to sell records, that its purpose is to "entertain" as many people as possible; entertainment is then defined as anything to which this large audience will listen. The BBC, in short, provides a hybrid form of broadcasting: its format and musical content are derived from Top 40 radio, rest on assumptions about the youth market, and reflect that market's record-buying behavior; but its attitude to its audience derives from a vaguer concept of entertainment, a vaguer assumption about the needs of "the general public."

I've spent some time describing the BBC version of pop radio, because it puts American commercial radio into perspective—in Britain itself, when legitimate, land-based commercial stations started broadcasting in 1973, in most respects they resembled the BBC more than American stations: by law, they had to provide "a general service" to all members of their communities as well as attract an audience "acceptable to our advertisers." But while their pop programming tended to draw "younger adults," their audience concern was more specific than the BBC's, and their programming more restricted, more conservative. It rested specifically on "a desire not to be offensive," for, as one of the new station's "music advisers" put it:

> Punk records are bought by people under 20, and they don't have the money to spend or the interest in the consumer durables we advertise—unless, of course, we start advertising safety-pins. The last thing I want is for a listener to hear a record he doesn't like and say "What the hell is that?" and switch off.[12]

In America, rock 'n' roll and Top 40 radio developed together in the 1950s, rock and FM radio in the 1960s, as program directors began to make consumer markets out of youth cultures. In Britain, American-style commercial radio—Luxembourg to some extent in the 1950s, the pirates certainly in the 1960s—were used in the same way: radio became an organizing part of the experience of musical community. Nineteen-seventies radio rarely offered that experience and, again, a comparison of commercial radio to the BBC is instructive.

BBC Radio 1 is a background for adult as well as youthful activities; it is used in factories and shops, on building sites and motorways. The paradox is that because young people are the only Radio 1 listeners who care enough about what they hear to buy the records for themselves, it is mostly their music that everyone else hears in the background—as long as it is not *too* punky or progressive or raucous. As a result, Radio 1 puts youth music into a setting that drains it of its significance, transforms it into Muzak. The BBC is not concerned with rock as a cultural form; its interest is confined to the music's ability to sooth and cheer a mass audience.

Commercial radio programmers have never been interested in music as music either. Merchandising factors have always determined musical policy—a "successful" radio station is judged a success in ratings terms, and one of the most obvious aspects of the 1970s rationalization of rock was the rationalization of rock radio. As stations got an increasing proportion of their income from *national* advertisers, so their Arbitron rating figures (a market research measure of numbers and types of listeners) increasingly determined exactly what share of the advertising market they'd get, what prices they could charge. The pursuit of particular demographic combinations became more organized, the design of the necessary programs more scientific, the musical rules that record companies had to follow more precise. Radio was central to the way in which music was divided into genres, the way in which the rock experience became an experience of familiarity and confirmation rather than a challenge or surprise. Records were being promoted on the air, but they were not being *sold*—commercial stations were no more willing than the BBC to work *on* an audience, to risk too agitated a listener response.

But then commerical radio stations never really have been in the business of musical education; they've always shifted their music out of context, suburbanized it, turned it into a shopping-mall soundtrack. When music-radio has mattered musically it has almost always been coincidentally—for a moment a music community is, at the same time, an advertising community; for a moment leisure needs are defined by a radio station's commerical concerns. Nineteen-seventies radio rarely mattered this way (though disco radio had its moment), not because it had changed, not because rock had changed, but because the listeners themselves had changed, as had the place of music in their leisure. Radio doesn't determine the meaning of music, but, rather, what music means to people determines how they use and listen to the radio. Radio's magic moments have been when that meaning was open: rock 'n' roll radio, early FM, the British pirates, were each part of a process in which the "consumption" of rock was given *new* meanings.

# MEDIA TIE-UPS

Individual consumption is not records' only fate as commodities; they are also used as the "inputs" for other media. This is most obviously true for radio, which, as we have seen, has a symbiotic relationship with the record industry; but even when the media are not so closely joined, the record industry can be a means to further profits. Television has very successfully created its own teeny-bopper record stars, for instance, and the association of *any* product with a popular record has been found by advertisers to help sales—non-music companies have even sponsored rock groups (on tour, for example) in return for these groups' advertising support—the old baseball/shaving cream endorsement with a new angle. The most profitable multimedia use of rock currently is the film/record tie-up. Youth-aimed Hollywood films have long used rock 'n' roll on the sound track, and most of Elvis Presley's career was committed to the simultaneous promotion of films and LPs; but it was the astounding sales of *Saturday Night Fever* and *Grease* at the end of the 1970s that suggested the untapped possibilities of "crossover marketing." The films sold the records, the records sold the films; the usually separate promotional strategies turned out to complement each other so well that a vast new volume of consumers was reached. As the 1980s began, a number of record companies were following Polygram, Robert Stigwood, and the Who (whose *Quadrophenia* employed the same record/movie tie-up) into film production.

Records can also be used more directly, as a means of entertainment in themselves. Discos and dance halls use them to draw customers, obviously enough, and these days there are few public places without permanent background music. The earliest use of records as background was on jukeboxes—a crucial part of service life which accounted for an appreciable proportion of records sold and helped to encourage the emergence of rhythm and blues and country music; in Britain, jukeboxes, now concentrated in pubs to provide "youth atmosphere," still account for about 15 percent of all singles sold. In a sense, records feed into live music too, into the basic entertainment provided by clubs and cabarets and hotels: there are tens of thousands of unrecorded musicians whose livelihood depends on their ability to reproduce, week after week, recorded sounds—what their public wants is good copies of past and present hits. But the purest use of records for collective consumption and entertainment is, obviously, by discos.

## DISCOS

Clubs with records as their only means of entertainment came to Britain and America (from France) in the early 1960s; before then deejays and records had been used in ballrooms not as alternatives to live music but to fill the gaps between sets. Initially, discos served obvious in-crowds—rock aristocrats seeking exclusion, dance addicts; but by the late 1960s, as live rock became increasingly undanceable and expensive, as rock concerts became major events or sit-down affairs, local clubs and discos took on more general significance, as places where a lot of record buyers were hearing a lot of records. Record companies began to notice inexplicably high sales for records which they had long since ceased to promote. In Britain the disco became a prominent aspect of the mainstream leisure of working-class teenagers (while a smattering of "northern soul" clubs continued to serve dancers who were exclusively committed to mid-sixties mod soul music). Record companies began to change their promotional tactics. In the words of Jonathan King:

> Discotheques have two great advantages: one, exactly the sort of person you're selling a record to goes to a discotheque, and two, you get your record played at massive volume which is how a lot of records ought to be heard. And a third thing is that that class and that type of person is the all-time spread-the-word person—they've got nothing else to talk about except football. [13]

In America discos were important as well for an older dancing clientele, for gays, blacks, singles—people who wanted to enjoy themselves casually, frantically, without hassles, with friends and possible partners. Discos were a new sort of music club.

Payola in discos is not illegal, and at first glance there is no reason why a record company shouldn't just pay a disco deejay to play its records. But disco deejays, too, are constrained by their own purposes: their job is not to sell records but to entertain a crowd.

A deejay puts on a show and it's for the show that the records are selected. His choice can't be determined by record companies; he has to be able to respond to the immediate demands of a particular dancing audience. The record companies' way into disco was, therefore, more subtle: companies had deejays mix and make the records themselves. The old payola wheeze—paying radio deejays as "release consultants" (obviously they'd play the records whose release they'd been paid to recommend)—was thus given substance by record companies' new disco departments. What was at issue was not the manipulation of an audience but its efficient servicing; the disco deejays were being employed to offer expert advice.

The relationship between disco music and the disco market is an example of the *dialectics* of "giving the public what it wants." The most important disco gatekeeper, the disc jockey, is employed to mediate the disco public's tastes back to the record companies as well as to select (and sell) the resulting records to the disco public. In the public's use of disco music (just as in its use of radio music) there is no moment, in fact, in which records are "passively" consumed, simply used up. Music is too volatile, carries too many meanings. It is actively consumed, *used,* in contexts of leisure and pleasure that are not easy to control, that set up relationships between musicians and audiences in which meanings as well as money circulate. I'll return to this point in chapter 7. First, though, I want to look at the problems posed by the peculiarities of musical consumption for the record companies' own concern—the pursuit of profit.

# CHAPTER 6

# MAKING MONEY

The ancillary uses of records—on jukeboxes and sound-tracks, as sources of radio and disco entertainment—are a vital source of income for the record industry, and the licensing and the copyright arrangements involved draw attention to music's special status as a cultural product. The normal principle of commodity production is that the owner of the means of production owns the commodity produced; its value may reflect the labor that has gone into its production, but the laborers are paid directly for their labor time and have no legal claim on the product whatsoever. The capitalist can do what he likes with both it and any proceeds of its sale. For most of the workers concerned with record-making the same relationship holds: they are wage laborers, paid for their time, without any economic interest in the product on which they're working. But cultural goods also use artistic labor, and artistic services are rewarded with a cut of the final profits—royalties act as an incentive to artists whose creative skills cannot otherwise easily be controlled by their purchasers.

In the recording industry we have to distinguish the work recorded from the record itself. Copyright law asserts (this is the British wording) that "a musical work (and any associated lyrics) acquires copyright protection immediately it is committed to paper or fixed in some other material form, such as recording."

Recorded rock needn't have lyrics, needn't be written down, may be improvised on the spot, but a recording is, legally, always a recording of a specific piece of music—a song—and song recording involves a crucial figure in music money-making—the song publisher.

# PUBLISHING

The broadside publisher was the original commercializer of popular music, and song publishers were the central figures of the music industry before the development of recording. Although the publishers' role has changed since then, they remain important.

Publishers are songwriters' employers, subsidizing them until their songs are successful (as Dick James subsidized Elton John and Bernie Taupin, and Ray Davies's company subsidized Tom Robinson), using them to produce songs for the song market, acting as the link between writers and recording artists. Freddie Bienstock, for example, rounded up songs for Elvis Presley: "He would not look at a song before I had seen it first, which didn't mean that I would pick them, I would just screen them for him, and then out of those that I had screened, he would make his own selections."

The publisher places his clients' work with record companies, advises recording acts on possible hits. The latter job is often a matter of giving advice on previously published material—a publisher's back catalogue is a permanent source of potentially re-recordable songs; the former job involves supporting and promoting new writers. In theory the publisher acts for the writer—bringing his or her work to public attention; in practice many rock songwriters have begun their careers working for a publisher, writing songs to order. Carole King remembers writing pop songs in the early 1960s:

> Every day we squeezed into our respective cubby holes with just enough room for a piano, a bench and maybe a chair for the lyricist if you were lucky. You'd sit there and write and you

could hear someone in the next cubby hole composing a song exactly like yours. The pressure in the Brill Building was really terrific—because Donny Kirshner [a music publisher] would play one song-writer against another. He'd say: "We need a new smash hit"—and we'd all go back and write a song and the next day we'd each audition for Bobby Vee's producer.[1]

In either case, in order to sell and place their songs, publishers have to make their own "demo-discs"—an approach pioneered by Kirshner—and are usually therefore obliged to develop their own independent production companies.

The publisher is the administrator of a song's rights after it has been recorded and performed. Even when musicians are recording their own material and don't need a publisher to provide or place songs, they do need someone to ensure that their rights are protected, that they get the income due from their songs' sales and use. Publishers provide the necessary legal and administrative expertise and help promote and market their clients' material in other forms: sheet music, live performances, and cover versions by other artists.

---

# COPYRIGHT

The copyright on a song (which means tune and lyrics combined) lasts until fifty years after the death of the author and entitles the copyright holder to payment on every copy of the song sold, whether in sheet music or recorded form (which can include its use on a soundtrack, commercial, segment of Muzak tape, etc.). The copyright holder is usually the song's publisher, who has his own contract with the songwriter, but the various rights available to the publisher are administered differently, according to whether they are mechanical or performing rights. Mechanical rights are the royalty rights on the use of a song as a recording, and the mechanical rights resulting from record sales are the most significant (a percentage of list price in Britain, a flat rate in the USA). Performing rights mean that "whenever a song is performed in public or broadcast on radio or TV the writer and publisher must be paid."

Public performance rights are assigned by publishers and composers to the Performing Rights Society in Britain, to ASCAP or

BMI in the USA (non-profit-making organizations funded by the publishers themselves), and these bodies license the various public uses of music and collect and distribute the resulting fees. How they do this varies from organization to organization, but, in general, the returns are divided equally between a song's publisher and writer. The legal principle underlying performing rights is the same in both countries:

> Music is a kind of property belonging to the composer, so that by controlling certain uses of his music he may earn a living. Thus one of the provisions of the law is that when you buy a record or some sheet music you may use it to play the music at home, but it does not give you the right to perform the music publicly—unless the composers' permission has been obtained.[2]

Composers' ownership of their compositions was established originally in Copyrights Acts at the beginning of the century (1909 in the USA, 1911 in Britain), which clarified the rights of all authors. The subsequent development of recording raised a new issue: Could the publishers of a sound or a performance claim the same rights as the publishers of a written text? British and American courts and legislators came to different conclusions on this. In Britain records cannot be copied, heard in public, or broadcast without permission; in America, the purchaser of a record (whether a private citizen or a radio station) is its owner and can do what he or she likes with it; even the 1976 amendment of the American copyright laws, which gave companies protection against unauthorized copying or bootlegs, did not give them performance or broadcasting rights. In Britain broadcasters have to get a license to play records, have to negotiate "needletime agreements" and pay the record companies' licensing organization, Phonographic Performance Limited, for their use of records at the same time that they are paying the PRS (Performing Rights Society) for their use of songs. American record producers (unlike American song publishers) have to be satisfied with the 2 percent of net revenue royalty which the National Committee for the Recording Arts negotiated with broadcasters in 1967.

## THE STAR SYSTEM

Underlying the various public uses of records and the substantial fees involved, is, as we saw in the last chapter, the assumption that music is an effective means to other ends—listening and viewing figures, gates, circulations, sales—and that some of the money brought in by music should go to its authors. It is not just rock on record that is a means to further profit—so are rock stars. The attracting power of stars is symbolized by their fan clubs. As I mentioned in discussing promotion, the biggest acts are able to exploit their success by licensing the use of their names or images. The *New York Times* reported in 1957 that

> retailers of soft goods last year sold more than $20,000,000 worth of Presley products. Such items as pre-teen and teen-sized jackets, skirts, T-shirts, jeans, hats, nylon scarves, charm bracelets, sneakers and nylon stretch bobby sox, all bearing the Presley insignia, are big sellers in the nation's stores.
>
> Chain, drug and novelty stores now feature lipsticks in autographed cases bearing color names for such Presley hit tunes as Hound Dog orange, Love You fuchsia, and Heartbreak pink.[3]

The music business doesn't only turn music into commodities, as records, it also turns musicians into commodities, as stars. When, in 1964, two Chicago businessmen bought the pillowcases on which the Beatles had slept in a Kansas City hotel for $1,000, cut them into 160,000 one-inch squares and sold the squares for one dollar each, the profits reflected the "value" that the Beatles, as stars, brought to every object they touched. Stars' record sales in particular are guaranteed, almost regardless of content. Record companies (like film studios) seek to reverse the "rational" relationship between stardom and music (or films)—if acts become stars because people like their records, the commercial object is to get people to buy their records because they are stars. The biggest stars, in fact, provide by themselves the major part of record companies' profits—whether Elvis Presley for RCA or Elton John and Olivia Newton-John for MCA. The Beatles remain the most dramatic example of this. In 1963–64 the turnover from Beatles music leapt from nothing to £6 million; by the middle of 1964 Beatles records were bringing in £500,000 a month, and that year EMI's pretax music profits rose 80 percent. Over the next ten years the Beatles sold the equivalent of 545 million singles, and even in 1973, long after the peaks of Beatlemania, it was estimated that the sales on two Beatles anthologies would account for 28.6 percent of EMI's pretax music profits, 16.7 percent of its total profits. When Allen Klein renegotiated the Beatles' contract with Capitol (EMI's American subsidiary) in 1969, he got their royalty rate raised to 25 percent (the average in the business was then about 10 percent), confident in the knowledge that the group had, for years, accounted for at least 50 percent of Capitol's sales.

Stars make record promotion easy, and it is in the star system that the "symbiotic" relationships of the different music-using media can be seen most clearly. The importance of stars for *all* sales means that papers will publicize them as much as they can, radio stations play their latest records as soon and as often as possible, magazines litter their pages with their pictures. Record sales rise without the record companies having to lift a finger, and the companies' business is not just more profitable, but easier; "what the public wants" becomes a known, fixed quantity, and the buzz associated with big stars rubs off on little stars, and so on down the rock line. The most common music business cliché, when sales are slow, is that what is needed is a "new Beatles," someone who is "guaranteed platinum."

The star system lay behind the rise of "musician power," discussed in chapter 4—it was as they became superstars that rock artists were able to define the commercial terms of music-making. "Stardom" describes a relationship between performer and audience, and in rock this relationship can take on a cultural life of its own. Rock's youth setting gives the fans' identification with the stars a material edge, and, partly for this reason, the most important rock event is the *live* performance, where performers and audiences genuinely react to each other (in the way film stars and their fans in the Hollywood star system never did). Rock is a record medium, but the music's meaning derives from the meaning of live performances—high-school hops, barroom brawls, stadium spectacles. Rock records, however privately used, take their resonance from public leisure, from the public ways in which stars are made.

# LIVE PERFORMANCE

Live performance involves the cooperation of two more "gatekeepers"—the agent and the promoter. The agent is contracted by artists to get them gigs (for a percentage of the fee he can negotiate) and acts as the link between musicians and the theaters, ballrooms, clubs, and colleges that are their regular employers; the promoter puts on the shows, hiring the venues and the musicians (getting them from an agent), organizing the stage, the publicity, the ticket sales, etc. Clearly the promoter's risk lies in whether or not an act will draw a crowd, and the obvious source of promoter security is an act with a hit record—the record acts as promotion for the performance. In Britain in the 1960s, for example, Robert Stigwood organized huge packages of acts from the Top 20 whose positions on the bill changed as their records changed places in the charts; and even today small British promoters, such as colleges, are predominantly interested in acts that have already shown their drawing power by selling records.

But in America live performance has always been equally important as a form of promotion in which record sales are the end rather than the beginning. Dick Clark's Caravan of the Stars tours, for example, which began in 1959, were co-promoted with local radio stations (which used the stars to sell themselves). The performers were paid very little, but their records were guaranteed intensive airplay. Such tours were a way of publicizing acts in regions they hadn't previously sold to; and in the late 1960s Frank Barsalona started the Premier Talent Agency specifically to *break* rock acts, to launch new performers. His plan was to use tours to build the market for a group, and one aspect of the resulting system—which dominated American rock in the 1970s—was its consolidation of promotional devices. Live rock became routinized: an album release a year was tied in with a tour, with a coordinated promotional effort in each locality, as groups did their bits for radio, retail stores, the press, TV.

There can be no doubt of Barsalona's influence on American rock. Previously it had been difficult to book rock 'n' roll groups into decent venues (in terms of size, comfort, acoustics—cities' premier concert halls had been reserved for "respectable" pop and classical performers with "well-behaved" audiences), and they were hassled even after they were allowed in to play. Now they were stadium owners' safest bet—Barsalona had changed the meaning of promotional risk. He might not have needed a hit to take on an act, but he did expect "professionalism"—he looked for suitable management and record company support, the right sort of musical temperament and efficiency. He expected his acts to take advice on their shows—how to present themselves, how to pace an evening. Live rock developed its own form of routine spectacle, its own way of "guaranteeing" a good night out. It became increasingly expensive to stage as sound effects had to reflect the developed technology of the studio and as musicians adopted increasingly sophisticated standards of showmanship—acts whose reputation rested on pomp and melodrama couldn't afford to disappoint fans with anything less pompous or dramatic on stage. It became impossible for the biggest rock groups to make a profit on ticket sales alone. The Rolling Stones' 1976 European tour, for example, cost about £2 million to present—its purpose was less to make money than "to add 300,000 to 400,000 copies to the sales of the latest album."

For acts like the Stones or the Who such concerts are automatic sellouts and thus involve a new relationship with their promoters. The latter have changed from entrepreneurs, risking their capital against box office receipts, to experts, laying on a service for a fee and leaving the record or management company to carry the costs from its promotional budget. Promoters are increasingly being paid for their professional ability to design a show, to provide a team of specialists—roadies, carpenters and electricians, lighting men, stage managers and sound mixers. The stage crew for a major rock tour is as elaborate and as expensive as that of a theater company, and major rock concerts are, these days, really put on by the record companies themselves.

# BIG BUSINESS

The 1970s rock business was marked by the development of musicians' power and by the use of an increasing number of independent professional experts to produce records, mount shows, manage careers, and orchestrate sales appeal. This marked, superficially, the loosening-up of the music business as promised by the original rock stars in the mid-1960s—the old controllers of concert halls, record companies, and radio stations had all been replaced by youth. But in financial terms, this description is misleading. Rock is certainly produced by a diverse collection of companies, but this division of professional labor conceals the extent to which overall control of the business has remained in the hands of the major entertainment corporations.

Even in the 1950s record business "independence" was something of a misnomer. Finding someone else to press their records had been a problem for small record companies since the 1920s. There were small manufacturing plants but they were often fully booked, and it was difficult for small companies to use them *flexibly*—to time their releases precisely, to respond quickly to an unexpected burst of consumer demand. Not surprisingly, most "independents" have ended up working through the major companies, and by the end of the 1970s, indeed, the majors in the USA (CBS, RCA, WEA, MCA, Polygram, Capitol) accounted for more than 90 percent of the record market in terms of both volume and sales; the "independents," had a smaller share than at any time since the beginning of the 1950s. Where capital investment was important the majors still had no rivals. In Britain, EMI, Decca, Pye, Phonodisc, CBS, and RCA manufactured and distributed most of the records that were issued (EMI alone manufactured one in four of all records sold, and distributed one in three); in America record manufacture was dominated by CBS, Capitol, and RCA (CBS alone pressed more than half of all American releases). The major record companies (like film companies but unlike book publishers) have their own manufacturing facilities (manufacture represents about one-fifth of the cost of record-making) and when, during the 1973 vinyl shortage, RCA and Capitol both stopped making other people's records in their pressing plants, there was nowhere else for the small companies without their own pressing facilities to go. Even large companies had to rethink their position: WEA began work on their own American pressing plant (the expense involved can be gauged from the fact that CBS spent $50 million on a new manufacturing plant for themselves).

The majors' control of distribution is the second factor in their continued domination of the music business—they can decide what not to distribute (as well as what not to press). Rock records are sold in shops (rather than via mail order or the sorts of consumer clubs that are so important for book sales), and in Britain the major record companies have always been directly in charge of their own retail distribution—they don't work through wholesalers. There are several independent distributors handling small company records, but the rack jobbers handle only budget lines. In America the situation is more complicated. In the 1950s the major record companies primarily employed independent distributors to promote and place their records, or they sold, at discounted prices, to "one stop" wholesalers, originally set up to service jukebox operators but now servicing retail outlets too. Record companies had to sell their goods to their distributors before they could sell them to the public—even record covers were designed with record sellers rather than buyers in mind (early Motown LPs, for example, kept artists' pictures off the sleeves in order to get them into white stores in the South), and by the 1960s most records were being bought in the ever-expanding department stores and supermarkets. These were not specialist record outlets, and they increasingly relied on the rack jobbers to stock and service their limited record space (the jobbers pay a store to let them keep a rack of records on its premises; they split the proceeds, and the jobbers are responsible for what is stocked). By the end of the 1960's such racks accounted for about three-quarters of American record sales, and the jobbers had grown enough to buy directly from the record companies. The rise of the rock LP led to a merger of the rack-jobbing and one-stop service, as well as to a declining role for the independent distributor (the same process was to affect bookselling in the 1970s).

The problem with this system for record companies was that there were contradictions in their own retail needs: on one hand they wanted to use shops as a way to break acts or records, on the other hand they wanted to consolidate sales, maximize the volume of hit record turnover. Rack jobbers were fine for the latter task— they had a wide consumer reach, they concentrated their stocks on guaranteed sellers—but not for the former—they couldn't respond easily to local promotion campaigns, they were unwilling to risk unknown names or titles, they didn't draw the necessary *rock* buyers. To reach them the major record companies in the 1970s set up their own "branch distributors," which functioned like the original independents but handled only company products. Simultaneously there was a consumer move back to large, discounted record retail chains like Tower (set up, often enough, by the rack jobbers themselves, whose share of the market, by 1976, was down to about 50 percent). The problem of overproduction remained though—evident in the cut-out bins and record returns—and in 1979 the big record companies began to modify the 100 percent sale or return deals they'd been doing with retailers since the 1950s, under which shops could return any unsold records in return for credit on new supplies. Stores, not wanting to be landed with records they could neither sell nor return, began to be more cautious in what they ordered; the record companies increased their control over shop policy.

The 1970s reassertion of distribution control by the American majors was a response to the rock boom (the new volume of sales, the new styles of promotion and marketing), but its effect was disastrous for record companies that couldn't afford their own distribution—the independent distributors suddenly lost custom, capital, and effectiveness. By the end of the decade, EMI had taken over UA, MCA had taken over ABC, and numerous smaller companies had vanished (like Private Stock) or were in deep financial trouble (like Capricorn). Even A&M, the biggest of the independents, had to sign a manufacturing and distribution deal with RCA.

In the 1970s the majors swallowed up numerous other areas of the music business besides distribution and manufacture. The most dramatic example of the extension of record company control in Britain came in 1969 when ATV (which had controlled Pye Records since 1966) took over the Beatles' publishing company, Northern Songs, for £10 million, despite the Beatles' well-publicized attempts to prevent it. ATV had already lost one publishing takeover battle in 1968, when Philips bought Chappell, and in 1969 EMI joined the chase, buying Keith Prowse. EMI hadn't had any publishing interests at all until 1958, when Ardmore and Beechwood was formed. This sudden flurry of record company interest in publishing at the end of the 1960s was, initially, a response to the huge profits that rock had brought publishers, despite their displacement from the music's creative center. By the mid-seventies all the major record companies were also major publishers and many of the apparently independent publishers, with their fanciful names, were actually, like their equivalent record labels, part of a huge combine. The continuing importance of publishing, even in its traditional form, was reflected in the fact that EMI got more than half of its considerable publishing income (an estimated 20 percent of world publishing revenue) from its newly acquired back catalogue (in its biggest deal, in 1976, it bought Screen Gems/Columbia, owner of all the old Brill Building hits, for $23.5 million), and throughout the 1970s ATV got 60 to 65 percent of its publishing income from Lennon and McCartney's 1960s songs. The majors, through their control of such catalogues, were in a position to exploit nostalgia to the maximum. Publishing was, indeed, a very safe investment—there were virtually no production costs, and songs had a much longer life than records—the money kept coming in.

The most successful conglomerate record company presently is Polygram, based on the interlocking relationship of Phonogram (owned by the Dutch company Philips Electrical) and Polydor (an offshoot of Deutsche Grammophon, which is in turn a subsidiary of the huge German electrical corporation Siemens). Polygram now owns Mercury in the USA, Decca in Britain, and, through its controlling 50 percent stake in RSO and Casablanca, was an early beneficiary of the tie-up between film and record production. In 1978 the company became the first in the music business to top $1 billion in worldwide sales.

By then Polygram had been joined in the world music markets by Bertelsmann, the second largest book and record publisher in Germany, which had established Ariola in both Britain and America, taking over Arista Records in the process. But for my example of interlocking entertainment interests I'll take the British company EMI, which before the arrival of Polygram claimed the title of "the world's biggest recording company."

EMI's growth is best dated from 1954 when it was being outsold by Decca; at that time Joseph Lockwood was appointed managing director. His first act of rationalization was to sell EMI's radio and gramophone-manufacturing interests to Thorn; thereafter the EMI story was about expansion. Its most publicized takeover came in 1969 when it acquired the Associated British Picture Corporation and thus Thames Television. I won't describe here EMI's far-flung empire (its overseas companies, its medical and defense interests), but merely point to the impact of that empire on the particular process of record-making. What was interesting, in this respect, about EMI's takeover of ABPC was that through the takeover it got control of a chain of cinemas and theaters that is one of the major British circuits for promotional rock tours (and which neatly complemented EMI's existing network of clubs, dance halls, and discos).

Following our way through the complicated web of EMI's in-

terests we find not just a publishing empire but also Britain's leading distributor of musical instruments; not just Capitol and UA
Records, American recording companies, but also Audio Device, an
American manufacturer of recording equipment; not just HMV, a
chain of British record and tape shops (stocking, of course, Emi-
tape), but also an American rack-jobbing company and a highly successful record shop-fitting service regularly employed by HMV's
high street competitors. EMI controls a network of talent and artist
agencies, concert promotion companies, ticket outlets, even a Muzak
library. The mutually advantageous relationships among these different aspects of the music business were essential to EMI's growth
as an entertainment empire; the ironic conclusion to its story came
in 1979, when EMI was, in turn, taken over by Thorn, the television
manufacturing and rental company to which EMI had sold its radio
interests twenty-five years previously. Thorn-EMI is a leisure company for the 1980s, a combination for the video age: Thorn makes
and distributes the hardware, EMI will make and distribute the software.

A similar picture could be drawn of Britain's other major leisure company, the Associated Television Corporation, which owns
not just ATV, Precision Records (formerly Pye), and Northern Music, but also its own chain of theaters and halls, Britain's biggest
supplier of Muzak, and various other musical enterprises. The major
American record companies are even more wide-ranging in their investments. In America the building of entertainment corporations
began in the 1920s and 1930s as radio manufacturers and radio stations merged and took over theaters and theatrical agencies, as the
developing film companies took over music publishers (to guarantee
their cut and control of film musical hits and themes) and established their own record companies and radio networks, and as the
two groups merged to form today's conglomerates, whose interests
cover all the mass media, all leisure activities, all youth concerns—
CBS for example, owns the Discount Records retail chain and the
rock instrument manufacturers Fender and Rhodes.

By the late 1960s the high profit and growth rate in rock was
attracting non-media conglomerates too. Kinney bought and put together WEA and combined its new musical interests with numerous
other investments in publishing, sports, and education. The development of video-recording has involved even more complicated business tie-ups. There are now three groups competing with each other

to determine the pattern of future leisure technology: EMI-Thorn/ Japan Victor, RCA/CBS, and Philips/MCA.

The object of record companies is profits and the size of their profits depends, in accounting terms, on the difference between their costs and their revenues. But throughout the 1970s record company profit strategies rested less on attempts to cut costs than on attempts to absorb them—hence the logic of vertical integration: if a company controls every aspect of record-making, then many of its costs will return as income; the object is not just to control production and distribution but also to make the instruments the musicians play, the equipment the producers need, the record players the consumers use.

The major record companies, in short, benefit from the *activity* of consumers. The average amatuer rock group has spent thousands of dollars before it is even ready to play, and popular music history is intimately linked to the development of popular musical instruments. Piano-based ragtime developed at the end of the nineteenth century because keyboards became available to black families under hire-purchase deals; rock music-making, similarly, has always depended on secondhand instrument shops and credit agreements. Record sales booms have always meant, too, booms in the sales of musical instruments. One effect of the technological development of rock in the 1970s—the increased sophistication of sound systems, the use of electronically complex instruments—was to raise the costs of making the right noise (let alone the right music); one of the catalysts of the new-wave sound of the end of the decade was the relative reduction in the price of synthesizers and recording equipment (and the huge increase in the volume of their sales).

The record industry is, similarly, a branch of the hi-fi and electrical goods industry: the more people who have record players, the more who will buy records, and vice versa. The development of progressive rock albums in the 1960s was made possible by the marketing of cheap stereo record players—the developing tastes of stereo owners had a clear effect on rock styles and recording techniques. In general, indeed, hardware developments precede software innovations. Record companies have always been slow to see the musical possibilities in technological change: they resisted, as a pop medium, both the LP and stereo (changes in recording techniques have always been pioneered by record companies' classical music divisions) and have yet to do much of interest with videodiscs. This partly reflects the economic logic of record companies as branches of multinational entertainment corporations. Traditionally, the multinationals have concentrated, for example, on exporting hardware rather than software; the object has been to control another country's record companies and pressing plants rather than to flood its market with foreign-made records directly. Thus, while American rock 'n' roll had an obvious impact on Europe in the 1950s, there wasn't much export of records—European companies could be successful with their own versions of the music (in terms of world sales Elvis Presley made more money from his films than from his records).

Rock did, to some extent, change this. From the late 1960s there was a rapid expansion in the world market for Anglo-American records and a sharp shift in market shares—by the end of the 1970s the USA accounted for about 40 percent of world sales, Japan and West Germany for 10 percent each, France for 8 percent, and Britain for less than 6 percent. And the records being sold in the different world markets were much the same. In Sweden, for example—a country with its own record industry and a government policy of cultural nationalism—more than 60 percent of the records sold are imported British and American rock LPs; in an English-speaking country like New Zealand, less than 5 percent of sales are of records originating in the country itself. The majors these days are, in other words, world majors, and most records sold in the world are, somewhere along the line, processed by the majors (thus Jamaican reggae reaches its biggest market, West Africa, by way of British, American, and German record companies).

Records are now increasingly made with the world market in mind, and the terms of record company competition have been altered. This is most obvious in Britain, where the worldwide impact of the Beatles can now be seen to have been an extraordinary and unrepeatable business event. The hard fact now is that British companies have to look to the American market for satisfactory sales, while American companies don't have to take much account of the British market at all—its share of the world market is small enough that record makers are more likely to be concerned with an act's potential Japanese and German appeal than with its likely British sales. In economic terms America still dominates the sound of world pop (thus disco made money in a way that punk did not), and the statistics are revealing. In 1975, 50 percent of American chart places were occupied by American artists; by 1979 the figure had reached 84 percent, and EMI, once the world's biggest record company had less than 10 percent of the U.S. market. In Britain, by contrast, CBS, WEA, and Polygram accounted for more than half of the records sold; UK companies for less than 40 percent.

Faced with such developments, it is not surprising that the independent rock entrepreneurs have felt their own need to expand and diversify. In the 1970s music publishers, for example, became independent producers, set up their own studios, packaged their songs as demo-discs, were involved in management and promotion. Independent record companies, meanwhile, expanded in the opposite direction, establishing their own publishing companies and studios, or taking them over. We can find examples of diversification from every possible music business base: promotion (the origins of Robert Stigwood's RSO records), recording studios, management, agencies, even retail (Virgin Records started as a mail-order firm).

The Who are perhaps the most interesting example of how an entire business can be built out of one group's success. In 1968 the Who's status as one of rock's most successful live acts was confirmed by the large sales of *Tommy*, which gave the group the money both to pay off its debts and to invest. Their first move was to cut the costs of constant touring by buying, rather than renting, their stage equipment, lights, and transport. Having bought them—and the space to keep them—they began to hire them out to other groups, in order not to waste resources when they were off the road. The Who's roadies thus became experts, selling a service that was increasingly specialized—repairs, electronic advice, stage design, lighting invention; they pioneered the use of lasers and began to manufacture some stage items under license from their American originators. A similar logic saw the Who move from renting rehearsal space to buying it to developing and renting it out as specially designed rock-tour rehearsal space, complete with stage, lighting banks, etc. By the end of the 1970s the Who owned Shepperton, one of Britain's three remaining film studios. They had originally bought a part of it for storage space, then installed video, dubbing, recording, and rehearsal studios, invested in holograph research, and expanded to take over the whole space. They had their own video and film production companies, their own publishing and record production companies—and this had all been achieved by reinvesting their post-*Tommy* earnings. Interestingly enough, the Who did not form their own record company (most groups' first move)—Polydor could do that job for them quite well enough.

One result of such diversification is the remarkable mobility of personnel within the record industry not just between companies but between roles. A&R men reach their positions from every possible music-biz background—they have been pluggers, promotion and advertising men, engineers, critics, musicians, deejays; managers emerge from agencies and studios, from bands and press offices. If people fail in a new role they move back to an old one; if they succeed they move on in the hope that their magic will rub off elsewhere.

# PROFITABILITY

Another result of this diversification is that it becomes difficult to measure the profitability of the record industry—profits are generated at so many levels. The final results on a company's balance sheet reflect a very complicated balancing act. In general, the steady and occasionally spectacular expansion of the record industry over the last twenty years has generated a huge income, and record companies have benefited accordingly. In 1953–54 EMI, for example, had pretax profits of £1.1 million, by 1976 the pretax profits of its music division were £11.5 million—and EMI was one of the decade's less successful music companies.

Such figures conceal the number of ways in which record companies make money; an alternative way of assessing the profits of record-making itself is to look at the costs involved. There are a variety of production costs—studio and session fees, manufacturing, packaging and distribution charges, and promotion expenses. There is a minimum below which such costs can't fall, but their percentage of total costs is reduced dramatically as the number of units sold rises. There are, secondly, a variety of royalty costs—a portion of the retail price of each record goes to the recording artist, to the songwriter and publisher, possibly to the producer or engineer; there is a cut on every sale to the retailer and the taxman. Record company profit is realized when the returns from sales after the deduction of royalties are greater than the production costs. The difficulty in determining this break-even point is that the production costs vary so greatly (and it must be remembered that such costs are usually charged to the artists rather than absorbed by the record company).

By the end of the 1970s the average "rock 'n' roll album" cost between $70,000 and $100,000 in studio time, and any rock "sweetening" (adding strings, for example) could add another $50,000 to the bill; promotion budgets began at around $150,000 and rose rapidly. But even these figures conceal the accounting decisions really being made. At the beginning of the decade there was still some sense of "normal" production costs, "normal" sales, "normal" profits (in Britain the break-even sales figure cited for LPs was usually about 23,000). But soon the decision was being made the other way around: the object became platinum sales—a million copies as starting point. Company bosses began to turn their noses up at gold records—500,000 sales; studio and promotion costs were established at whatever would ensure platinum. In this context, "break-even" calculations are almost impossible—there are such huge differences, in both investment and return, between the big sellers and the rest. The platinum strategy reflects the fact that once the break-even point is passed, the accumulation of profit is stunningly quick: a million sales of an expensively made record is far more profitable than 50,000 sales of a cheaply made one (record companies would always prefer to sell 500,000 copies of one release than a total of 500,000 copies of ten releases); and time further complicates matters—albums can build sales over a long period of release and rerelease. Despite the difficulties of the calculations, though, most business commentators agree that about 10 percent of all records released (a little less for singles, a little more for LPs) make money.

The ratio of hits to releases seems remarkably small (Paul Hirsch once calculated that more than 60 percent of singles released are never played by anyone), and for all the professionalization of rock record making and selling, the market remains hard to control: one reason why it is so difficult for independent record companies to compete with the majors is that to achieve the necessary cash flow they have to have a much bigger hit-to-release ratio, they have to be much more single-minded in their pursuit of hits from *every* release. The majors not only benefit from their manufacture of other people's hits, but their capital resources also provide them with their own safety net: the size and range of their back catalogue gives them a continuing source of income, no matter what is happening to their new releases. Budget LPs and TV compilations (anthologies of old hits sold through TV commercials) command, between them, about half the LP market in Britain, for example; and if the big money is in rock best-sellers, the steadiest revenues come from the "middle market," which can be used to solve the problems of capacity utilization and stock control.

The majors can take a long-term view of their investments—they don't only use singles as promotion for albums, but also use the first album as promotion for the second. In the pattern of rock success that emerged in the USA in the 1970s, record companies could expect losses on albums and tours for anything up to three years until a record achieved its sales breakthrough—a breakthrough which often led to the artists' back catalogues selling too, so that in the long run these initial records weren't, in fact, failures. Only the majors have the capital to sustain such long-range investment planning.

If the cost of staying in the rock market was rising, so was the cost of entering it as the demands made by each professional within the system—artist, producer, studio, etc.—rose. The majors could meet these demands and, indeed, helped to escalate them by raising the costs of the competition. When CBS drastically increased its advances to musicians in the early 1970s, for example, it also increased the numbers of sales necessary for break-even and thus, also, the amount necessary to spend on promotion. Independents found the overall costs of success ever inflationary, even if they could solve the problems of manufacture and distribution. However good they were as talent spotters, they couldn't afford the advances necessary to attract future stars and were unable to promote them sufficiently even if they did sign—even Warner Brothers needed Kinney's cash to become a proper rock label. And the advances necessary didn't just reflect artists' greed; they rested on a realistic assessment of the costs of the equipment, transport, and studio time necessary for rock recording. Six-figure advances to unknowns with potential became routine, and the higher such an advance, the greater the loss on failure. It was, of course, a vicious circle: as the capital investment rose so did the break-even point; as the break-even point rose so did the necessary investment to reach it. Even if independents could keep studio costs down, the pressing charges had to be met; and the more copies of a record that it was necessary to press—

to get it into enough shops, to achieve more than regional sales, to prevent cover versions and fleeting interest—the greater the manufacturing charges.

Thus, internal as well as external pressures forced many independent companies to seek capitalization from the majors—not only in the licensing deals already discussed, but also in more covert arrangements: they got loans in exchange for exclusive distribution or publishing options (George Martin's AIR studio and label, for example, which opened in 1970 at a cost of £350,000, depended on such a deal with EMI). Independents in this situation are always vulnerable to changes in their majors' policies, changes which can bankrupt or squeeze them out of business almost instantaneously (as WEA effectively shut down Radar Records in 1980).

In the business as a whole, a large amount of money is always changing hands internally, regardless of the success of the final product—recording studios, for example, get most of their revenue from the costs of making records that never sell a copy; but the point that needs to be stressed is that the returns on a successful act are hugely different from those on an "ordinary" act—this is the reality of a mass medium and of the profits that come flowing in once a product starts selling millions of copies. It is the prospect of these returns that sets rock costs rising—successful groups notoriously spend vast sums of money in the studio, and the often startling rises in royalty rates at contract re-signing times reveal what huge profits record companies have previously been getting from their best-sellers.

The dependence of record company profits on artistic productivity leads to bizarre disputes, as companies seek legal and financial control of supposedly spontaneous genius. WEA, after waiting two and a half years for the Eagles' follow-up to *Hotel California,* offered them a cash bonus to bring the tape in by a certain date. But, reported *Fortune,* "the deadline has passed, and the album still has not been completed. 'You're dealing with people who have so much money,' says WEA Chairman Joe Smith, 'that there is no financial spur.' He adds with a touch of exasperation, 'We even sent them a rhyming dictionary.' "

There was a similar problem in the Northern Songs/ATV battle—at least part of the bid was for Lennon/McCartney's artistic potential. When Paul McCartney subsequently asserted that his wife had become his coauthor and was therefore entitled to half his new songs' copyrights (a half in which Northern Songs would have no share, as she was not signed to them), ATV counter-asserted that she had "never written music before her marriage" and therefore could not have made any significant contribution. The law was brought in to make an aesthetic judgment (did the songs reveal Linda's contribution or were they all Paul's own work?) on which depended a substantial income.

The problem for ATV (as for all rock capitalists) was precisely that it couldn't *determine* either the music McCartney made or its popularity—all it could hope to do was exploit, to the full, whatever successes occurred and not waste too much on failures. The paradox of the massively successful rock business in the 1970s was that all its strategies—the incorporation of the independents, the expansion into the world market, the development of multimedia sales techniques, the professionalization of its personnel, the routinization of its sounds—were developed because of the problems of overproduction, sloppy musicians, unpredictable audiences. Rock, despite everything, retained its capacity to surprise; its meaning could still be changed.

# CHAPTER 7

# MAKING MEANING

The rock story I've told so far has been a success story, an account of how rock brought new wealth to the record industry, and how the record industry learned to manage and increase that wealth. The story has a relentless logic—exhilarating for the record companies, depressing for radicals like Chapple and Garofalo. But the story is *not* without contradictions, and they emerged publicly in 1979, when the music boom stopped. World sales had expanded from $4.75 to $7 billion between 1973 and 1978, but in 1978–79 there was a 20 percent drop in record sales in Britain, an 11 percent fall-off in the USA. EMI and Decca, the dominant British record companies for thirty years, were both taken over, and if, in America, none of the majors got into trouble that was that bad (only MCA actually made a loss), their employees did feel the pinch—hundreds of them were fired.

I don't want to exaggerate this "crisis." Companies compensated for declining numbers of records sold by increasing cover prices; much of what was going on reflected a general shift in the power of companies, in terms of international competition, as the American majors and Polygram consolidated their world status at the expense of EMI (and even the latter was back in profit by the end of 1980). Nevertheless, the growth rate in the rock business—a rate which had reached 25 percent per year by 1976—was down to 5 to 6 percent and likely to stay that way. There was a real decline in the numbers of records sold (in the UK, for example, the Rolling Stones' *Emotional Rescue* reached the number-one spot in the LP charts with sales of only 75,000 copies—it would have needed 200,000 sales the year before). Record companies simply could no longer operate on the assumption of an ever expanding rock market. Short-term calculations had to be pruned: expected 5 million sellers became expected 3 million sellers; record companies stopped wondering what mineral came after plutonium.

Such changes had significant ripple effects. As sale or return deals with retailers were cut from 100 percent to 20 percent, so stock orders became more cautious; as promotional budgets were cut, so the concert business was squeezed—groups didn't get subsidized unless there was already a sign of record success. There was a move back to small venues, cheap bands, local scenes. The industry had become cost-conscious again, prudent in its signings, restrained in its marketing. Mistakes and failures had become dangerously expensive if platinum successes could no longer be taken for granted.

Most of the reasons why people weren't spending so much money on music pointed to factors outside record business control. The recession, the growth in youth unemployment (particularly dramatic in Britain) meant that people had less money to spend or were, at least in the USA, spending what they had on gas, not albums. There isn't much evidence that the demand for particular records is price-elastic (people don't buy Ted Nugent rather than Billy Joel just because his record is cheaper), but there does seem to be a general price above which people are reluctant to go (especially if, in their cost-cutting efforts, record companies sacrifice pressing and sound quality). This brings us to the record companies' perceived villain of the 1980s: the cheap cassette tape.

Record companies equate each blank tape sold with a record not sold. Counterfeiting and bootlegging (serious problems in international terms) don't affect the level of sales (just who gets the proceeds). Home taping, by contrast, could have a permanently disruptive effect on the record business. The most buoyant sector of the electrical goods industry by the end of the 1970s was stereo cassette manufacture, and, the record companies argued, their purchasers must use them to tape something. Despite a number of panicky surveys, though, the commercial consequences of taping remained unclear: people do tape LPs—from the radio, from friends' collections—rather than buying them, but home tapers buy records too, more than anyone else in fact. Home taping, in other words, has become, along with record buying, another aspect of what it means to be a rock fan.

The record industry's hostility to home tapers was reminiscent of its original hostility to radio; missing from the simple argument about unfair competition was, again, any sense of how records work in leisure. By the end of the 1970s the rock business had, indeed, a very conservative concept of music. This was reflected in its dominant selling strategies. The obvious policy was to maximize the volume of record sales by aiming them at the widest possible market. As Al Coury of RSO Records (who could claim to be the most successful music salesman of the decade) put it, "We try to design the music in the album to the widest demographics possible." This strategy meant pursuing worldwide sales, using movie tie-ups, TV advertising. Music was being made for multimedia settings, aimed at an undifferentiated market (in which even youth was not particularly significant), and only certain acts could be so marketed—rock was being redefined as "professional entertainment."

This has been a recurring aspect of the development of music as mass culture—a style developed for a particular audience is sold to a general audience—and it has had recurring musical effects. In the 1950s *American Bandstand* had dress rules for its dancing teenagers—they had to look clean and smart, acceptable to the mass of viewing parents; and Dick Clark confined the audience to fourteen- to eighteen-year-olds who had the right degree of "malleable enthusiasm." In 1978 Don Kirshner attributed the success of his TV rock concerts to their safety—kids whose parents wouldn't let them go to live rock shows could watch his show. The effect of fitting rock 'n' roll into a medium like television is to make it safe, to deprive it of some of its significance—an undifferentiated audience *can't* be a rock audience.

Historians of black music have documented how the rise of the mass media led to the exclusion of black performers from mass American culture. This was only partly an effect of direct racism—

assumptions about what the mass white audience would be prepared to watch and hear. It was also an effect of the difference between the standardized forms of mass entertainment and the vital, spontaneous, personal basis of black entertainment. Hence, for example, the destruction of the vernacular black dance tradition by television, with its emphasis on planned, routinized choreography; if 1950s television variety shows (Jackie Gleason, Steve Allen, and so on) took off from vaudeville, they ended up with bland, television-created acts like the June Taylor Dancers. Richard Peterson has made a similar argument about country music. The emerging presence of country on radio and television in the 1960s led to new definitions of what country should sound like—"urbane, sophisticated and lively"—and to new sales targets—country superstars could go platinum, too. This, as in rock, led to higher production and promotion costs, to the pursuit of ever bigger "crossover" markets, until country ceased to be distinctive in terms of audience, musicians, or sound; it had become another label for MOR pop. In the mid 1970s Olivia Newton-John was able to be, simultaneously, a British pop performer, the American country singer of the year, and the star of the mass teenage film *Grease*.

The pursuit of a mass market does not necessarily mean boring, bland, bad music—*Saturday Night Fever* was a good film and record as well as a marketing triumph. But the pursuit of a mass market does change music's context, the way it works culturally: it involves an undifferentiated audience that is not a music audience as such. The music business can't rest on TV-promoted nostalgia packs, and *Saturday Night Fever* was an exceptional phenomenon— the Bee Gees, for all their sales, never became cultural superstars like the Beatles. If the pursuit of the mainstream market has to be, in the end, at the expense of the rock market, then the pursuit of the rock market, in the end, has to be the normal concern of record companies.

The rock sales strategy is to exhaust the spending power of a number of particular markets. Record companies minimize their risks by dividing the rock market into a number of genres, each with its own set of institutions—radio, concert halls, press, and so forth. Each new release then just has to be fitted into its institutional slot—in the 1970s even "crossover" became a genre in its own right. This approach to music is, again, essentially conservative. It rests on a sophisticated assessment of what particular audiences want, and means giving them that, over and over again. The aim is to eliminate surprise—no surprise profits, but no surprise losses either; everyone, musicians and audiences too, knows what to do, what to expect. The record company question became not what to put into its packages, but how to get them to their market; and one consequence, as we have seen, was the shift in the financial power of the musicians involved. In the last ten years the average royalty rate has tripled, and these days record companies rarely get unexpected windfalls from low-royalty unknowns. They have changed musicians from one-hit wonders into careerists, expecting to use their unknown years as a period of *grooming.*

By the end of the 1970s, record companies were obviously restricted by their routines. The majors, for example, initially resisted disco (while for those companies that did go with it, like Casablanca—an "independent" controlled financially by Polygram—the returns were huge: it was cheap music to make and promote, and it had no superstars—royalty rates were low or nonexistent). What was happening seemed to fit the usual accounts of pop music history: the majors had standardized rock; new sounds, disco and then punk, came from independents, and were, in their turn, standardized and co-opted into new record company divisions.

But we should be wary of reading too much from a survey of record company balance sheets. Neither punk nor disco (nor any other musical taste) is *just* a market; both involve active leisure interests, the uses of music by audiences with their own account of what records are for. Punk music-makers, in particular, developed an ideology of "independence" that wasn't just a matter of economics but articulated, too, an argument about rock consumption.

# INDEPENDENCE

In the first six months of 1980 ninety new labels appeared in Britain. Independent record companies have always had a British presence—particularly for minority musics like jazz and folk—but since 1977 there has also been an explosion of independent rock music-making activity. This was less a response to frustrated consumers (unsatisfied by the limited musical choices made available by the majors) than the expression of frustrated producers, excluded from record-making by soaring studio costs and by the new "professional" conventions of the rock industry. By 1976 a lot of "cheap" music was being made—on the pub rock circuit in particular—by amateur performers or failed professionals in whom record companies had no interest. New companies, like Chiswick and Stiff, were formed to record it and the punk rock that it became. The punk-independents had a new ideology: they weren't just the labels of on-the-ground entrepreneurs, recording bands whose live popularity was evident; they were also, increasingly, formed by musicians who were recording themselves, going public via do-it-yourself production (even if they had to borrow money from local entrepreneurs to do so). While the average costs of recording rock had been rising, as record companies referred to the costs necessary to reach the mass market, the minimum cost of record-making had been falling: punk musicians could use small, front-room studios without any reference to sales at all; their music sounded fine through four-track tape recorders, and there were soon as many street-corner, amateur records being made as there had been in New York in the late 1950s.

The problem was to transform such local activity into a national presence, and the solution was provided by a number of independent distributors like Rough Trade, frustrated record shopkeepers for the most part—frustrated by the unavailability of local records, frustrated by the irrelevance of most of the majors' products. National distribution helped local labels' sales and eased the problems of cash flow, but did not mean large profits. Sales of much more than 20,000 still needed full promotion, access to department store racks, capital enough to cover the initial pressing costs; independent labels with that sort of ambition, like Stiff, had to make distribution deals with the majors. Nevertheless, between them the unambitious independents sold enough to establish a viable "alternative" record business, with its own network of studios, shops, clubs, charts.

The majors had to take this alternative presence into account in both their A&R and marketing policies. They treated the independents as talent and trend spotters and tried to formalize such arrangements financially. At a time when British rock companies were in trouble, the punk independents, however small, had the authority of their own idealism. They moved attention back from markets to musicians, to the ways music works to symbolize and focus communities. They articulated an explicitly anti-professional attitude to record-making, a concern for music as a mode of survival rather than as a means to profit. They brought a new tension into rock practice, a new concept of ambition, a new challenge, particularly for those musicians—the majority—who continued to sign with the majors, to abandon local love for mass success.

The American tradition of independent record-making involves rather different considerations. In the heyday of small R&B and rock 'n' roll labels in the 1950s, the impetus came from unmet consumer demand: jukeboxes, radio stations, and stores all wanted music the majors weren't making, and the object was to find, record, and sell that music (financially, the independents probably treated their musicians worse than the majors would have done). Even Motown was set up not to record Detroit music but to use Detroit musicians to make a new sort of pop radio sound. By the mid-1970s there were local music-makers, rock experimenters, punks whose only way onto record was to do it themselves, but their labels did not have the same impact in America as in Britain. To reach the national market (and so make the majors take notice) required a much greater outlay, and radio access was more limited (British independent records relied heavily on John Peel's BBC show for national success). As in Britain, the American majors sought to absorb punk as commerce, and they were more effective in excluding punk as ideology—licensing deals (like A&M's with Miles Copeland's IRS) were straightforwardly commercial. The "alternative" rock questions were confined to local areas, specific audiences.

And it was there that they had their effects. By 1980 concert promoters and venue owners wanted, for their own reasons, cheap musicians—cheap to equip and stage and record, musicians who were not careerists but obsessives. In good times such musicians make less than the stars, but in bad times they lose less, and these were bad times. There was another point, too, that record companies began to brood about. In the words of Tony Wilson of Factory Records, "In a time of recession, the only people who will buy records are kids to whom music means more than money." The question of what the music meant—for its makers, for its consumers—had not mattered much during the rock boom. Now it did because underneath all the demographic expertise was a nagging problem: Is rock essentially a youth music, recreated by each new generation? Or is it only the music of 1960s youth, developing with them into middle-aged affluence? American record companies had opted for the

1960s (while dully servicing the 1970s too) and now, as the rock generation approached its forties, the doubts arose. Who was buying records and why? Punk, in Britain at least, offered some answers.

## THE CASE OF PUNK

Within a few months of its public appearance in 1977, virtually every radical commentator in Britain agreed that punk was a Good Thing. Three arguments were used in punk's support: first, the music was taken to represent the consciousness of working-class youth; second, punk seemed to challenge capitalist control of mass music—there was an emphasis on do-it-yourself, on seizing the technical means of music production; third, punk raised questions about musical meaning, it suggested new sounds, new forms, new texts. One way or another, punk eased the doubts of rock's left-wing critics and revived the hopes of rock's original, 1960s, dreamers: it seemed to be different from previous mass music in terms of how it was made *and* how it was used *and* how it meant.

The first argument drew on subcultural theory. The music was taken to articulate the values of a punk subculture which was read, in turn, as a form of working-class consciousness—"an oblique challenge to hegemony," in Dick Hebdige's words. In many ways the punks' music was not much of a departure from rock 'n' roll tradition—punk consciousness was just a new variation of an established gesture of teenage bravado—but radical commentators described punk, nevertheless, as rank-and-file music which broadcast directly the way things were.

Even in terms of reflection theory (punk as a spontaneous sign of lived experience) this argument did not make much sense. The pioneering punk-rockers themselves were a self-conscious, artful lot with a good understanding of both rock tradition and populist cliché; their music no more reflected directly back on conditions in the dole queue than it emerged spontaneously from them. The musical "realism" of punk was an effect of formal conventions, a particular combination of sounds. It was defined through its aural opposition to the "unrealism" of mainstream pop and rock. The real/unreal distinction depended on a series of musical connotations—ugly versus pretty, harsh versus soothing, energy versus art, the "raw" (lyrics constructed around simple syllables, a three-chord lack of technique, a "primitive" beat, spontaneous performance) versus the "cooked" (rock poetry, virtuosity, technical complexity, big-studio production). The signs of this musical realism, this form of "unmediated" emotion, were, in fact, drawn from well-known rock 'n' roll conventions—conventions which had been established by American garage bands, even if they had a rather different cultural currency in the context of British rock ideology.

The punk argument about music production was drawn directly from 1960s debates. Punk opposed commercial music in two ways. First, it denounced multinational record companies with a version of the assertion that "small is beautiful"—punk music was, authentically, the product of small-scale, independent record and distribution companies. Second, punk demystified the production process itself—its message was that *anyone* could do it. One effect of this was an astonishing expansion of local music-making, but the most important strand in its development was a people's version of consumerism, the idea that record buyers had a right to maximum market choice, that record buying should involve customer expression rather than producer manipulation. Just as Britain's hippie entrepreneurial spirit found its most successful expression in the shop-based Virgin Records at the end of the 1960s, so the most enterprising punk company—Rough Trade—was, symptomatically, based on a shop. Such consumerism led to the creation of an "alternative" production system that both paralleled the established industry (alternative shops sell records made by alternative record companies and featured in the Alternative Charts) and was integrated into it. But "independent" records, made by do-it-yourself companies, remained commodities.

Independence in this context seemed to refer primarily to the question of artistic control: the punks, like hippie musicians before them, assumed an opposition between art and business, with honesty on one side and bureaucracy on the other. And this involved not only the mass culture argument about commodities but also a more romantic argument about creativity. Musicians were not seen as workers, as cultural employees, but as individual artists. Their music was progressive because it involved the direct expression of the people-as-artists; the punk task was to make everyone a star. Punk messages could be distorted by the process of commercial production, but only if this process was in the wrong hands (multinational bureaucrats, boring old farts). Punk truth could get through, but the means of music-making had to be kept under control—by the musicians, by the kids.

The original punk texts had a shock effect. They challenged pop and rock conventions of romance, beauty, and ease. Punks focused their lyrics on social and political subjects, mocked conventional rock 'n' roll declarations of young virility and power, disrupted their own flow of words with their images and sounds. It soon became apparent though, as the shock wore off, that punk was constricted by its realist claims, by its use of melodic structures and a rhythmic base that were taken to tell-it-like-it-was just *because* they followed rock 'n' roll rules—the 4:4 beat, shouted vocals, rough guitar/bass/drums lineup.

The result of these limits on experimenting was the emergence, after 1977, of a clear split: punk populism versus the punk vanguard. The punk populists remained locked in their original position. They read teenage gestures and heard punk forms as the spontaneous expression of anti-hegemonic youth; the political problem was to develop youth consciousness and prevent its symbols from being commercialized. The punk vanguard became more interested in musical meaning itself, in the stylistic assumptions that bound subcultures together. These musicians—the Gang of Four were the most articulate—began to explore textual structures in ways familiar in other media (in Godard's films, for instance), distancing themselves from their own performances, juxtaposing terms from different genres (musical montages of rock/reggae/funk). They sought to undermine the populist assumptions of transparency and subcultural identity, to mock the idea of a direct line from social experience to musical form, to expose the subjective claims deeply embedded in all rock music.

Music is a medium in which the expression of emotion is so direct (performers talk straight at us) that powerful conventions of "subjective realism," truth-to-feeling, have developed. Rock musicians drew on both blues and folk devices to establish their "authenticity," and these devices were important for punk musicians too—they lurk behind their realist claims.

In daily discourse the voice *is* the person, it is our means of representing our "selves" to other people; and while we can lie with language and fake the emotions expressed in nonverbal sounds, communication depends on trusting the voice as the expression of the person. Thus the punk vocal was the clearest sign of punk intentions. Punk singers like Johnny Rotten developed an explicitly working-class voice by using proletarian accents, drawing on football supporter chants, expressing an inarticulateness, a muttered, hunched distance from the words they plucked from the clichés of public expression. These devices, startling in aural terms, worked in fact to present punk singers in the traditional rock way—their emotions were expressed openly, directly. The original punks were all personalities.

Rock critics have always defined art in terms of subjective expression. Music, according to the reviewing principles developed by *Rolling Stone*, for example, is meant to be honest: critics value a performance if they can hear it as the authentic expression of feeling, and the clearer and more intense the feeling, the better. At the most naive level this means listening to lyrics as if they were about their singers' own experiences, but even sophisticated critics listen for sincerity. Rock creativity, in describing an individual sensibility, is contrasted to the soulless formulas of pop.

This approach did not make much sense of the punk vanguard which was, in a sense, "objective." These musicians challenged the suggestion that music works as an emotional code, that individual sensibility can be read from musical output; they developed punk's mannered, chanted vocals into an argument that the singer must be detached from the song—the voice is a tool to sing with, not through.

There was a parallel emphasis on electronic devices, machines that couldn't be seen or heard emotionally. The electric guitar, central sound of rock, has always been treated personally: the archetypical rock image is the guitar hero—head back, face clenched, his feelings visibly flowing through his fingertips. Electronic machines can't be played or symbolized like this: armed with the right program, anyone can make *exactly* the same sound, regardless of individual "feel." For electronic musicians, the spontaneous moment of a sound—*the* creative moment in live rock—is less significant than its preplanning; self-discipline and calculation are more obvious musical virtues than strength of feeling or passion.

The terms subjective/objective refer to emotional realism, truth to feeling. The other set of rock critic assumptions challenged by the punk vanguard concerned social realism, truth to experience. We take it for granted that sounds go with social conditions, that musical effects carry direct social meanings—we hear a tone of voice as "sexy," a chord change as "aggressive," a guitar sound as "harsh." But by the end of the 1970s there was no music a rock musician (however young) could make that did not refer back, primarily, to previous rock readings; the music was about itself now, whether it liked it or not—this was obvious even (perhaps especially) in the work of a skilled rock naturalist like Bruce Springsteen.

The punk vanguard turned such musical reference into artistic purpose: they queried the "naturalness" of musical language. Beginning from the assumption that all music is constructed, they sought to strip it down to its foundations; they juxtaposed rules and regulations from different genres; listeners were invited to notice the musical presence of effects that were previously inaudible. These musicians valued the pop quality that rock fans most despised—artificiality. They were concerned with rhythmic rules (with disco, funk, reggae) because rhythm is the musical element least easy to describe in subjectivist or realist terms—drummers aren't heard to express *themselves* like guitarists or singers, and the social meaning of pop beat is usually functional—it makes the music easy to dance to.

Rock analysts relate sounds to their immediate conditions of production—to the record industry, a subculture, an artistic vision. The challenge thrown up by the punk vanguard was to develop a general account of rock's means of signification. Musical effects are not biologically given, even if in any particular culture people communicate through music as naturally as they communicate through language. What is said normally matters more, to musician and audience alike, than how musical terms come to be established—black American musicians, for example, take the social significance of the blues for granted. The assumption of an unproblematic relationship between social experience and musical expression works well enough in cultures in which everyone, in one way or another, practices music; the problem of mass music is that the sounds that fill our lives are always made *for* us. In musical cultures people learn the language through using it—they know how musical meaning is made because they make it themselves. In mass cultures we hear music as natural and think nothing about how it came to be made that way.

After their initial burst of spontaneous anger against the ways of the rock establishment, a surprising number of British punk musicians began this more systematic, theoretical exploration of how to make music differently. Many of these musicians came out of art school or college; they had a grasp of similar debates in other media, they drew their ideas not just from film theory but also from the "new sobriety" of Weimar culture, the 1920s reaction to Expressionism which, in John Willett's words, emphasized "objectivity in place of the previous intense subjectivity, self-discipline in lieu of passion, skepticism and dry humor instead of solemnity and faith."

This could equally be a description of the punk vanguard's response to rock. The result was not art for art's sake, but a new approach to the question of *how* music grasps, copes with, and intervenes in experience. These musicians were still determined to rock and roll. They wanted, in Robert Christgau's words, "to harness late industrial capitalism in a love-hate relationship whose difficulties are acknowledged, and sometimes disarmed, by means of ironic aesthetic strategies: formal rigidity, role-playing, humour."

Rock "spontaneity" had depended on a taken-for-granted and therefore unheard, unthought-about, structure. The question now was what this structure expressed. We cannot, in practice (and despite a common critical theory), judge musical quality simply in terms of how the music was produced—by reference to the good intentions of the artist, the bad intentions of the profit-takers; musical effects are a property of the music itself, and from the musicians' point of view the most interesting decisions are not what contracts to sign, but what notes to play. If the latter decision is not (another common critical theory) a matter of pure inspiration, spontaneous emotion, some "natural" essence, but instead the result of thought and intelligence, then theoretical knowledge opens the range of musical possibilities; rock doesn't have to be, in Keith Richards's formulation, "music for the neck downwards."

The punk vanguard itself was most inspired by reggae musicians because reggae seemed to suggest a quite different way of musical being. It opened up questions of space and time in which musical choice—the very *freedom* of that choice—stood in stark contrast to the thoughtlessness of rock 'n' roll; it implied, too, a homelessness—this was choice as terror. The music itself—its lack of a hierarchy of sounds, its depth of pulse—was the moment of cultural analysis; it didn't express something else, some prior reality, but *was* the structure of experience, for musician and audience alike.

# MUSIC FOR PLEASURE

Roland Barthes has challenged "the stock idea that what is not expressive can only be cold and intellectual," the assumption that abstraction is, by definition, a counter to sensuality. This assumption derives from the conventional bourgeois account of musical pleasure: music is taken to be descriptive of something else—the sign of an experience rather than an experience in itself. The resulting aesthetic rests on an "intimidation of detail": a series of discrete signs—words, notes, beats, sounds—accumulates until we are overwhelmed by, overcome with, emotion. Such an aesthetic, Barthes suggests, effectively innoculates us against the pleasure of the music itself, which is reduced to an already coded set of experiences, explained (its uniqueness thus denied) by reference to what can already be said. Music criticism has always been a matter of adjectives.

Barthes argues that to interpret music is to deny "the pleasure of the text." To get at this we must change the object of critical discourse. The task is not to pin down the details that make up a musical experience but to respond directly to its "surface." Barthes uses the example of the voice: the pleasure of singing, for the listener as well as for the performer, comes not just from the words or notes involved but also from the *grain* of the voice itself, from "the materiality of the body" in it. Singing is a physical pleasure, and we enjoy hearing someone sing not because they are expressing something else, not because the voice represents the "person" behind it, but because the voice, as a sound in itself, has an immediate voluptuous appeal.

The pleasure of rock texts (combinations of words and music) has always derived from the voluptuous presence of voices, and rock fans, unlike high art aestheticians, have always known that music's sensual truth isn't dependent on rules of expression. We respond to the materiality of rock's sounds, and the rock experience is essentially erotic—it involves not the confirmation of self through language (the mode of bourgeois aesthetics, always in control), but the dissolution of the self in *jouissance*.

Barthes argues that what is involved in musical pleasure is not significance but *signifiance*—the work of signification; our joyous response to music is a response not to meanings but to the making

of meanings, and *jouissance,* like sexual pleasure, involves self-aban-
donment, as the terms we usually use to construct and hold our-
selves together suddenly seem to float free. And if this sounds like
an unlikely way to treat rock 'n' roll pleasure, think of Elvis Presley—in the end this is the only way we can explain his appeal: not
in terms of what he "stood for," socially or personally, but by reference to the *grain* of his voice. Elvis Presley's music was thrilling
because it dissolved the signs that had previously put adolescence
together. He celebrated—more sensually, more voluptuously than
any other rock 'n' roll singer—the act of symbol creation itself.

In chapter 2, I quoted Lester Bangs's point that we listen to
rock music to hear passion expressed. My point now is that such
passion can't necessarily be described as something behind or beyond the music: musical pleasure involves not just the expression
of passion but also the passion of expression. People are inspired
by their records to make music—to speak—for themselves. And
even this argument doesn't exhaust the issues at stake in the ideology of rock. "Rock and roll," writes Robert Christgau, "is not
something that you believe in, in that onanistic, self-reflexive way
that has vitiated so much modernist art. It is something you do to
get somewhere else."

## THE MUSIC PRESS

The ideology of rock—the arguments about what records mean,
what rock is for—has always been articulated more clearly by fans
than by musicians (or businessmen). In a sense, rock matters more
to fans—rock as fun and pleasure is a more difficult idea to negotiate than rock as career or business. The paradox is that rock, for
all its emphasis on community and culture, is for most of its fans,
most of the time, a personal experience—people listen to their records at home, develop private fantasies about their stars—and they
need all the help they can get. Hence the importance of the professional rock fans—the rock writers. Music papers, indeed, are important even for those people who don't buy them—their readers act
as the opinion leaders, the rock interpreters, the ideological gatekeepers for everyone else.

The specialist pop press has a much longer history in the UK than in the USA, and Britain still, remarkably, supports four consumer weeklies (with a combined circulation of 600,000 to 800,000). The oldest of them, *Melody Maker,* started in 1926 as a trade paper for the growing number of jazz and dance-band musicians and, for a long time, provided the only informed and regular coverage of the popular music scene—it was soon used as a consumer's paper too. The paper initially heard rock 'n' roll as the antithesis of its readers' concern for "good taste and musical integrity." "For sheer repulsiveness coupled with the monotony of incoherence," commented one reviewer, " 'Hound Dog' hits a new low in my experience. How much further can the public be encouraged to stray from the artistry of an Ella Fitzgerald, or the smooth swinging musicianship of a Frank Sinatra?" *Melody Maker* was not a youth paper, and as early as 1952 it had been joined by the *New Musical Express,* which while not much more enthusiastic about rock 'n' roll, was aimed at the new market of teenage record buyers.

In the 1950s the British music press was uncomplicatedly a facet of the music industry, and its growth reflected the increased importance of records and record sales (as against songs and publishers) in that industry; even *Melody Maker,* which continued to provide a specialist service for musicians and jazz fans, became centrally concerned with record publicity (and thus did, once its popularity was established, acquiesce to rock 'n' roll). The papers were important because there was no alternative source of information and advertisement, no pop radio except Luxembourg. The British papers' business function was symbolized by their charts: in 1952 *NME* established the first regular and reasonably accurate list of British record sales, and soon *Melody Maker,* too, compiled a hit parade, from a "secret list" of retailers' returns. These charts had a noticeable effect on stocking and promotional policies—the job done in the USA by a trade paper, *Billboard,* was done in Britain by the consumer press.

In general terms, even if their final ends were different (circulation versus record sales), the British music papers and record companies saw themselves as having the same interests. Music press "news" was news of the latest recording stars, the latest entrants to the charts; all such stars were equally important and their importance lasted precisely as long as their chart success. The papers published press-office handouts and conducted quick interviews (arranged by the growing band of publicists) in order to fill out com-

pany bios with their own human-interest details: "What is your favorite color?"

The 1950s music papers functioned like the film fans' magazines of the 1930s, and they served their purpose competently
enough, keeping pop fans informed of who was doing what and
where. Their American equivalents were the monthly teenage picture magazines which, complemented by pop radio, didn't have to
be so topical or informative. Such publications provided no perspective on the music they covered; they had no developed critical position (except that what was popular must be good); they showed no
curiosity about where records came from or where they went. The
music papers presented the industry's own public view of itself and
were written, accordingly, in a breathy, adman's prose. Their success was entirely dependent on their readers' interest in the stars
they covered: the *NME* sold more than *MM* in the 1950s because
it provided better news of the current chart stars:

> We give the kids what they want. We write about their current
> idols. And we're not so much a jazz paper, like the *MM*, as a
> pop paper. A lot of our competitors write about stars who have
> dropped out of the charts, why they've lost their popularity,
> etc. And they write about up-and-coming singers who are going
> to be the stars of tomorrow. It's the stars of today the kids want
> to know about, not the stars of tomorrow.[1]

By 1964 the British music papers had reached unprecedented circulation heights (*NME* was selling nearly 300,000 copies per
week—another aspect of the Beatles phenomenon), but their music
coverage was little affected: they continued to assume that their market was working-class teenagers with a limited, immediate interest
in the latest pops. The Beatles' success, from this perspective, was
a matter of quantity rather than quality. The TV show *Juke Box Jury*
continued to encapsulate the music papers' own view of rock—a
mixture of show-biz condescension to the youngsters' tastes and the
assumption that music criticism was the same thing as the assessment of sales potential.

As the Beatles phenomenon went on and on these assumptions
were challenged on two fronts: first, it became clear that the Beatles'
market was not just working-class teenagers; second, arguments began to be made that did not relate the Beatles' value simply to their

sales. There had always been non-teenagers interested in rock 'n' roll and even non-teenagers concerned about showing that some rock 'n' roll records were more valuable than others according to noncommercial criteria. But such writers' interests had been in teenage culture as a social fact; they were outsiders, and their critical judgment usually involved rescuing particular performers or records from their teenage context, placing them in some tradition of "proper" music—thus William Mann's famous review of the Beatles in *The Times* in 1963 (which put rock 'n' roll for the first time onto the arts pages) used the critical vocabulary of classical musicology. What began to happen after 1965, though, was an attempt from *within* the rock world to develop an account of the music as art, and for the emerging progressive album-buying rock market of 1966–67, the music papers' pop approach was inadequate. The new rock audience had attitudes that weren't expressed in their pages—the basis of the *MM*'s coverage was still the excitement generated by action in the singles charts—Esther and Abi Ofarim! Don Partridge!—and *NME* was even more clearly a teenage pop paper. The new rock fans had to publish their own papers to articulate an alternative music ideology, and they found this ideology in the USA.

In the 1950s and early 1960s, the USA had no music papers between the trade press on one hand (*Cash Box* and *Billboard*) and the teeny-bop magazines on the other (*Hit Parader* was the nearest thing to a pop newspaper). America's rock press emerged from two other sources.

First, there was the underground press proper. This had its origins in the *Village Voice*, but its real foundations were laid by the *LA Free Press* and *Berkeley Barb* in 1964, papers that were not concerned with music as such but with life-style, with "dope, sex and revolution," with, in the words of the White Panthers' subsequent slogan, "revolutionary motherfucker armed love." Music was valued insofar as it could be connected with these interests, and it soon became important as the most fertile source of underground income—whether the money came from record company advertisements or musicians' benefits. Rock turned out to be the basic form of underground culture, but in becoming so it was imbued with an ideology that was at marked variance with previous notions of pop: rock was valued for its political stance, its aggression, its sexuality, its relationship to cultural struggle. The music that was most despised and mistrusted by the underground press was precisely the commercial, successful, teenage pop that had been essential to the development of the British music press. Rock was defined as the music that articulated the values of a new community of youth; it was opposed to the traditional values of show biz; and as the appeal of the underground spread from its original bohemian roots so did this notion of rock. In 1967 the Underground Press Syndicate was formed, and by 1969 it was claiming 125 member papers in continuous publication and 200 other papers in "erratic" appearance.

I don't intend to trace the history of the underground press, and I don't want to exaggerate the extent of its readership; my point is that underground papers were important as the source of what became the dominant ideology of rock. This ideology was confirmed and developed by a second American event, the creation of new, specialist music magazines: *Crawdaddy* began publication in 1966 and was followed over the next few years by *Mojo-Navigator, Fusion,* and *Creem.* These magazines varied greatly in their format, style, success, and concerns, but they had in common the serious treatment of rock as a cultural form, and they made, from their side, the same connections between rock and life-style that the underground press made from theirs.

The most important of the new music papers was *Rolling Stone,* a San Francisco fortnightly the first edition of which appeared on November 9, 1967. Its founder, Jann Wenner, "wanted the publication to focus on rock music, but it was also to cover everything else in the youth culture." The magazine's intentions were made clear in the first issue:

> You're probably wondering what we are trying to do. It's hard to say: sort of a magazine and sort of a newspaper. . . . We have begun a new publication reflecting what we see are the changes in rock and roll and the changes related to rock and roll. Because the trade papers have become so inaccurate and irrelevant, and because the fan magazines are an anachronism, fashioned in the mold of myth and nonsense, we hope that we have something here for the artists and the industry, and every person who "believes in the magic that can set you free." *Rolling Stone* is not just about music, but also about the things and attitudes that the music embraces.[2]

For the first four years of its existence, *Rolling Stone* experienced tensions and conflicts over the successful achievement of its proclaimed role. The paper found a disjunction between the available ideology of rock, an ideology drawn from the concerns of the underground, and the demands of rock promotion, demands coming from a record business that was slowly beginning to understand the new market and was exploring ways to reach it. The contradictions involved were symbolized by CBS's famous advertisements—"The Revolutionaries Are On Columbia" and "The Man Can't Bust Our Music"—and in 1969 the tensions of the situation had a British expression: Jann Wenner opened an English office to publish *Rolling Stone* in "a regional edition," but his English editors followed too closely the practices and policies of the underground and were dismissed (they founded an English underground paper, *Frendz*).

In America, meanwhile, *Stone* slowly established itself as by far the most popular of the new publications by developing a style of in-depth reporting of youth cultural events; but the excellence of its coverage of, for example, the Woodstock and Altamont festivals increased the tensions inherent in its role, rather than resolving them. As the paper which most clearly understood the new youth culture, *Rolling Stone* had the hopes of both the record industry and the rock ideologues focused on it. By 1971, after numerous crises and staff changes, it had become clear that it was record company hopes that would be satisfied; *Rolling Stone* became integrated into the American music business.

Chet Flippo argues that Jann Wenner's own approach was consistent from the start: "exhaustive coverage of the superstars, inside information on the performers and the music industry, and competent, often excellent, reportage of anything of interest to young people." What this meant in practice was, in the words of one of the staff who left, "a tastefully executed fan magazine." The music was treated seriously—readers were not teeny-boppers—but *Rolling Stone* did not, in the end, represent any fundamental break from the traditional show-biz conception of stars and selling and consumption. The paper had its own version of news and gossip and "in-depth" interviews with the stars, had its own sort of cynical treatment of the latest singing sensation; but its dependence on the concerns of the music industry was soon as obvious as that of the British music press, and if, in its early years, this was tempered with an emphasis on rock as politics, this idea became less evident in the 1970s as staff were sacked for "negative" reviews, for failing to have "the proper attitude toward the artists."

*Rolling Stone*'s ideological dependence on the music business reflected its material situation. It was supported through the various financial difficulties of its early years by record companies. WEA loaned the paper $100,000, CBS helped with distribution and administration, record companies supplied virtually all of *Stone*'s considerable advertising revenue from its beginning. They believed that "the paper was good for music" and agreed with Clive Davis of CBS—if *Stone* "blasted us occasionally" it was simply "to protect itself against the charges of 'selling out'" from its "allegedly anti-establishment readership."

In August 1973 *Rolling Stone* changed format and became "a general interest magazine, covering modern American culture, politics and arts, with a special interest in music." But by now *Stone*'s readership—twenty to thirty-five years old, mostly male, white, affluent, interested in rock even as they settled down and lost their youthful fanaticism—was precisely the same market in which the record companies were interested, and *Stone*'s move away from music made no difference to its advertising revenue or to its importance to the record industry. In the words of Howard Bloom of Famous Music, "Within this business all anybody cares about is an article in *Stone*. It has more impact than any other magazine."

Much the same description of progressive integration into the rock business could be made of America's other music magazines, whatever their origins, and an appreciation of this process can help us to understand the apparent differences between the British and American rock press—while *Rolling Stone* was becoming, from nowhere, the dominant paper in the American music business, nothing much seemed to happen in Britain at all. In 1976 the British music press was much the same as it had been in 1966—the same weeklies with their massive circulations, the same lack of "alternative" publications. Numerous such magazines had been launched but few had survived long, and none had reached a circulation comparable to that of the weeklies. Instead the "alternative" approach to music was, by the mid-1970s, to be found in the pages of the traditional weeklies themselves.

In 1968 *Melody Maker* began to go "progressive." Its features got longer, its interviews more serious; the core of the paper became the album and concert reviews. In 1971 the paper's circulation overtook that of the *NME* (between 1968 and 1972 it doubled from 100,000 to 200,000) and the editor commented that

the scene we report, reflect and interpret is now accepted as a great deal more serious and creative than previously catered for by a "bubblegum philosophy" of popular music. It's a subject that requires careful, sympathetic analysis. And the *Melody Maker* is the thinking fan's paper.[3]

The thinking fan now dominated the market, and in 1972 the *New Musical Express* was reorganized too. A new team of writers was recruited from Britain's own underground press, from *Oz* and *IT* and *Frendz* and *Cream*. Their immediate effect was on the paper's style rather than on its content; their writing was hip and knowledgeable, their cynicism about the rock business was up-front. By 1973 the effects of these new attitudes on the paper were obvious even to its most casual readers: on one hand, the *NME* had developed a calculated eccentricity in its layout and subheads and picture captions—the paper knocked itself in a zany way derived from the American rock magazine *Creem;* on the other hand, music coverage was beginning to stretch beyond the latest chart sensations into a critical vision of rock and its history that went beyond sales figures. The underground argument that rock was only one part of youth culture was expressed in the extension of coverage to nonmusical matters—film and science fiction and comics and drugs. By 1974 *NME* was back to 200,000 sales. It had, successfully, gone up-market, switched from its old pop audience—single-buying, chart-concerned, star-struck—to the new rock audience—album-buying, hip. Like *Rolling Stone, NME* had embedded the rock ideology of the 1960s in the rock business of the 1970s.

There are, nevertheless, differences between the papers. *NME* (like *Creem* in America) tends toward a sociological response to rock, valuing music for its effects on an audience rather than for its creators' intentions or skills: the meaning of rock consumption for *NME* writers lies not in the goods themselves, in their properties as music or art, but in their consumers' participation in a particular form of culture. *Rolling Stone* (and *Melody Maker* in Britain) make, more clearly, an artistic response to rock: music is valued for its complexity, musicians for their intensity of feeling.

Today the music papers' general approach to rock is based on an appreciation of the importance of their readers for the record industry: they are the section of the population most likely to invest in hi-fi, to buy records and attend concerts, to influence what the rest of the rock public does. Just as in 1950s Britain, the music press has an important role in record-marketing. News and interviews are still determined by companies' publicity and promotion plans, timed to support record releases and concert tours, initiated by the press office. There is still little coverage of the rock business as a business (*Rolling Stone*'s reporting expertise is, these days, usually applied to non-music stories). The main task is to make each week's stars seem significant, and once somebody's been done they're put back in the files until the next tour, when the same sorts of question from the same sorts of people get the same sorts of answer. Who to write about depends on the editors' judgments of their readers' tastes, and if these judgments are no longer so exclusively determined by the charts as they once were, they are still a response to popularity, an effect of the rock star-making machinery. Music papers and record companies work together not because the papers are "controlled" by the companies' advertising, but because their general images of the world, their general interpretations of rock, are much the same.

Most rock writers are, in consequence, almost completely dependent on the record business. Their news, their interviews, their access are provided by record companies; music writers' lives necessitate the constant consumption of company-provided resources— free records, free trips to concerts, lunches, drinks, receptions, parties, weekends in Jamaica; virtually everything writers do is covered for them. In America the result is hundreds of free-lance writers, poorly paid by their eventual publishers, but surviving on the perks they get. In Britain, where most rock writers are full-time employees of the music weeklies, the result is a cheap (and profitable) form of magazine production. In both countries there is continuous job mobility between rock journalism and rock publicity—record company press departments recruit from the music papers, music papers employ ex-publicists; it is not even unusual for writers to do both jobs simultaneously.

The most interesting position in this press/industry tie-up is occupied by the review. In the 1950s pop press, reviews were little more than news of releases plus predictions of success. Reviewers didn't expect to influence readers' opinions and probably didn't influence them. But for the readers of the rock press, album choices are matters of identity and status, and reviews are of crucial importance—they arouse by far the majority of the responses on the music papers' letters pages. An album or concert review is read equally carefully by record companies. Reviews rarely have a direct effect on sales—popular acts are not harmed by poor notices, unpopular acts aren't often pushed to success by press praise alone—but they do influence companies' promotion strategies. A strong review at the right time can enhance an act's status with its record company, make it more credible to agents and promoters: Jon Landau's Bruce Springsteen rave was effective in squashing CBS's doubts about him and in committing the company to a major promotional effort; Greil Marcus's *Village Voice* praise for James Talley's first LP made no difference in its sales, but it did change the way both Talley and his record company thought about his music and its possibilities. Reviews are most important, in other words, for unestablished acts, for those people whom no one is quite sure yet what to think about—everybody knows who and what Led Zeppelin are for; no reviewer is going to change that.

From the record companies' point of view, the music papers serve a double purpose. First, they're a promotion vehicle: they can be used to break acts, get a buzz of publicity going; the stories written don't even have to be favorable—it's the space and the photos that matter. But second, the papers are also part of the rock-filtering process: they give record companies an early indication of public taste, useful advice on which releases to push, which to drop; and, in this context, it's the writers' independence from record company influence that gives good reviewers their authenticity. Bad reviews (and they are numerous) don't lead to reduced advertising revenue (A&M withdrew its advertising from *Crawdaddy*, for example, not because of a review, but because the magazine had criticized the company).

Like deejays, rock writers have to establish their credibility for their readers; their reviews reveal their standards, their individuality; and rock writers (unlike their pop predecessors) claim criticism rather than puffery as the essence of their job: their distance from the producers is part of their self-definition. What such criticism actually means, though, remains confused, as writers seek simultaneously to provide a consumer guide, to comment on a culture, and to explore personal tastes.

Such confusion reflects the history of the music press. In his study of American rock writing, Chet Flippo argues that because in the late 1960s rock was an integral part of a youth culture, writing about it automatically involved writing about a variety of other issues. In the 1970s the culture dissolved and the writers' role was reduced to servicing one or another of two consumer markets. On one hand, there was the 1960s generation, older now, interested in rock only as a form of entertainment akin to *Playboy*, a movie, or television; it was this generation at which *Rolling Stone* had always been aimed, and as it grew into a general-interest magazine, its music coverage became little more than a hip consumer guide—you'll enjoy this record, you won't like that. On the other hand, there was a new rock 'n' roll generation, using its music and idols just as the teenagers of old had, also wanting a consumer guide, but wanting it in the form of an old-fashioned, if a little more sophisticated, fan mag—hence *Circus* and *Creem*.

A similar argument could be applied to the British music press. The details are different—Britain has less obviously developed a generation of thirty-year-old rock consumers, *NME* is closer to *Creem* than to *Rolling Stone*—but the basic distinctions are the same. On one hand is *Record Mirror*, a teenage fan mag that has hardly changed its concerns for twenty years; on the other hand is *Melody Maker*, a progressive consumer guide for the thinking fan. But there are difficulties in lumping all the music papers together as consumer guides: the different consumers *use* rock differently, and the concept of "consumer guide" needs better definition.

The essence of fan mags is that they *respond* to tastes. Their consumer service is the provision of information, gossip, and pictures of the stars whom their readers have already chosen or the promotion of new acts that seem to fit established tastes. Their function is not to explain or assess or criticize their readers' preferences, nor even really to influence them; rather, it is to reflect them. Their commercial function, in other words, is *purely* promotional.

There is an aspect of this sort of service in all rock papers, including *Rolling Stone*. It also provides information about and pictures of the musicians whom its readers are known to like; it, too, confirms taste, offers a sense of hip community. In this respect the music press specializes in serving particular markets (just like radio). But the consumers of the up-market rock press make other demands of their magazines. They don't just want to know what they do like, they also want to know what they might like and even what they ought to like. For them a consumer guide is a guide to rock value. What they like *matters*.

I've been assuming that rock writers are opinion leaders, that both record-sellers and record-buyers take notice of them, put some trust in their judgments. Their position only works, though, if their values do represent those of their readers: there may be disagreements about particular records, but reviewer and reader must share an account of what rock means, have the same criteria of rock worth, and it is in this context that we can observe the continued resonance of rock's original, 1960s, ideology.

*Rolling Stone* writers, for example, tend to judge records according to their relevance for a rock community that no longer exists. Because that community—1960s youth culture—is gone, the critical question becomes: Can this artist, this piece of music, provide the experience of that community *in itself?* Hence the emphasis on artistic purposes and skills, the equation between emotional intensity and rock excellence. This approach has two consequences. First, it is essentially conservative: it looks to music to recreate the past—the most important rock cultural figures for the paper are the same now as they were when it started; Jann Wenner has even used his editorial power to reaffirm the importance of the rock greats when his reviewers have appeared to doubt it. Second, it is essentially mystical: the rock experience—"the magic that can set you free"—is never described but endlessly referred back to as some mythical adolescent moment against which all subsequent rock moments can be judged. Punk, for example, was eventually welcomed by *Rolling Stone* not for what it said, not for its political or social stance, but because it offered the authentic rock 'n' roll buzz—the Clash were just like the Stones! *Rolling Stone's* readers trust its judgments because they share its tendency to conservatism and mysticism. What they value in music is its ability to infuse hedonism with a sense of community; rock is defined by a particularly nostalgic use of leisure—it is old people's youth music.

*Rolling Stone* can be contrasted to papers like the *New Musical Express* and *Creem,* which have a continued teenage readership. Their critics assume that a youth culture still exists and assess records according to their contribution to it: the explanation of a record's value lies not in the organizing art of its maker but in its authenticity as a youth cultural product; music is "false" (however complex, sensitive, artful) if it does not emerge from or articulate a youth community. If *Stone* reviewers interpret texts, *NME* reviewers interpret audiences, and, as sociologists, become *de facto* spokesmen *for* youth cultures. More obviously than *Stone* critics, they try to influence how their readers *use* their music.

The rock press, in short, operates as an opinion leader in two modes. Some papers are consumer guides for adults. Their readers want to consume a particular sort of rock experience—their 1960s experience of youthful community—and the critics' job is to find the musicians who provide this experience, to explain the skills with which they do it. The result is the ideology of rock-as-art: it is the art that guarantees the community. Other papers are consumer guides for teenagers. Their readers want to consume another sort of rock experience—one which articulates their present sense of being young—and the critics' job is to find the records which are the signs of that experience, to explain how they work as signs. The result is the ideology of rock-as-folk: it is the community that guarantees the art.

And there are, finally, rock "fanzines" (initiated in the 1960s by Greg Shaw's *Who Put the Bomp*, currently represented by "avant-punk" papers like the *New York Rocker*). Fanzines accumulate rock facts and gossip not for a mass readership but for small coteries of cultists, and they are *belligerent* about their music. Many fanzines are, indeed, belligerently reactionary—they are the house journals of musical preservation societies—but the more important ones (*Crawdaddy* in the 1960s, *Sniffin' Glue* in the 1970s) are belligerently progressive. Their stance is oppositional: they claim their music to be better than what most people like and they want to *change* people's ideas of how music should work.

The rock press is, like rock itself, mostly a mass medium. Its readers are mass consumers too, and the music papers have to *construct* their sense of rock community. This is a diffuse, contradictory process (most of the time, for example, there are obvious gaps between writers' tastes and those expressed by the charts) and in it fanzines have an unexpected significance. Their importance is not commercial (they don't have the mass market record companies are after—their readers buy their records anyway) but ideological. Fanzines, fanzine writers (and the important critics in the mass music papers share the fanzine stance) are the source of the arguments about what rock means, arguments not only about art and commerce, but also about art and audience. Rock ideologues rest their case, as we have seen, on assertions about the place of their music in youth cultures, in experiences of sex and class and growing up. It is these experiences I will now examine.

THREE

# ROCK
# CONSUMPTION

# CHAPTER 8

# YOUTH

Rock is the music of youth, and the question I want to answer in this chapter is straightforward: What's so special about the young? In sociological literature there are two approaches to this problem and two descriptive categories: teenagers and youth (or Elvis Presley and the Beatles). These different terms partly reflect different historical moments, partly different concerns, and they often overlap. "Teenager" is a 1950s concept, "youth" and "youth culture" come from the 1960s; "teenager" refers mostly to the working-class young, "youth" suggests the insignificance of class distinctions at this age, but is usually, implicitly, applied to the middle-class young. Both concepts must be examined in detail.

## TEENAGERS

In 1959 Colin MacInnes's novel *Absolute Beginners* was published. He captured better than anyone else the mood of frenzied celebration that marked the public emergence of teenagers onto British city streets:

> This teenage ball had had a real splendour in the days when the kids discovered that, for the first time since centuries of kingdom come, they'd money, which hitherto had always been denied to us at the best time in life to use it, namely, when you're young and strong, and also before the newspapers and telly got hold of this teenage fable and prostituted it as conscripts seem to do to everything they touch. Yes, I tell you, it had a real savage splendour in the days when we found that no one couldn't sit on our faces any more because we'd loot to spend at last, and our world was to be our world, the one we wanted and not standing on the doorstep of somebody else's waiting for honey, perhaps.[1]

The important thing about "teenager" as a concept was that it described a style of consumption. In his influential 1959 study of "the teenage consumer" in Britain, Mark Abrams, having defined teenagers as young people from the time they leave school until the time they are married or reach twenty-five, turned immediately to the teenage market and showed that this market was dominated, in money terms, by young male workers: the aesthetic of the teenage market was a working-class aesthetic. There was a distinction, in the words of sociologist J. B. Mays, "between a culture largely based on working-class peer-group solidarity and the commercialized entertainment world, on the one hand, and the individualistic, middle-class, high school and university career system on the other." Teenagers lived in the former world and, in Britain, the resulting class distinctions among the young were taken for granted. As one grammar-school girl put it:

> The coffee bars and snack bars etc., are the main congregating grounds for other teenagers, but I personally do not patronise these establishments, preferring to drink hot Nescafé at home rather than cool insipid liquid to the blaring of a juke box at eight pence a time in a howling hole of humanity.[2]

This stress on leisure and pleasure has been retained in accounts of working-class youth ever since. Jeremy Seabrook, for example, in his angry 1971 study of a northern British town, suggested that the only real difference between the life of its teenagers today and that of previous generations "is a greater sense of hedonism, a commitment to enjoying life." He described the young's "preoccupation with self-gratification" and argued that "the only really new feature in the lives of the young is the intensity and resolution of their devotion to pleasure, a commitment to enjoyment and consumption."

A teenager is the conspicuous consumer par excellence, and for the intrigued 1950s public the teenage world was the world of teenage consumption objects, "the world of coffee-bars, motor-scooters and jazz-clubs," to quote the blurb of *Absolute Beginners*. But once this world had been described, once its basis in the relative affluence of young workers had been established, once teenagers' lack of obligations (especially, in Britain, after the end of National Service) had been stressed, questions remained: Why did these teenagers consume the way they did? What was the basis of their leisure choices?

It is in the responses to these questions that we can see how fearful a notion the teenager originally was. One fear was that the young consumed without any values at all, that they were the passive victims of market manipulation. From this perspective the "teenager" was simply a commercial creation, and the result was a nihilistic culture, a generation without any concerns save for flashy, instant pleasures. Professionals concerned with young people, teachers and youth workers, worried about the consequences; conservatives pointed to the young's "private hedonism and lack of public and community sentiment"; liberals feared a generation of depoliticized, "never had it so good" workers.

For the media the problem wasn't the banality of teenage life, it was its possibilities for sex 'n' violence. Fears of a world of youth unpenetrated by adult interests and dominated by peer group norms had been around since at least the beginning of the century (the boys' club movement was one result), and the image of the adolescent city gang had long had blood-chilling potency. In the 1930s this youth problem was exacerbated by economic depression. "Roosevelt Roosts" were established, work camps for juvenile hobos, for the transient teenagers who'd been driven onto the road by the lack of work, who relieved their parents' money difficulties by running away from home. But such adolescents were made invisible by their very mobility and, as Paula Fass has put it:

The problem of youth was a problem of outsiders, of juvenile offenders, young prostitutes, children of the ghetto and the slum. The victims of exploitation and neglect, these youths needed to be assimilated or reformed and integrated into the wholesome norm of society.[3]

What the notion of the teenager did in the 1950s was blur this distinction between the normal and the abnormal, between the ordinary and the violent kids—the suggestion was that *all* teenagers lacked a moral code. This is the blurb for *Teenage Jungle*, an American paperback published in 1957:

Here is a frightful indictment of youthful crime and vice in the U.S.A. It shows how the violence and sex-crazed teen-age cult exists in a living nightmare of ruthlessness and depravity.

These are the ordinary kids you read about every day of your life—"ordinary," that is, until they shoot a store-keeper, assault a girl, torture a bum or wind up dead in a ditch.

Teddy boys were Britain's first visual symbols of the fearful possibilities of the teenager, and, if it was not their delinquency that was new but their aggressive and exclusive sense of youthful style, the effect was still to identify style with trouble—"teenager" and "delinquent" became associated terms.

In Britain the teenage issue was clearly related to the decomposition of the prewar working class. Children in the 1950s had different experiences from their 1930s parents, derived from new leisure opportunities. Teenagers had money to spend and new goods to spend it on; they became part of a mass culture that went beyond neighborhood or class concerns. One important aspect of this process was an "Americanization" of British youth culture. The American influence had begun with music and films in the 1920s, but it was now made material in the coffee bars and dance halls and clothing styles of the 1950s. British teenagers were trying to move like, look like, play like their American models. The teddy boy look, for example, was derived more clearly from a Western movie image— the city slicker villain's string tie, sideburns, and frock coat—than from its supposed local aristocratic model; chronologically, the teds' look predated ted music and rock 'n' roll, but these teenagers were already committed to a fantasy of hillbilly cool—the move from Tennessee Ernie Ford to Elvis Presley was no more peculiar in London's Elephant and Castle than it had been in Tennessee itself.

For the British, then, the very idea of the teenager was American. British teenagers were recognized by their American music, their American idols, their American dreams. What sense did Americans, meanwhile, make of their teenagers?

Many of the social changes that marked the liberation of British working-class teenagers in the 1950s had been significant in the USA since the 1920s. The car began to be used as a means of escape from family supervision, and dating ceased to be adult-chaperoned and controlled; make-up and fashion clothes and cigarette smoking ceased to be the mark of a "bad girl." Movies sparked off new ideas and daydreams, offered new insights into adult hypocrisy and convention. Robert and Helen Lynd quote a Middletown press account of a Sunday film-showing to emphasize the effect of the new mass media on small-town mores:

> Sheiks and their "shebas" sat without a movement or a whisper through the presentation. . . . It was a real exhibition of love-making and the youths and maidens of Middletown who thought that they knew something about the art found that they still had a great deal to learn.[4]

These cultural influences and consuming possibilities emerged simultaneously with shifts in youth institutions: the accelerating separation of home and work; the decline of parental influence over their children's marriage and job possibilities and consequent loss of authority (this was particularly true in the big cities, where even by the 1920s few adolescents spent much of their free time at home); the growing importance of the high school as the new hub of adolescent social life. Between 1900 and 1930 there was a 650 percent increase in the population of American high schools; by 1930 more than 60 percent of the eligible age range was at school.

From the 1920s, then, youth choices were opening up—choices about work and education, about sex and marriage, about leisure and consumption. The mass media were, simultaneously, changing people's assessments of the risks and possibilities of these choices, and the school-based peer group was challenging the family as the source of guidance and precedent in the decision process. By the time of their second (1937) Middletown study, the Lynds could write of "a self-conscious subculture of the young."

Before we equate this subculture with 1950s teenage life, I need to make a point about class: in many respects the choices and institutions and leisure styles described thus far were confined to middle-class adolescents, were a problem only for middle-class parents and teachers and counselors. It was *their* children who seemed to be developing a new morality. Working-class children often lacked even the resources for change—playing and dancing, dating and driving cost money and time (working-class children were less likely to be at school, more likely to be at work). In some respects, indeed, the immediate effects of the diffusion of mass culture and consumption on the working class were to strengthen the family unit, as leisure activities moved off the street and into the family car, as the family radio came to dominate the living room. The possibilities of teenage life glimpsed by working-class girls and boys in the 1920s were obscured by the economic pressures of the 1930s (which also had their dampening effects on college culture) and were only finally realized in the 1950s. By then working-class teenagers, as in Britain, had both money and time to devote to the teenage goods (the radio stations, films, clothes, music) that were aimed at them.

In Britain, 1950s teenage culture was so clearly associated with the working class that middle-class youngsters were excluded from it by definition. Class cultures are less sharply defined in the USA (where other sorts of distinctions—big city/small city, urban/rural, east/west, black/white—have more significance), but American sociologists, too, distinguished working-class (peer- and commerce-based) and middle-class (career- and education-based) youth cultures. In America, though, much more clearly than in Britain, *both* these cultures were an aspect of the teenage phenomenon; both were aspects of a teenage definition that was ideologically fought for.

The adult fear associated with the concept of teenager was, in the 1950s, primarily a fear of working-class adolescents, and it had two components: first, a fear that teenagers had no proper norms at all; second, a fear of corruption, that "bad" teenagers were leading the rest astray, supplying the missing norms themselves (hence the anxiety that the distinction between ordinary and delinquent juveniles was breaking down). One of the obsessions of American sociologists of youth in the 1950s was to discover the *difference* between delinquent and nondelinquent youth—why did one group of working-class youngsters choose to be deviant and another group choose to conform? In A. K. Cohen's classic 1956 study, *Delinquent Boys,* a distinction was made between the "college boy," conformist, quietist, happy at school and work, responsible at play, and the "corner boy," bored and demoralized at school and work, bursting into delinquency in leisure in order to compensate for his alienation and achieve a sense of status.

The language of this distinction between good and bad behavior—the college versus the corner—is significant and was, indeed, a cliché in the teenage media themselves (it remains the central theme of stories of the 1950s like *Grease* and *Happy Days,* though the hoodlum figure is now, with the usual reversal of nostalgic distance, the hero), but it wasn't a distinction that came naturally. If the teenage problem was normlessness, if this moral vacuum was in danger of being filled by delinquents, then the adult response had to be intervention—parents and educators had to *compete* with the street. This was done not by denying the power of teenage culture but by institutionalizing it, by making it middle class, drawing on the models of adolescent behavior that had been developed in colleges and high schools in the 1920s.

This makes some sense of the confusion with which American teenagers were treated by the mass media in the 1950s. On one hand were the rebel images—knife-flicking gangs, leather nihilists, corner boys; on the other hand were the all-American college boys and girls, the sports stars and cheerleaders, the high-school hoppers, the petting-party goers who always knew *exactly* when to stop. And if the delinquent image reflected the exaggerated lines of a moral panic, so the high-school image was a carefully constructed ideal, part of a systematic attempt to make teenagers *nice.* Paula Fass quotes an educator suggesting as early as 1920 that school dances should not be discouraged, but that they offered "an exceptional opportunity for training." And by the 1950s, child-rearing experts (doctors and psychiatrists, teachers and high-school authorities) had given a lot of thought to the problems and possibilities of *controlling* the culture of their pupils—encouraging certain sorts of sport, certain sorts of society, certain sorts of fun, certain sorts of conformity.

The mass media, too, were concerned to promote the responsible use of teenage products, to root teenage consumption in the framework of the ideal middle-class family—small, intimate, rational, mutually respectful. Dick Clark's 1959 book *Your Happiest Years* is a fascinating example of this concern. Clark—"a much-listened-to figure in the teenage world"—offered advice on parents, dating, careers, marriage, manners, health, and looks, advice designed to ensure that his teenagers would become "tomorrow's adults" with the minimum possible disruption to middle-class assumptions about sex roles, competitive work, individual effort, collective quiescence. "There are many different opinions about just what is the most exclusive club in America these days," begins Clark.

> We all seem to have our own ideas on that subject, and no matter who you are, I'm sure that in your school or community you can name at least one organization that you think is tops, and that you would "give anything" to join.
> One thing, though. In all of those clubs you'll notice that, after signing, you are handed a set of rules that must be obeyed if you are to stay in good standing. For instance, for the sports club you have to keep in trim and spend long hours practicing your jump shot, your curve ball, or your blocking and tackling; otherwise, you'll end up merely a spectator. Same thing holds for the dances—with a little bit of work you can be a wallflower, and with a lot of work you can be a much-sought-after dance partner. Getting into the club can be the easiest thing you have ever done; staying in it may be pretty difficult, but it's worth it when you consider the reward.
> That is true also of the membership requirements for what I like to consider the most exclusive—and important—club in these fifty United States. It's the "Teenagers of America, Inc."[5]

Dick Clark's book provides the rules for the teenage club and advice on "the perils and pitfalls, the excitement and happiness of those wonderful years," and in these words (from the blurb) a tension is apparent: the suspicion arises that these years are wonderful and exciting because they are *not* rule-bound.

Sociologists of the American working-class family in the 1950s discovered a marked ambiguity in the attitudes of parents to their teenage children. On one hand, there was an omni-tolerance: youth was a time for sowing wild oats, when boys will be boys and girls should get some good times while they can. On the other hand, there was a sour intolerance: the young were layabouts, delinquents, oversexed and underdisciplined.

Such a mixed attitude to youth has a long history. Ever since nineteenth-century changes in relations of production and domesticity opened up a stage between childhood and adulthood and made the problems of puberty public, adolescence has been both celebrated—as a time of innocence and idealism, a time when all life's choices can still be made—and condemned—as a time of anarchy and hysteria, irresponsibility and selfishness. The rise of teenage culture between 1920 and 1960 made these problems social, and as teenagers developed their own institutions, their own means of expression, they became both more envied and more feared, more celebrated and more subject to control. By the end of the 1950s, indeed, teenagers had become, in themselves, symbols of a much wider set of arguments about work and leisure, responsibility and fun.

## YOUTH CULTURE

Even before the Beatles, the more astute adult observers of the British teenage scene were remarking on the development of a culture that was specifically young but not specifically working-class. The hero of *Absolute Beginners* commented that

> the great thing about the jazz world, and all the kids that enter into it, is that no one, not a soul, cares what your class is, or what your race is or what your income is, or if you're boy, or girl, or bent, or versatile, or what you are—so long as you dig the scene and can behave yourself, and have left all that crap behind you, too, when you come in the jazz club door. The result of all this is that, in the jazz world, you meet all kinds of cats, on absolutely equal terms, who can clue you up in all kinds of directions—in social directions, in culture directions, in sexual directions, in racial directions. . . . in fact, almost anywhere really, you want to go to learn.[6]

And George Melly, analyzing the class significance of British dialects and language in 1963, claimed:

> Scratch the rebel, art student, beatnik, CND supporter, jazz musician, and you'll usually find a lower middle class background. The suburbs have thrown up most of the young people

who are in conscious revolt. . . . Their only sin, and it's a minor
one, is sometimes to lie about their origin. They pretend to be
working class.[7]

These were early intimations of what was to develop as British
"youth culture," a culture that was apparently classless and rebellious, but which rested on the gradual middle-class adoption of the
trappings of working-class teenage life. In the words of one historian:

The lack of a firm class sense was one of the most notable
things about a great many of the young. The working-class lad
was no longer swallowed up into the beery fug of the working
class pub. In the new coffee bars, jazz cellars and youth clubs,
grammar school and modern school rubbed Italianate shoul-
ders; "fish-and-chip" girls and Acacia Avenue girls alike em-
braced the new informality of "separate" and drove holes into
the floor with stiletto heels of approximately the same sharp-
ness. A teenager was a teenager.[8]

Youth was an ideological concept: American sociologists noted
that middle-class children were deliberately adopting lower-class
*values*—"toughness, excitement, chance-taking, indulgence, 'con-
ning,' autonomy and hardness"—and were thus making a conscious
decision to oppose the values of their parents (unlike working-class
teenagers who were, it seems, simply indulging themselves on their
way to a life of conformity).

The development of youth culture in the 1960s became associated with the development of the student movement and the
"counterculture." The great symbolic event happened in France in
May 1968, when students and young workers came together in an
act of political and cultural opposition to the state. Even usually
hardheaded observers were carried away and proclaimed a "crisis
of industrial society" as the new student generation, recruited from
the ruling class itself, seemed to reject the terms of their parents'
rule. Sociologists began to devote more time to deviant middle-class
children than they ever had to deviant teenagers. Journals and con-
ferences and textbooks pored over "Alienated Youth," "The Making of the Counter Culture," "The Greening of America." Most of
this literature read strangely once the youth "revolt" of the late

1960s had become the hedonistic apathy of the early 1970s, and Tom Bottomore suggests, cynically, that the student movement's connection with "youth culture" had been one of its weaknesses: pop music and drugs had "very little radical significance at all."

But to make sense of youth culture we have to examine it in a wider context than the rise and fall of the 1960s student movement. Youth culture, after all, emerged first in the 1920s, in "the Jazz Age." How did 1960s youth culture differ from that of the 1920s?

Paula Fass defines 1920s youth culture as "a tangle of work and play, career preparation, and mating games," and, rather than repeating her complex analysis of this tangle, I want to stress just three points.

First, 1920s youth culture was a peer-group culture: it developed in the specific setting of college life and was expressed through college institutions—fraternities, sororities, athletic societies, and so forth. It was a culture based on competition and exclusion; conformity, in Fass's words, was "the glue of campus life," and even the minority of bohemian rebels, who slummed it in city jazz clubs and dabbled with marijuana and lived "wildly," did so as campus rebels, rather than in any expression of solidarity with non-students. This culture was, in other words, precisely that organization of campus conformity, isolation, and smugness against which 1960s youth culture became a gesture (a gesture which had its roots in the 1950s, when campuses had an influx of older working-class students under the GI Bill, and, for the first time, an active bohemian presence with the rise of the beats).

Second, 1920s campus culture was not, even at the time, an expression of generational conflict—difference yes, hostility no. Campus youth in the 1920s were politically inactive and remained firmly committed to the capitalist economy, the party political system, bourgeois family life. The shock effects of this youth movement lay in the areas of consumption: the flappers symbolized a faddish pursuit of instant gratification, an obsession with fashion and style and image. The dominant value was personal liberty—sexual pleasure, for men and women alike, became part of the definition of love and marriage, and campus youth took full advantage of the new leisure possibilities of travel and friendship and drink.

Such a life-style was limited in its effects: premarital sex still led, conventionally, to marital sex; the pursuit of personal pleasure was still equated with the accumulation of wealth and property. Indeed, the youthful approach to consumption—the concern for fashion and change and up-to-dateness, the use of style to establish in-group membership—became the model for *all* consumption. It is from the 1920s that we can date a consumer culture in which continuous purchase is encouraged with the suggestion that you are buying something that makes and keeps you young. Youth, far from being a threat to society, became its ideal. "The path of the damned," in Paula Fass's words, became "the way of the beautiful."

The third point follows directly: this middle-class way of leisure became the model for working-class youth too. The immediate expression of this was a spate of campus movies and stories and books: college fashions set the models for shop girls, campus clubs featured in the weekend fantasies of clerks. More importantly, though, the organization of the campus became, as we have already seen, the long-term model for high school organization too: the conformist conventions of 1920s students became, in an even more restrictive context, the conformist conventions of 1950s teenagers.

We can now see how genuinely radical 1960s youth culture was. The class relation was reversed: middle-class teenagers were deliberately adopting lower-class values and styles that, by now, had a power and a glamour of their own. And they were doing this as an aspect of an explicit opposition to both peer-group and adult middle-class norms. Nineteen-sixties youth culture was still campus-based, but in rejecting the rules of fraternity and pantie raid and the Big Game, student rebels had to draw on values from outside campus, from a wider context of generational struggle against the established political, economic, and sexual system (hence the radicalizing role of the civil rights movement, for example).

The student movement, in other words, far from being sapped by its association with "youth culture," depended on it for its original radical thrust, and the questions raised by 1960s student radicals must be considered seriously: Was there a set of activities and attitudes and values which, on one hand, distinguished young people from adults and, on the other hand, gave them an identity that transcended their own class differences? Did youth culture have any political significance?

The affirmative answer to these questions rested on an argument originally developed by Karl Mannheim. He suggested that young people find themselves in a particular set of occupations and roles in most societies and consequently develop a sense of themselves as an age-group; but only rarely is this consciousness of shared age developed not just with respect to the immediate problems of self-definition, but also with respect to history, as a consciousness of generation.

In certain historical situations, though—Mannheim referred to periods of profound social change or political instability—an age-group does become a generation and youth culture does become political; the positive accounts of 1960s youth culture involved such a historical analysis. Emphasis was placed on the capitalist boom of 1952 to 1968, the effects on the young of full employment, the expansion of secondary and higher education, the developing importance of tertiary and scientific work, the decline of unskilled labor. The object was to show that 1960s youth experience was both something new and something that differentiated the young, as a group, from the old. The Weathermen, for example, tried to organize a Revolutionary Youth Movement; their assumption was that all young people were similarly exploited and oppressed. Students, draftees, the unemployed were all involved in the "absorption" of surplus value, were all used as a solution to American capital's problems of overproduction; their oppression was even more obviously shared—all young people found their leisure pursuits, their sex and drugs and rock 'n' roll, threatened by the police, whether on campus, the streets, or in the barracks.

RYM recruited few members. Political movements can't be based on abstractions, and solidarity depends on shared experience, on a belief that collective action can change things. Most young people in the 1960s, it turned out, did not *feel* similarly exploited. The police and the drug squad were a common enemy, but the defense of private pleasure was not a basis for a lasting political organization, and RYM confused the general experience of powerlessness experienced by young people long before the 1960s with the specific problems of play in Berkeley and Oakland, San Francisco and Leavenworth. Youth culture, whatever the common feelings of restlessness and frustration, remained differentiated by class and race and sex, and by the 1970s the norms of both 1920s campus culture and 1950s teenage culture were being restated, if in the context of new styles of consumption (drug consumption, in particular), new notions of personal freedom (particularly sexual freedom), and a more critical understanding of "the system." Nevertheless, there had been experiences that marked a generational consciousness, experiences that can't be separated from the meaning of rock 'n' roll.

First, there was Vietnam. It was the war (and the draft) that, above all, fueled American student radicalism and made 1960s campus culture political; the ending of the draft meant the dissolution of the radicalism. But the point I want to make is a wider one: wartimes, for all its gathering together of young people, is not usually a time when youth cultures flourish or can even be identified as such. But the Vietnam war was experienced as a youth event, both by those people who survived the endless tedium, pointlessness, and fear of active service with drugs and rock 'n' roll, and by those people who had to come to terms with their personal desperation and political determination not to be drafted. In the 1960s there was a *generation* of male Americans who had to define and evaluate their lives in terms of Vietnam, whether they fought there or not.

Second, there was 1968: the cluster of events in Paris, Czechoslovakia, and, in different ways, in the rest of Europe and America made it seem, for a moment, that societies and institutions and people could be liberated. The actual effect of that experience has become clearer since, through the process of "normalization." The experience of abnormality is rare, and 1968 changed people's lives in unexpected, private ways—whatever the public effects of normalization, after 1968 nothing personal *had* to be the way it was before. Nineteen sixty-eight was a more diffuse youth experience than Vietnam, less exclusively youthful, but only the young responded to its events with a spontaneous gasp of excitement, without the simultaneous shadow of doubt about disrupted order and routine that even the most dedicated revolutionary, after years of quiescence, must feel. Rock was the sound of 1968 too.

I'm stressing a generational basis for 1960s youth culture, rather than the more obvious signs of shared tastes, because, in the end, it is history, not sociology, that must account for the emergence of a youth culture and for its fragmentation. Young people in the 1960s had experiences (experiences of war and politics) that intensified the conflict between public and private obligations, between freedom and responsibility, and it was these problems that rock, more than any other form of expression, addressed and made plain. But the 1960s were exceptional. The 1970s meant a normalization of youth and rock too, as college students expressed, once more, a sober concern for grades and careers, as teenage culture was re-established around the new conventions of drug use and sexuality, as youth leisure, on campus and off, became again simply a matter of partying. Youth was still being experienced (just as it had been in the 1950s) as a stage on the way to adulthood; it no longer seemed to be a permanent gesture of defiance (particularly since so many aspects of 1960s youth style—from haircuts to marijuana to rock 'n' roll itself—turned out to be effortlessly absorbed into adult success stories). Even if the generational experience of the 1960s had shaken up young people's sense of class, sex, and racial divisions, these divisions still remained—and, in the 1970s, were sharpened. Nineteen-sixties rock politicized leisure—gave public, collective expression to usually private issues of risk and pleasure and sex. Rock music in the 1970s, as we have already seen, was in many ways routinized: music makers became professionals, the music market was divided into taste publics, musical consumption became once more a matter of leisure itself. But the issues of risk and pleasure and sex didn't therefore vanish. Leisure—not politics—was the problem, and youth leisure—not youth politics—still focused this problem.

Most sociology of youth leisure looks not at generational and historical experience, but at structure and function. The sociological argument is that youth leisure culture is a solution to the common problems of adolescence: *all* young people occupy a similar transitional position as they make their move from the family in which they were brought up to the economic and social system into which they must eventually fit; *all* young people have, in other words, a marginal social status. Whether at school or college, in apprenticeships, or in and out of unskilled work, they are not fully integrated into the economic structure; they have emerged from one family but not yet formed another; they are not integrated fully into the social structure. Societies have a series of preparatory institutions to control the transition period, not just formal organizations like schools, but also informal leisure organizations that provide training in "adult orientations"; and whatever the other differences between them, young people share an experience of powerlessness.

Shared experiences make for shared needs: adolescents seek a stability to balance against their time of change, they seek a sense of autonomy and status and self-esteem to balance against their time of insignificance. Hence the role of peer-groups (something between the family and society) and their symbols of pride and self-assertion, membership and exclusion. Peer-group values are not opposed to adult values, but are a preparation for them. The young become a social problem only when they refuse to grow up, and the refusal to grow up (this was a common sociological theme in the 1960s) is not a political act but an Oedipal one.

The historical objection to this argument concerns its abstraction: the experiences of different class and sex groups, occupying different economic and family positions, having different amounts of power, different access to educational and social rewards can't be similar, subjectively or objectively, even if all the members of these groups are the same age.

# YOUTH AND PRODUCTION

Youth cultures have always been described—whether by media or academic commentators—as leisure cultures, revolving around particular styles of consumption. What is taken to bind youth together despite class or sexual differences is a shared taste. The youth problem is, then, interpreted as a problem of choice, and the sociology of youth has become a sociology of choice, whether youth cultures are explained in terms of class values, subcultures, psychosocial needs, or commercial pressures. The analytic task is to explain youth styles by reference to the values they articulate and then to search for the origins of these values. But once we start considering the *differences* between youth cultures, it then becomes obvious that they reflect not just consumer tastes and values but also forces of production, forces in the labor market. In Britain, for example, a number of obvious distinctions can be made.

First, an increasing number of young people are not at work at all, but are engaged in full-time education until the moment of adulthood (the major difference between British and American youth cultures in the last thirty years has been the difference in the size of their college populations—a far higher proportion of Americans continue full-time schooling after the age of sixteen). The general statistics on students conceal differences—between home-based and campus experiences, for example—but the points I want to stress here are these: first, involvement in full-time education effectively segregates students from young workers socially—this separation is obvious in leisure and is illustrated by the rarity of cross-educational marriages; second, being a student means being subject to a different form of control, different patterns of discipline and freedom, from those faced at work.

Among young workers themselves, the most obvious distinction is sexual. In Britain girls still have limited career possibilities (few are involved in occupations that have a long-term future), and it is the lack of training facilities for female workers, rather than unequal incomes, that is now of most concern to investigators of sexual inequality. For a large proportion of girls marriage is still the only career choice available, the only source of long-term economic opportunity; girls still, in the words of one researcher, "regard homemaking as their vocation." Numerous surveys have shown the extent to which marriage and work aspirations are complementary—low aspirations for the future go with a commitment to early marriage and the traditional female role; marriage is seen as the way out from educational failure and work dissatisfaction (a way out not available to boys).

At first glance, a comparison between the occupations of girls now and their situation before the war suggests marked changes. In 1931, for example, almost a quarter of fourteen- to seventeen-year-old British girls at work were still indoor domestic servants, though this had been a declining source of occupation since 1900. Nowadays few girls become servants of any sort—hence the belief that this century has meant a steady increase in teenage girls' freedom and independence. But even today, most of the few girls who get apprenticeships get them in hairdressing, most of the few who get professional qualifications get them in nursing, and most girls are, anyway, employed in shops and services and offices. The basic pattern of girls' employment—their lack of involvement in training schemes, their exclusion from skilled jobs and careers—remains similar: as it was in 1900, marriage is the crucial occupation for girls not in higher education. Teenage girls know that marriage is still the most significant and vital career choice.

The largest group of young male workers in Britain are apprentices. There are distinctions within this category—notably between apprentices preparing for careers as skilled factory workers and apprentices preparing for careers as self-employed artisans—but some general points can be made. First, apprentices, whatever the length of their indentures, are involved from the outset in a lifetime career—their future is known. Second, the importance of formal training in their jobs means that they experience forms of work discipline which resemble those of schools as much as those of the adult work place. In some ways apprentices seem to fare worse than their untrained peers—they are paid less, have low status at work, are subject to more authoritarian control—but, on the other hand, they are also much more stable in their jobs, their situation is regarded as desirable by fellow workers and blends more easily into the work habits and attitudes of adults.

The separation of apprentices from other young workers and the resulting social distinctions between skilled and unskilled labor have a long history. The preindustrial labor hierarchy survived the industrial revolution, if in changed form, and in the latter part of the nineteenth century the differentiation of labor became even more rigid. John Gillis, in his history of youth, suggests that the "second industrial revolution," at the turn of the century, not only increased the number of unskilled jobs for teenagers ("boy labor" in distribution and transport, for example) while the number of available apprenticeships declined, but also established the pattern of unskilled jobs being, immediately, much more financially rewarding than skilled jobs. The young unskilled worker could expect something approaching an adult wage at a time when an apprentice was getting little more than a pittance. This reinforced the differences within the working class—the poorer section needed wages as good as their children could get at once, those better-off could afford to invest against the future. Apprentice/non-apprentice labor divisions became imbued with "respectable"/"rough" cultural divisions.

Contemporary researchers suggest that "the striking difference" between the skilled and other young workers lies in their degree of commitment to their jobs. Apprentices are "stabilized" by their employment situation, by their immediate involvement with adult work institutions such as unions; white-collar workers make a similarly realistic assessment of the long-term value of their training. But for the young unskilled, the pressure to be a "steady worker" comes only with marriage.

The unqualified and unskilled have a special relationship to production. Job changing is frequent (occupation changing too, among boys), and the highest job level is reached by age twenty, even if maximum wages are not; unskilled workers are always at risk of being replaced by younger, cheaper labor, and the job mobility of unskilled boys reflects both their own readiness to leave when "fed up" and their employers' readiness to sack them for "disciplinary problems."

It is from this sector of the young work force that trouble has always been considered to come; theirs are the occupations of young "roughs," from nineteenth-century scuttlers to 1980s skinheads. The sociological explanation here is "anomie": the young unskilled worker has not yet settled down at home or at work; he is aimless, floundering around for job satisfaction, a prey to bad influences, whether criminal or commercial, a problem for social workers. Irresponsible leisure derives from dissatisfaction at work—we're back to the corner boy/college boy distinction.

Although there can be no doubt that the skilled/unskilled work distinction has an effect on the use of leisure, it is less clear that what is involved is simply a difference of *attitudes* to work, a difference in job satisfaction. Apprentices are bored and frustrated by their daily tasks, look to leisure for their thrills, and the unskilled, equally, understand the implications of their job choices. Their occupational "floundering" is often, in fact, perfectly controlled— from their point of view being young and having a good time is part of the process in which they know they will marry and settle down. It is a good interlude rather than a bad one.

Different leisure patterns reflect different opportunities rather than different values. This is obvious in the context of youth unemployment, which now dwarfs all others as *the* contemporary youth problem (in the USA and Europe sixteen- to twenty–five-year-olds bear the brunt of the recession). Unemployment is a labor market problem rather than a result of individuals' attitudes, and, these days, the young unemployed and the young unskilled cannot be treated as separate categories—they are part of the same statistic.

In the past, the pattern of casual, intermittent employment of young workers was possible because there were plenty of jobs to be done by them (some which could only be done by them, because of their very toughness and irregularlity). But employers are, increasingly, looking for a quality of steadiness, a mature, responsible attitude toward work; in the long run, such a shift in the work available for the young will have a profound effect on their leisure too. The steady decline of casual unskilled labor means a decline of the group that has traditionally been seen as forming the core of hedonistic teenage culture, and, at the same time, the expanding sector of the young suffering long-term unemployment means an increasing number of young people who have no leisure at all.

It has been suggested that punk-rock was the first expression of these "dole queue kids," but before examining the relationship of the various youth groups to music, I want to make one last comment on the teenage "boom." The affluent teenagers of the 1950s and 1960s were affluent because their parents were; what was involved was disposable income. Before then, in the 1930s, for example, earning youngsters earned to help their families stay above a bread line, to pay their parents back for their "kept" years. One reason for teenagers' good times from 1950 to 1970, one reason for their sudden independence from the family, was that their parents were fully employed and relatively well-off. Such independence is not necessarily permanent.

I've been describing the British social structure because I live in it—when I was a schoolboy and student in the 1960s I knew perfectly well both that I shared tastes with children at other schools (who would leave them long before me) and that our lives were quite different, that shared tastes did not mean a common culture. But the same distinctions—student/worker, male/female, skilled/unskilled, employed/unemployed—are significant in the USA (with the further complications of ethnic and regional differences in work experience and opportunity), and youth choices in America, too, can only be understood by reference to opportunities and restrictions.

The sociology of youth, however, remains a sociology of choice. Even the subcultural theorists of youth who (beginning in Chicago in the 1920s and ending in Birmingham in the 1970s) sought to understand youth in terms of class, focused on the class basis of *values*. Youth subcultures were identified by their styles; young people were watched at play, isolated from the routines of work and family; their concerns were derived from ideological processes—a class tradition, a cultural transmitter. Juvenile delinquents were explained in terms of labeling—attention was focused on the labelers, the police and courts and press, on leisure signs and symbols. Subcultural theorists took young people's ability to choose what to do for granted; the academic task was to *interpret* these choices.

My argument is that for youth, as for everyone else, leisure consumption and style involve a relationship between choice and constraint. The problem is that the young, since the 1920s, have come to symbolize leisure, to embody good times. Youth seem to be freer than everyone else in society, partly for the standard sociological reason—they are in a marginal position; they are not bound, like their elders, by the routines and relationships of family and career. But it is because they are *not* really free that this matters. The truth of youth culture is that the young *displace* to their free time the problems of work and family and future. It is because they *lack* power that the young account for their lives in terms of play, focus their politics on leisure. Youth culture matters for the old too: it is young people's use of leisure that raises the problems of capitalist freedom and constraint most sharply and most resonantly. Youth is still the model for consumption.

CHAPTER 9

# YOUTH AND MUSIC

 Elizabeth Hardwick remembers her adolescence in prewar Kentucky this way:

At our high school dances in the winter, small, cheap, local events. We had our curls, red taffeta dresses, satin shoes with their new dye fading in the rain puddles; and most of all we were dressed in our ferocious hope for popularity. This was a stifling blanket, an airless tent; gasping, grinning, we stood anxious-eyed, next to the piano, hovering about Fats Waller who had come from Cincinnati for the occasion. Requests, perfidious glances, drunken teenagers, nodding teacher-chaperones: these we offered to the music, looking upon it, I suppose, as something inevitable, effortlessly pushing up from the common soil.[1]

Popular music was tangled up in the experience of growing up, as it had been since the beginning of the century when the dance craze swept American cities and British music halls were dominated by "young men," shop assistants and clerks, putting on a weekend style. In Middletown in the 1920s music and radio topped the lists of interests of boys and girls of all classes, and dancing was, in the Lynds' words, "a universal skill among the young; their social life is increasingly built about it."

By the 1930s remarks on the "independence" of the young were journalistically commonplace, and jazz, as a dance music, was seen to have a special appeal to them. But neither it, nor any other form of pop, was heard as an *expression* of a youth culture. The music was, as Elizabeth Hardwick suggests, just *there.* Where it came from, what it was made for, were not questions that mattered much to the adolescents who danced and dated to it. It was music made by adults, and there were adults, too, at dances and jazz clubs (even high-school events were just an imitation of more sophisticated affairs to come); in working-class families, at least, radios and phonograph records were still family goods. The young, the leisured young, set the consuming styles and music dominated their play. But it was not yet their music.

In the first survey of British leisure after the war, Rowntree and Lavers described the continued importance of dancing, but also noted that the dance halls were now dominated by the very young— "mostly between the ages of sixteen and twenty-four, drawn from the working and lower middle classes." Rowntree and Lavers were disturbed by the consequences:

> Modern ballroom dancing may easily degenerate into a sensuous form of entertainment, and if self-control is weakened with alcohol it is more than likely that it will do so, which might easily lead at least to unruly behaviour and not infrequently to sexual immorality.[2]

This was an early recognition of teenage culture in which pop music and youth consciousness were integrated in a process eventually symbolized by rock 'n' roll. The young had always had idols—film stars, sportsmen, singers like Frank Sinatra and Johnnie Ray; the novelty of rock 'n' roll was that its performers were the same age as their audience, came from similar backgrounds, had similar interests; and the rise of rock 'n' roll meant a generation gap in dancing, as dance halls offered rock 'n' roll nights or became exclusively rock 'n' roll venues. Rock 'n' roll records and radio shows were aimed exclusively at the young (in Britain, for example, the most visible setting of the new world of teenage consumption were the self-service "Browseries" and "Melody Bars"), and by the end of the 1950s most pop records were being bought by the young. James Coleman's massive 1961 survey of American adolescents confirmed that music was their most popular form of entertainment and that rock 'n' roll was their most popular form of music. The importance of music in young people's lives had become a given of youth research. Teenagers' interest in pop was found to determine the television programs they watched, the magazines they read, the cafés and dances they went to, the "necessary tools" (transistor, record player, tape recorder, guitar) they sought to own.

Sociologists in the 1960s and 1970s continued to replicate Coleman's arguments that pop was central to the teenage social system. A recent survey of the literature on British adolescents, for example, concludes that "music is in many ways the central activity of British youth culture from which many subsidiary activities flow." It is still the presence of "their" music that attracts young people to pubs and discos and youth clubs; "homemade entertainment" still means music-making or listening to discs; market researchers continue to monitor the concentration of teenage expenditure on dancing, on musical products generally. This pattern of youth and music is not even confined to capitalism: if in the USA and Britain it was the advent of rock 'n' roll that signaled the arrival of a musical youth culture, it emerged in most other European countries too, East and West, after the success of the Beatles in the 1960s.

I've been laboring the obvious, but it is because young people's interest in music is so taken for granted that the necessary questions about it don't get asked. The surveys I've cited are descriptive: music's presence in youth culture is established, but not its purpose. Many observers, from Coleman on, have implied that if music is a universal teenage interest, it is also a superficial one—the impression left by most sociological research is of a culture in which music is always heard but rarely listened to. It is this assumption that I will examine in this chapter by exploring the following questions: What does music mean to the young? Why is growing up a musical experience? How does rock affect and articulate this?

# THE USE OF MUSIC

In 1972, I conducted my own youth survey, interviewing 105 four-teen- to eighteen-year-olds at school in Keighley in England (and talking too to their older college friends). Keighley is a small indus-trial town lying on the edge of the textile conurbations Leeds and Bradford in the north of England. Its own economy is based on the surviving nineteenth-century woolen mills and on more recently de-veloped light engineering works, but its population also spills into the surrounding mill villages where the textile business has always been combined with small farming (one of these villages, Haworth, is where the Brontë sisters lived—the local moors still provide a viv-id sense of *Wuthering Heights*). Keighley is, in short, a small and concentrated enough community for everyone to know each other's place in it (the children all attend one or the other of the two high schools), while being near enough to the leisure facilities of two big cities (and universities) for local youth to fit into the mainstream of mass culture.

My research confirmed that the rock experience was common to all young people, whatever their background, but the findings that most interested me were the different patterns of music use and taste within the customary teenage framework. First, there was a distinct "sixth form culture," a pattern of rock use shared by all the sixth formers (seventeen- and eighteen-year-olds) and students to whom I spoke (mostly, but not exclusively, middle-class). Under the English education system most people leave school for work (or un-employment) after taking their Ordinary Level or Certificate of Sec-ondary Education exams in the fifth form, at the age of sixteen; pupils who remain at school for another two years, in the sixth form, are almost all preparing for Advanced Level exams, the qualifica-tions for university entry. In most schools the distinction between academic and nonacademic pupils occurs long before the sixth form. On entering secondary school at age eleven, pupils are streamed (or banded) according to ability—the top stream contains the potential sixth formers. In my sample, these top-stream pupils bought albums rather than singles, had "progressive" rather than "commercial" tastes, were not much involved in the trappings of rock (the radio or the music press), and went to folk clubs or concerts rather than discos or dances. The ideological essence of their culture was individualism. Typical replies to questions about influences on tastes were:

> I like what I like, no one changes my opinions on music. . . .
> I like what I like, not what I'm told or influenced to like.

Choosing a record was an individual decision of some importance: albums were never bought spontaneously or on spec, and sixth formers rejected the idea that their records were chosen just to fit an image or group identity; they didn't accept that they had an image ("I am myself") or else accepted it only reluctantly ("I suppose I have although I don't readily admit it"; "I hope not"; "I do not *want* an image"). The role of the musically knowledgeable in informing and stimulating rock interest was acknowledged—boys were more likely than girls to play the role of opinion leader—but in the end musical taste was individual. Records were listened to, appreciated, and criticized in terms of their meaning—lyrics were important, but not the only source of such meaning—and music was praised in terms of its originality, truthfulness, and beauty and condemned for its triviality, banality, and repetition. "Rubbish" was the favorite pejorative word for "commercial trash which gets in your head and you can't escape and it does nothing for you except make you puke."

These sixth formers articulated youth culture as a set of values different from those of an older generation; they saw themselves as "rebelling against unreasonable ideas and conventional ways of doing things." Their fear was that even youth culture was not a true or meaningful expression of individuality:

> Rock music is unfortunately fashionable and its followers are exploited. It is very hard to separate true opinion from "conditioned response."

In sharp contrast to this was the lower-fifth-form culture of those pupils who were going to leave school at sixteen. They bought singles and watched *Top of the Pops*, went regularly to youth clubs and discos but rarely to concerts, emphasized beat and sound in their tastes rather than meaning, and identified with specific youth styles. Their standard mode of criticism of other tastes was abuse. In many ways, this differentiation of youth cultures was one of ideology, the way people talked about music, rather than activity, the way they actually used it. There was less difference than first appeared, for example, between sixth-form musical individualism and the cult identities of the lower-fifth formers. The latter were aware of the playfulness of their groups—"the image changes—it's just for laughs," and styles were usually a matter of convenience:

> I have assorted friends—some hairies [long hairs/hippies], some crombie boys and girls [skinheads gone "smooth," wearing Crombie overcoats]. I can sit and listen to both sorts of music and don't mind either. . . .
>
> I'm in between a skinhead and a hippie. . . . I wear "mod" clothes but I listen to both kinds of music. . . .
>
> I wear skinhead clothes, but I don't just like that type of music. . . .

And consider these two more extended comments:

> I don't know what youth culture means. I think it means what you are—Skin, Grebo [greaser/rocker/biker], or Hairie. I am none of these. Beat that, I thinks. The groups have different outlooks on sex, drugs and politics. The lot of it is different views to that of my parents. My brother was a skinhead gang leader for three years. Music is not important to any group, to me music is what I like not everybody else's opinion.
>
> I think that music makes up for 75% of youth culture and that the music you like depends on the cult you're in. This idea of cult is taken too far. Teenagers can't be split into hating each other with a few in the middle just because they have different view points. But they are.

On the other hand, one of the most militant groups among fifteen- and sixteen-year-olds was that of the future sixth formers, the self-identified hairies and hippies, with their missionary zeal for progressive rock and hatred of commercial pop:

> Rock music, progressive and heavy are fantastic. If they were not there life would not be worth living. They are the backbone behind music as a whole—showing us what it should really be like.

It was from this group that the most assertive statements of image and shared tastes came. If group identity is part of teenage culture for conventional reasons—"if you like soul or reggae music and they like rock, you will both wear different clothes and you may split up to go with your own group"—then even people with an ideology of individual taste become a group of individualists and need the symbols and friends and institutions to assert themselves as a group:

> I listen at home most of the time, in my room. I don't often go to parties. Don't go to clubs, 'cos I haven't anyone to go with and the clubs round here aren't the places which I enjoy going to. Dances are a bit like clubs, the people that go aren't the sort of people I mix with well. Discos are the same, my sort of people don't go there. I love concerts but it's difficult for me to get to them or get tickets. I go when I can. I listen alone or with a friend most. There's not a lot of people in our village which like progressive music.

One of the paradoxes in my survey was that the group which most stressed individual musical choice also most stressed the importance of shared musical taste for friendship—music served as the badge of individuality on which friendship choices could be based. One of the ironies was that because music was taken as a symbol of a cluster of values, the most individualistic groups were the ones most thrown by their musical heroes changing direction. This was particularly a problem for the hairies because they differentiated themselves from the masses as a self-conscious elite by displaying exclusive musical tastes. Their tastes weren't just a matter of identification, they also reflected a different—more serious, more intense—relationship to music. The hairies thought of themselves not as just another teenage style, but as people who had transcended the trivialities of teenage style. Their music *meant* something, and when one of their acts "sold out," became part of mass taste, there was great bitterness:

> What do you think of T. Rex? I do not usually think of them. It puts me off my meals whenever I think about T. Rex. They were once good when called Tyranasorous Rex—Next Best Thing to Beatles and Stones. T. Rex are very bopperish. It's

all the same music like Tamla. NB Marc Bolan and Micky Finn
are *Two of a kind.* Puff Puff Puff.

Class and academic cultural differences were interwoven with
age and sex differences. One aspect of the contrast between sixth
form and lower-fifth culture was that sixth formers were older. It
was clear in my survey that the maximum involvement in youth
groups and use of youth symbols occurred at age fifteen, when most
pupils had some such identity: by sixteen most were claiming non-
membership, and in the sixth form there were no admitted group
members at all. There were also obvious distinctions between the
sexes. Girls were more interested in dancing and tended to be more
concerned with lyrics, especially romantic lyrics. They were aware
of the special female features of pop culture—fan clubs, poster magazines, star personalities—even if only a minority were interested
enough to get involved in them. I will discuss the sexual division
of youth culture in a later section of this chapter, but I want to con-
clude this summary of my survey with a brief qualitative description
of the pupil cultures I found in Keighley.

Alison and her friends were a group of sixth formers and college students who had a busy and self-contained social life, meeting
weekly at the folk club (most of them picked at guitars themselves),
at parties in each other's houses, at concerts or the bar at the local universities, at selected pubs. The group tended to come from
middle-class backgrounds (the local professional and management
class), and this had some effect on the material basis of their leisure—they had access to cars, for example, which made them mobile—but they were not particularly well-off in terms of income,
spent a large proportion of non-school time studying, and were consequently at home a lot—working-class sixth formers fitted into this
culture without much difficulty.

Music was a background to their lives, radio and records were
always on. The records were LPs, chosen carefully and individually
and often purchased by saving money after hearing a friend's copy.
People listened to music together and often exchanged albums temporarily. Few people in the group had a large record collection, although a crucial musical role was played by older brothers and
sisters and friends who had more records, knew what was happening, and turned the group on to new sounds. The overall result was
an eclecticism of taste, with individuals developing their own spe-

cialisms—folk, heavy metal, singer/songwriter, avant-garde. They were aware of general rock trends but not particularly interested in them—they could pick up the rock knowledge they needed from one or two obsessive friends, from casual listening to evening radio shows, from an occasional glance at someone else's music paper.

This group was conscious of itself as a group that was clearly differentiated from the culture of their parents, but what really dominated its members' lives was a sense of possibility. They were all preparing to move on—to universities and colleges, to new towns and opportunities, to new sexual and social and chemical experiences; they were all aware that the group itself was transitional and temporary, that individuals had to maintain their individualism within it. They were articulate and self-aware and valued these qualities in music; they turned to music for support as well as for relaxation. They most valued music that was most apparently "artistic"—technically complex or lyrically poetic—and tastes here went with other interests, in the other arts, in politics, in religion. There were few direct restraints on the activities of this group except members' shortage of money; they were successful at school and at home and rarely clashed with authority. But their life was already a career and the importance of exams and qualifications was fully realized. The resulting tensions made music all the more important—as the context for bopping, relaxing, petting, falling in love, and shouting a temporary "Fuck the world!"

Craig and his friends were in their last year at school, fifth formers itching to get out. They would leave school without skill or qualification but had been used to failure for years, and school was not so much oppressive now as irrelevant. Their lives already revolved around the possibilities of (unskilled) work—most members of the group were already working part-time—and their leisure reflected this expectation. The group went out (why bother studying) to the youth clubs provided by the local authority or attached to local churches, to the pubs that would take them, to the fish-and-chips shop and the bus station and the streets. None of this group was a militant member of any particular gang, but they had skinhead friends and relations and could run casually with them and with the emerging groups of mods and crombies and knew which side they were on in a fight; Friday night, for example, was the traditional time for a trip to Bradford, the boys for a brawl, the girls for a dance at the Mecca.

This group had plenty of free time but little money or mobility, and their leisure was consequently focused on public places, putting them in constant confrontation with the controllers of those spaces—police and bus conductors and bouncers. But home wasn't much freer, and so the boys went out most nights, doing nothing, having a laugh, aware that this was their youth and that their future would be much like the past of their working-class parents. Music was a pervasive part of their lives, in their rooms and clubs, on the jukebox, at the disco. Sometimes, when they had the money, they'd buy that single that was really great, and they knew the big names and what was in the charts and what was good to dance to, though they didn't really follow it. The point really was that when they were in their group they had their music and knew what it was without thinking much. They also knew what they hated, that hairy stuff, heavy rock—"it's crackers the way it's arranged—isn't it?"— though that mattered more at school than on the streets, where they were grown-up already and went drinking with their brothers and their mates. Music was for the girls really, wasn't it? It was the girls who stayed at home and listened more and even had their favorites pinned on the wall and sometimes told the boys what to buy, for their girlfriends.

David's and Peter's friends were younger—age fifteen and in the fourth form—but were committed to the academic routine and saw their futures stretching out through the sixth form and college. This was how David's parents and teachers saw it too, though Peter's had their doubts. They were young and lacked the resources and the mobility and the freedom for student life, and in chafing about this they were more aggressively hip at school, in the youth club, and most of all at home, where they'd gather their friends and sit around the record player as if it were Moses, bringing messages from on high. It was important for this lot to distinguish themselves from everybody—teachers, parents, peers. They were hippies, hairies, in their clothes and attitudes and tastes and drugs; and they worked at it, read the music press, got passionate about their records and about the evils of commercialism. They were an elite, a group apart from the masses, even if they were in the same school and youth club and street.

Most of these kids made it into the sixth form with no sweat, and entered that culture easily, the greater freedom and success accompanying a looser hipness so that their interests remained but their expression was less aggressive. Some, though, did not. Peter failed his Ordinary Level exams and the school wouldn't have him in the sixth, regarded him as an academic "no-hoper"—they wouldn't even give him a reference for local technical college. He found his life-style incompatible with the unskilled work his father and brothers did and lived on the dole mostly, not articulate enough to say what he really wanted but hearing it in music, which seemed like the right life if he could get it together. He dreamed about that in the cafés by day and the hippie pub by night, did a little dealing and always turned-on his friends, whether at school or home for the vacation. He knew everything that was going on and believed more than ever what they'd all once believed, that "rock is a real boost from reality"; and he needed to believe it now, more than ever.

Peter wanted desperately to be an active rock consumer, and the meanings he found in his music, his commitment to it, were not the result of mass cultural manipulation but reflected his own situation, his complex experience of leisure as something both desirable and forced upon him. Music seemed to make sense of this experience, just as, in different ways, it made some sense of the leisure experiences of all Keighley's teenagers. The different youth groups' uses of music were different not because some groups were more resistant to commercial pressures than others, not even because some groups were more organized in subcultural terms than others, but because the groups each had their own leisure needs and interests—Keighley's youth culture patterns were an aspect of the town's social structure, its relations of production.

## MUSIC AND CLASS

I have described the teenage culture of a small English town at a particular moment, and I don't want to claim too much for this. Nevertheless, my broad distinctions of age, sex, and class are echoed not just by other sociologists in Britain but, as significantly, by the record companies' own market researchers. Their account of youth and music goes something like this.

The first decade of rock 'n' roll (1955–1964) established it as music for working-class teenagers. It was music for dancing, courting, and hanging about—silly love songs with a more or less insistent beat. This pioneering period (in which music got worse as record companies made formula teenage pop out of the original rhythms and passions) was succeeded by the golden age of teenage music, 1964–67. The Beatles and Bob Dylan met up with Elvis Presley; rock 'n' roll and teenage pop got mixed up with blues and soul and folk and protest; the resulting records were at once exciting, intriguing, and real, and the audience sat down to listen. By 1967 pop had become rock—no longer working-class teenage music, but a form of expression for youth in general, for a generation. Nineteen sixty-seven seemed to mark the end of the beginning—rock had become an art form which bound a community.

But, so the argument goes, this would have been a false conclusion. Nineteen sixty-seven was, in fact, the beginning of the end. The chart clues to the future weren't "A Whiter Shade of Pale" and *Sgt. Pepper,* but Cream's "I Feel Free" and Jimi Hendrix Experience's "Hey Joe." What the industry learned in 1967 was that rock could be marketed as a specific genre—not integrated with rock 'n' roll and pop, but sold in deliberate isolation from them.

The rock/pop distinction was established quite slowly and through two separate stages. Rock forms of production and consumption were perfected between 1967 and 1971, as an increasing number of bands and performers aimed their music at an album-buying market of hip, mostly male music freaks. This was the period in which Jethro Tull, ELP, Pink Floyd, Yes, and the rest of the rock super-groups established their popularity; it was the time when Led Zeppelin became the world's number-one live attraction and album band without releasing a UK single. Rock music meant lengthy studio workouts, rich and elaborate sounds; it was music made for expensive stereos and FM radio and campus concerts. This music was marketed without reference to mainstream teenage taste. It didn't meet the dancing needs of a working-class weekend; it sounded wrong on a cheap transistor radio; it offered few suitable idols for the teeny-bopper's bedroom wall. The resulting vacuum was filled in the 1971–73 revival of pop—the parallel success of T. Rex and Slade, the rise of manufactured teen stars like Sweet, Gary Glitter, Suzi Quatro, and teen idols like Donny Osmond and David Cassidy. Pop was sold in dance halls and discos, on *Top of the Pops* and Radio Luxembourg. It was bought by a mass market of dancing, chart-watching, female pop fans.

By 1972, the year I did my research, the rock/pop division seemed absolute, and the division of musical tastes seemed to reflect class differences: on one hand, there was the culture of middle-class rock—pretentious and genteel, obsessed with bourgeois notions of art and the accumulation of expertise and equipment; on the other hand, there was the culture of working-class pop—banal, simple-minded, based on the formulas of a tightly knit body of business-men.

This equation of class and taste was crude, a marketing rule of thumb, and there were obvious additional factors that entered into the assumptions: age (the pop audience was younger) and sex (the pop audience was more female). Nonetheless, these distinctions made sociological as well as commercial sense. Similar rules guided American record companies around their fragmented "taste publics." American sociologists, too, took for granted class distinctions within youth culture, "higher" and "lower" tastes within the "drugs and music" ideology. "*Rolling Stone* vs. *Sunset Strip*," was how Herbert Gans put it, and R. Serge Denisoff's 1975 study of the rock industry, *Solid Gold,* divided the rock audience into three broad groups: young, predominantly female, bubble-gum pop fans (singles and poster buyers, teen idols on their bedroom walls); older "punk-rockers" (rock as aggressive background music for the rituals of dancing, dating, and the stoned weekend); and collegians (followers of "folk-art-rock," concert-goers and LP listeners, their stars with something interesting to say).

American taste-publics are not the same as British taste-publics, partly because in the USA academic differences are less sharp, less static, less damning at an early age. Denisoff's punk-rockers, mixed-up elements of rock and pop, and rock itself, defined around the blues-based concert sounds of Cream, the Rolling Stones, and Led Zeppelin, brought together punks and collegians. In Britain, too, there were musical movements which resisted the marketing men's formulas: "glamrockers" like David Bowie, Roxy Music, Rod Stewart, and Elton John were successful in both rock and pop terms. And as the decade developed it became increasingly difficult to make sense of heavy metal as student music. Bands like Black Sabbath, Uriah Heep, and Deep Purple had their own armies of scruffy working-class fans, and the dismissive response of *Rolling Stone* to hard rock as a genre (and to all its exponents except its original 1960s founders) was symptomatic. The huge popularity of Grand Funk Railroad, in 1970–71, symbolized the arrival of a rock culture of working-class fans who didn't even read *Rolling Stone;* and the rise of Kiss later in the decade was an even clearer indication of how rock could be integrated into the traditional marketing modes of teenage *pop*. The result was a music which had no significance for "the intelligent" rock fan at all (or, for that matter, for the UK equivalent of a U.S. Kiss fan—pop fans are essentially provincial in their demands). From the record companies' perspective, this was the safest way of making money: to mark out the various consumer groups involved in rock—as they had for pop—and to cater to their tastes accordingly. The social fragmentation of rock consumers and the professionalization of rock producers described in chapter 5 were aspects of the same process.

## THE SOCIOLOGY OF TASTE

The problem with the concept of "taste-publics" is that tastes are not commensurate. The rock audience must be differentiated not just in terms of what people listen to, but also by reference to how they listen, what the music means to them. Class distinctions (as was obvious for Peter in my Keighley survey) are overlaid by issues of challenge and commitment. In the 1970s it became clear that rock could be as commercial, as easy listening, as any previous form of pop, and that musical commitment did not necessarily have anything to do with "intelligence." By the end of the decade it was obvious that the music that mattered most was created and survived in the *interstices* of the class structure.

The most common sociological explanation of the importance of music for youth is in terms of peer-group culture. Colin Fletcher, for example, describes how rock 'n' roll transformed Liverpool's street gangs into beat groups, as every gang nurtured its own musicians, provided its own fans, and started to assert its presence on-stage with "the wild and basic sound" of Mersey Beat. Allan Williams, the Beatles' original manager, suggests that the groups didn't replace gangs but extended their activities and, if anything, added to the violence—battles of the bands were fought more often by fans than musicians.

Music has always been particularly important for British youth as a means of distinguishing one peer group from another:

> What about me? I dig mod clothes but I don't wear them. I like the Beatles but don't rave over them. I listen to Blue Beat music but don't dance the Blue Beat way. I wear my hair long and

sometimes use hair lacquer, but I don't sport a Blue Beat hat.
I dig everything a mod raves over but I don't hunt with a Mod
pack. Recently I asked a typical mod boy what title I should
come under. Sizing me up he said, "You're not one of those
in-between Mods and Rockers called Mids. There's an Ivy
League style about your suits and your appearance differs from
the Mid. I would put you under the title of—a Stylist."[3]

From this perspective, musical tastes, like clothes, are simply
a matter of style, and American observers have always been amazed
by the detail of British youth cults:

> True skinheads always look neat. Their clothes are smart and
> expensive. Their boots are always polished to perfection. Their
> favourite clothes are Levi sta-prest, Harrington jackets, Jaytex
> (shirts), Bens (shirts), Crombies (coats), Bluebeats (hats), Doc's
> (Dr. Martens boots), Royals' (shoes), Monkey boots (girls'
> boots), Fred's (Fred Perry shirts), Toniks (two-tone suits).[4]

Youth groups in the USA have rarely had such sartorial self-
consciousness (though this may be just a matter of sociological ignorance—Alison Lurie noted in 1976 that it was junior high lore
that "freaks always wear Lees, greasers wear Wranglers, and everyone else wears Levis"), and the most clothes-obsessed young Americans come out of black and Latin cultures. There is nothing in the
USA to match the *precision* of white youth styles in Britain, where
the slightest differences between groups are matters of passionate
argument. The intensity of musical identity is most visible at a British show—everyone is dressed like the star.

Music is used, equally, to distinguish the young from the old,
to identify a place or time or occasion as youth's property. Music—
played on transistor radios, record players, portable cassettes—is
the easiest way for the young to signal their control of their rooms
and clubs and street corners. The demands made of it—noise, beat,
flash—are general rather than specific: if the noise is right, any
noise will do; music is the context rather than the focus of leisure.
This is obvious in the main institution of teenage culture, the dance.
Dances focus on displays, deals, the exchange and mart of sexual
partners (and such displays and deals long predate rock 'n' roll).
The music accompanies the activity without necessarily expressing

it, for, as a fifteen year old in my survey put it, "If the older people want to begin looking for a wife or a husband, they *have* to go to Bradford Mecca."

Music, according to sociologists, is an aspect of peer-group organization. It is in their peer groups that teenagers learn the rules of the social game ("achieve competence in the interpersonal domain") and develop sexual identity and social status; it is in peer groups that they learn how to publicly handle private feelings. In sociological terms, all adolescents have these problems, all adolescents pass through peer groups, all adolescents use music as a badge and a background, a means of identifying and articulating emotion. Youth culture is, from this perspective, classless. Whatever the material differences between young people, they still have more problems in common with each other than with the adults of their own class or sex—hence the resonance of rock music, a sound and interest for *all* young people, as the sales figures show.

They show differences too, though, as we've seen. My argument is that adolescence has different settings, peer groups play according to different rules. The broad class distinction of my survey—sixth-form culture versus the lower fifth—can be applied to adolescents more generally: the cultural distinction is the suburb vs. the street.

Suburban culture is home-centered, socially fragmented, a matter of family solidarity, as parents and children work out together their career plans. Suburban culture means sensible work at school, the constructive use of abundant leisure time and goods. The suburban young are taught about effort and reward and competition—success is the measure of self-worth; they have to be, simultaneously, satisfied and dissatisfied with their lot. Their peer groups are the setting not only for class competition but also for escape from the struggle, for irresponsibility, self-indulgence. Their music is a source of both an emotionally intensified sense of self (artists are heard to articulate the listeners' own, private, fears and feelings) and a collective excitement, an illicit, immediate sense of solidarity and danger, an un-bourgeois lack of caution, an uncalculated honesty. Part of the middle-class use of music, in short, is as a way into working-class adolescence; rock offers the fantasy of a community of risk (this approach to music has a long history: in the 1920s and 1930s middle-class adolescents were, for similar reasons, drawn to jazz).

The street culture that fascinates the suburban young is a romanticized version of the culture of working-class peer groups. Powerless and pushed around at home, work, and school, young proletarians have to claim their own space, literally; they must "magically" appropriate their material environment—streets and cafés and pubs and parks—from the "outsiders" who, in reality, control them. For these teenagers a sense of class *is* a sense of place: it is *their* streets that must be defended, their streets on which status is won, on which "them" and "us" is made visible. Street culture has, also, a long history, stretching back through a hundred years of city gangs—masculine (though dependent on the women at home), touchy, suspicious of strangers, committed to violence as the best expression of emotion. It is within such groups—more or less organized, more or less criminal, more or less desperate—that working-class adolescents solve their problems of status and identity, and music is little more than the background sound of their activities, "the small coin of social exchange," in Graham Murdock's words.

It is, nevertheless, the street experience of leisure—dance-hall drunks, doing nothing, tedium and laughs, fighting, male camaraderie—that, sentimentalized, distanced, focused as it is, fuels rock 'n' roll. Youth music celebrates street culture for its participants *and* for its suburban observers. American analysts in the late 1960s were prone to describe such celebrations in religious terms: rock concerts as a ceremony of the *spiritual* communion of youth. But this was to evade the complexity of the relationships between work and play, class and ideology, the fantastic and the real.

## SUBCULTURES

Ever since teddy boys appeared on street corners in the early 1950s, the most obvious difference between British and American youth cultures has been the obsessive focus of British working-class youth on style—after the teds came mods and rockers, skinheads, suèdes and smoovies and spikes, Bowie and soul boys, funkers, punks, rudies. If American youth cultures depend on myths of community (which means that America invented the hippie), British youth cultures depend on myths of difference. The response, in both cases, is to the problem of class.

The USA has, in fact, its own subcultures (various sorts of

gangs, Hell's Angels, surfers, and so on), and the corner/college boy, suburban/street distinction has always had a stylistic expression—in the 1960s every town had its separate leisure groups of surfers and greasers, frats and hitters, punks and dupers (it was these distinctions that were thrown into confusion by the arrival of the hippie). In America, though, in Bob Christgau's words, "our class system is afraid to speak its name," and only in Britain have youth subcultures been *explicitly* class-conscious, involving not just peer-group street norms, but also, in Dick Hebdige's phrase, "a struggle for the sign." British subcultures work *on* the ideology of class and youth, respond to the headlines, to the dominant definitions of who and what they are. Just as different youth groups become, for contemporary commentators, "signs of the times," so the groups themselves use the media's imagery of class and sex and age. The skinheads, for example, took on the look of the cartoon lumpen worker—shaved head as a sign of stupidity, work boots as a sign of drudgery, body moving clumsily as a sign of brute force, dumb surliness as a sign of menace. The whole ensemble was a proletarian caricature of a bourgeois joke.

The easiest way of analyzing subcultures is as variations of street culture. In their preoccupation with "toughness, excitement, fate, autonomy, and status," the teds, for example, were no different from other lower-class adolescents. It was their concern for style, their attention to the details of fashion and music, that made them interesting, and the teds, like most subsequent British subcultures, did not create their own musical symbols, but took them over from what was on commercial offer. Music "expressed" the subculture only indirectly; its meaning lay not in its production, its intention, but in its consumption, its position in a leisure style. Subcultural analysts argue that there is, nevertheless, a homology, a stylistic fit between youth groups' values and the musical forms they use to signify them; the sociological problem is to *decode* the styles.

There have been, by now, numerous subcultural readings, some subtle, some absurd, but all raising the same musical question: What is the relationship between rock as style and rock as activity? Against the early adolescent theorists' descriptions of a transitional street culture, i.e., music as background, the subculturalists pitch a theory that is both more romantic and more political: style represents the experience of class oppression in the individual; the moment of refusal is the act of symbolic creation itself. The problem is to reconcile adolescence and subculture. Most working-class teenagers pass through groups, change identities, play their leisure roles for fun; other differences between them—sex, occupation, family—are much more significant than distinctions of style. For every youth "stylist" committed to a cult as a full-time creative task, there are hundreds of working-class kids who grow up in loose membership of several groups and run with a variety of gangs. There's a distinction here between a vanguard and a mass, between uses of leisure *within* subcultures.

The most significant of Britain's youth cults were the mods of 1962–65. They established new terms for teenage fashion, music, drug use, mobility, exclusion. The teds had, in the end, seemed like losers, desperate for attention; the mods seemed to have a secret that made adults irrelevant. The mods were arrogant and narcissistic, cynical and tense; they came on like winners, and consumption was, for them, as much a playground as a last resort; the urge was movement—from shop to shop, club to club—speeding on pills, on dance floors, on the latest fashion coup. The mods became, indeed, the 1960s symbol of consumption generally. Mod style was exploited to transform shopping (the rise of the boutique), listening (the rise of pirate radio), and dancing (the triumph of soul music). Mod style eventually made its impact—via British beat and Los Angeles—on American youth culture too.

It is difficult to relate mod as street culture—gangs, fighting, intense transitory leisure moments—and mod as permanent obsession with looks and goods and knowledge; and the mods themselves, unlike their adult observers, were well aware of the distinctions within their community. The mod cult began in the early 1960s with the "modernists," a few petit-bourgeois kids, clothes-conscious children of Jewish rag-trade families, who met up with a few street-culture dropouts—semi-beatniks—in the coffeehouses of London's Soho. The concern of both these groups was to distinguish themselves from the mainstream, and they looked to America for stylistic inspiration (*On the Waterfront*, the beats, modern jazz) and France (Belmondo, the student look, intellectuals, a black beret). For the original modernists the point was exclusivity (ever more obscure tracks of R&B and ska) not solidarity; theirs was a self-conscious gesture against conformity of any sort. These mods were mobile, ambitious, and wanted out; they drove their scooters *through* the streets, cool in their fifteen-m.p.h. formations (they didn't stay *on* the streets or need spaces to defend).

Mod was routinized from 1962–63, then, not just in commer-

cial terms but in street terms too: mod/rocker battles became a ritual; the modernists became stylists and then moved on altogether.
In 1965, remembers Penny Reel, the Scene Club's coolest couple
arrived, "dressed in exotic Tibetan smocks, with Indian silk scarves
affixed to their wrists, sandals on their bare feet, wooden beads
around their necks, daisies in their hair, and looking for all the
world like, as one observer put it, two flecking gipsies. They proceed
to tell anyone who will listen that love is all what really matters."
The mods had become hippies and Penny Reel's point is that there
was more in common between the "stylists" of the various 1960s
youth groups than between such eccentrics and their conformist im-
itators.

Subcultural theorists usually distinguish between working-class
and bohemian groups (beats in the fifties, hippies in the sixties).
Jock Young argues that whereas "delinquent youth culture" is focused on leisure because its members are marginal to the labor market in terms of skill and opportunities, bohemian youth culture is
focused on leisure because its members have deliberately rejected
the rewards of work:

> Like the delinquent he focuses his life on leisure, but unlike
> the former his dissociation is a matter of choice rather than a
> realistic bowing to the inevitable. Moreover, his disdain for so-
> ciety is of an articulate and ideological nature. He evolves so-
> cial theories which uphold subterranean values as authentic
> guides to action, and which attempt to solve the problem of the
> domination of the ethos of productivity.[5]

Music, as I showed in my Keighley study, had a special importance for hippie (or hairy) culture—it didn't just symbolize the
group's identity but was heard to make a specific commentary on
the world against which the hippies were, in some respects, protest-
ing. Rock, in other words, was more than just hippie music by adoption. In Richard Mills's words, music was given a "missionary
purpose"; its task was to carry hippie values into the heart of the
commercial beast, to spread

> the ubiquitous notion of "turning on," the sudden intuition,
> the transcending of rational standards and structuring judg-
> ments (there was mystical illumination or there was nothing)
> and the explicit linking of mental and physical dimensions—

to be "smiling and bopping about and not questioning, to know what it is to be alive."

Music offered the experience of community as well as its expression:

> Pop groups thus held a key position within the culture. They helped minister and uphold that experience of transformation which underlay it, provided the forms and rituals through which its goals and values found expression, and, in the process, established the minimal degree of social and economic organization necessary to sustain them. All these factors gave them a position of leadership which partly strengthened, and partly itself flowed from, their final role, that of negotiating between the different realities of the hip and the straight.[6]

In the long run, this role, missionary in the commercial world, proved impossible for hippie musicians to sustain. In California, where hippie ideology was most powerful, the violence of the Altamont Festival of 1969 was taken by rock fans (including San Francisco's hippie community itself) as the final sign that a community could not be based on musical taste alone. But the proof that the world of the hip could only be the world of the commercial hip lay in earlier festivals: Monterey, which brought big business in; Woodstock, which dramatized the total separation of rock's performers and consumers.

The original hippies tried to use music to express their opposition to "the ethos of productivity." They had an articulate position on capitalism and the good life which was in sharp contrast to the inarticulate position of the working-class young. Teddy boys' music was, for example, "their most vivid link with contemporary culture," an area where they were "at one" with society. T. R. Fyvel suggests that if teds were against hard work and getting on:

> Sweat and toil to learn music is one of the few exceptions. A boy willing to devote every day to practice in a band is not derided for his pains. Even in the toughest Ted circles, musical ambition is generally regarded as legitimate.[7]

In the negotiation between the hip and the straight, the hippie was armed with an ideology, the teddy boy was not: rock 'n' roll wasn't a symbol of the teddy boys' independence but of their continued dependence on the world of the teenage consumer.

This class cultural comparison makes less sense of the mods. Whatever its resonance on the streets, their position prefigured the hippies, was an aspect of bohemianism. I have already quoted Reel's comments on this, and he goes on to describe Beardy Pegley, London "mod notability," like this:

> Not only is he the first guy I ever see wear hair lacquer and lipstick, but he is also the earliest on the scene with a pink tab-collar shirt, a grey crew neck jersey, knitted tie, scarlet suede jacket with matching leather collar, navy blue crombie overcoat, white half-mast flares, and candy-stripe socks, as well as being the first mod to sing the praises of Laurel Aitken, James Brown, the Pretty Things, the Flamingo Club in Wardour Street, Lawrence Ferlinghetti and marijuana, insult Eden Kane in the Chez Don, and is still the only guy I ever met who owns a pair of bright emerald green fur booties, all this circa 1962.[8]

It is not easy to put these symbols together as an expression of a *class* ideology. What they represent is an attitude to style, an argument that leisure is the only part of life that matters.

In my survey of Keighley it was clear that music was most important for pupils who rejected their class cultures, whether middle-class pupils who rejected success or working-class pupils who rejected work. In his study of working-class boys in London, Peter Willmott also discovered "another kind of rebel":

> He was alone, playing records by Billie Holiday and Miles Davis. He says of his parents, "They couldn't understand me in a hundred years. Like most ordinary East End people, their idea of living is to have a steady job and settle down with a nice little wife in a nice little house or flat, doing the same things every day of your life. They think the sorts of thing I do are mad." What sort of things? "Well, I might decide to take the day off and go up the park and sit and meditate. Or go round my friend's pad for an all-night session. A group of us drink whisky and smoke tea and talk about what's happiness and things like that." He says that he and his friends regularly take Purple Hearts too: "It may seem sinful to some people. But we're just young people who like to enjoy ourselves

and forget the Bomb." He reads Jack Kerouac, Norman Mailer, James Baldwin—"That's the sort of thing I dig. I suppose I'm really searching."9

Willmott writes that such "rebels" are rare, but their importance for rock should not be underestimated. Such local "hip" figures were crucial to 1960s youth culture not just in turning us on to blues and politics and poetry, but also as the link between the culturally adventurous of all classes. They provided the continuity of bohemian concern that runs from the beats to the punks. For most young people leisure is enjoyed not in opposition to work but as an aspect of it—work and leisure complement each other; only "rebels" read rock for alternative values, only for "rebels" is music not just leisure's garnish, but its point.

Some people are deviant not in the way they value music but in the way they consume it. They are fanatics, and their life revolves around an idol to the extent of imitation, sexual pursuit, a compulsive flaunting of their idolatry. There are musical fanatics too: in Britain and France, in particular, there is a long history of jazz and blues and soul freaks, scholars who work less as a group than as a network of communication. Such purists meet only to play and listen to their music, in their own clubs and pubs and halls. Britain is scattered with jazz clubs and folk clubs, rock 'n' roll nights and rockabilly weekends, old teds gathered to reminisce on Gene Vincent, Northern soul dancers on the floor all night to the *obscure* Motown sound, funkers forming human pyramids. For all these people, music is neither the casual accompaniment of leisure nor a subcultural sign; it is, rather, a hobby.

The different uses of music—background, ideology, hobby—reflect different uses of leisure, different ways in which people relate play to work; and the most significant of these differences reflect sex as well as class divisions. In chapter 8, I suggested that for teenage girls—working-class girls in particular—marriage is the most vital career choice. Domestic labor continues to be the organizing center of women's work. What we need to examine now is the effect of women's work on women's play, and the fantasies and realities that women, as young girls, bring to leisure.

# GIRLS AND YOUTH CULTURE

Boys' and girls' lives are different, and such differences can't be explained simply in terms of values—the choices involved reflect different opportunities, and the starting point for any analysis of the sexual differentiation of leisure must be that girls spend far more time at home than boys do.

There are three immediate reasons why girls stay home more. The first and most important is that parents exert control over them, at least in their early teenage years—forbidding them to go out every night, limiting where they go, with whom, for how long. This control is not exercised to anything like the same extent over boys and means that girls are more closely integrated into family life as teenagers. Children are prepared for different adult sex cultures from an early age, and the close family relationships in working-class homes are sex-bound—girls and their mothers, boys and their fathers. The women's world is the home; leisure outside the home is assumed to be a male preserve.

The second constraint follows from this. Working-class girls, unlike boys, have a role in the home from an early age (while they are still at school indeed); they have tasks to do—babysitting, for instance; they are expected, even if in a comparatively light way, to help with cleaning and cooking; they are a part of home organization, more economically dependent on their parents than their brothers, with less chances to make teenage money for themselves outside the house. (This is why mass youth unemployment in Britain has been, unexpectedly, a more aggravating problem for girls than boys: working-class girls, leaving school at sixteen, have always used full-time work as a means to temporary independence, a way of getting out of the home during work and leisure; on the dole, they find themselves still treated by their parents as dependent, expected to work in the home instead. Boys, by contrast, get the freedom of the streets whether they're working or not.)

The third constraint has a different immediate source but the same effect: girls spend longer than boys preparing to go out, with clothes and cosmetics and toiletries. Girl culture is also a culture of courtship—I'll return to this later.

Though girls are more confined to home, they are not as a result completely bound by the family or excluded from youth culture (though they are less visible at youth culture's most dramatic—and most frequently analyzed—moments). What they are excluded from is *street* culture—boys are on the streets, moving in and out of gangs, learning the rules of loyalty, bravado, and public leisure from an early age. For girls, "street walking" has very different connotations; instead, girls meet at home to listen to music and teach each other make-up skills, practice their dancing, compare sexual notes, criticize each other's clothes, and gossip. Their reasons for being at home don't prevent the home from being used as a youthful place— friends can share in tasks, girls are allowed out to friends' houses, even evenings with boyfriends are acceptable if they end, not too late, together at home.

Girls at their youngest and least free stage are teeny-boppers. Teeny-boppers are very young (ten to thirteen year olds), and if the focus of teeny-bop culture is usually a pop star (such teeny stars come and go in three-year cycles), the cultural symbol is less records (though girls are more likely to buy singles than boys) than magazines—idol-related products like T-shirts and tea trays sell as well as the records anyway (David Cassidy's records, for instance, only accounted for about one-fifth of his earnings). At this age girls' youth cultural activities are heavily concentrated on what is immediately accessible in the home, and TV is more significant than radio, the sight of the star more important than his sound. Teenage girls' magazines (in Britain they started with *Marilyn* in 1955, *Jackie* is now the most important; in America the most influential of the thousands of such mags has been *16*) have always shown "a dominant interest in pop stars and the pop scene," but their interest has been less in music than in chat and clothes and possessions and pictures. The circulation of such magazines is heavily dependent on the potency of the *image* of the latest teenage idol, and for teeny-boppers, seeing an idol in person is less important for the power of the actual experience than for the status it confers. In every group of girls, one or two can now swagger a little more proudly, and the occasional public sense of teeny-bop identity can, just as in male street groups, be violent and aggressive and funny. The most abusive mail I've ever had as a rock critic was after a David Cassidy review: "How dare you put Donny Osmond in the same column as David Cassidy?" wrote one girl. "Maybe his suit was tight fitting," wrote another, "but he has some balls to show. I'm sure you haven't."

Girls grow out of the fantasy sexuality of teeny-bop as they begin to date and dance and go out more seriously, but the relationship between music and the bedroom continues. Their public use of music might be much the same as boys' (for background and dancing), but girls' home use remains different, with a continued emphasis on personalities. Girls' magazines feature rock stars rather than rock music and the lack of female interest in "serious" rock is revealed clearly in the readership patterns of the music press and the audience patterns of radio and TV. Even within sixth form and student culture, girls have less interest in music than boys: they may potter about on guitars, but while the boys are investigating electronics, it's the lyrics the girls get into, singer/songwriters and rock as angst— in my Keighley sample the girls in all groups were far more interested than the boys in rock words, the boys far more interested in performance. They were relating to rock through different discourses of sexuality.

In male music, cock-rock performance means an explicit, crude, "master-ful" expression of sexuality (the approach is most obvious in the singing style that derives from Led Zeppelin's Robert Plant, in the guitar hero style that derives from Led Zeppelin's Jimmy Page). Cock-rock performers are aggressive, boastful, constantly drawing audience attention to their prowess and control. Their bodies are on display (plunging shirts and tight trousers, chest hair and genitals), mikes and guitars are phallic symbols (or else caressed like female bodies), the music is loud, rhythmically insistent, built around techniques of arousal and release. Lyrics are assertive and arrogant, but the exact words are less significant than the vocal styles involved, the shrill shouting and screaming. What's going on at such "hard rock" shows is a masturbatory celebration of penis power: girls are structurally excluded from this rock experience: it "speaks out" the boundaries of *male* sexuality. The cock-rock image is one of the rampant traveling man, smashing hotels and groupies alike (groupies, in this account, standing for the male sexual fantasy of anonymous, ever available female flesh, no emotional strings attached), and cock-rock music adds a relentless public push to the physical frankness of rhythm and blues. Cock-rockers' musical skills are synonymous with their phallic skills; stud and guitar hero are, with performers like Ted Nugent, integrated aspects of the same sales appeal.

Female music, teeny-bop, is, by contrast, a confidential, private discourse. It sets up, in Jenny Taylor and Dave Laing's words, "a relationship between singer and listener which implies a 'hidden truth' of sexuality to be revealed." The teeny-bop idol's appeal is based on self-pity, vulnerability, and need. The image is the ideal boy next door: sad, thoughtful, pretty. Teeny-bop songs are about being let down and stood up, about loneliness and frustration; teeny-bop music is less physical than cock-rock, drawing on older, romantic, ballad conventions. Sexuality is expressed as a kind of spiritual yearning, carrying only vague hints of physical desire. The singer wants someone to love—not a bedmate but a soul-mate; and if cock-rock plays on conventional concepts of male sex as animalistic, superficial, just-for-the-moment, teeny-bop plays on notions of female sex as serious, diffuse, implying total emotional commitment.

These discourses are not exclusive, neither do they exhaust rock's sexual meanings; but they do have a general resonance and they are predicated on general sexual divisions: if male consumers identify with rock performers and do so publicly, collectively (concerts are, in this respect, reminiscent of football games and other occasions of male camaraderie—the euphoria experienced depends on the symbolic absence of women), female consumers are addressed, by contrast, as individuals, the potential objects of the performer's private needs. And male identity with the performer is expressed not only in sexual terms but also as a looser appropriation of the musicians' dominance and power, confidence and control. It is boys, as we have seen, who are interested in rock as music, want to be musicians, technicians, experts. It is boys who form the core of the rock audience, become rock critics and collectors (girl rock fanatics become, by contrast, photographers). The rock 'n' roll discourse constructs its listeners in sexually differentiated terms—boys as public performers, girls as private consumers.

Girl culture, indeed, starts and finishes in the bedroom. Romance always ends with the heroine getting married, her girlhood over; but, in fact, girls move from the organization of one household to another with a much less abrupt process of "settling down" than their male peers. The problem is to find a husband—hence the significance for girl culture of dancing. In Britain, more young brides, of all classes, still meet their husbands at dances than in any other way; and the most dramatic change in female leisure is the abruptness with which women give up dancing once they are wed. The point (and this applies to the USA, too) is that if marriage is a girl's career, then her leisure before marriage is her work, is the setting for the start of her career, the attraction of a man suitable for marriage. The postwar development of married women's work hasn't really changed this situation. Marriage and motherhood may once have been seen as an alternative to work, but working-class girls don't now regard work as an alternative to marriage and motherhood. Domestic and non-domestic labor are, rather, complementary—the job has to fit into domestic obligations, and most girls still work and play with marriage in mind.

The process begins at home, with the job of making oneself generally attractive—market researchers continually emphasize how much of girls' income goes to clothes and cosmetics. The work of dressing and making-up, staging the feminine show, is girl culture's central secret; and if artificial faces and tissue-paper breasts are added in the privacy of the bedroom, the girls' toilet is the public space where they can work and plot and laugh together. Nevertheless, all this female activity, whatever its fun and style and art as a collective occupation, is done, in the end, individually, for the boys' sake. It is the male gaze that gives the girls' beauty work its meaning. As Dick Clark explained to his teenagers in 1959:

> The fellows have no aversion to makeup, if it is used in the correct way. The correct way, of course, is to bring out your natural beauty (and you all have some) and not to be noticeable while doing it. It's easy for some girls, difficult for others. The difficulty lies in knowing just how much to use before it becomes apparent. The trick is to don lipstick, powder, etc., and still convince the fellows that it isn't makeup at all but the real you.[10]

Boys are fashion- and appearance-conscious too, of course, but their look, however elaborate, is essentially narcissistic, and also seeks confirmation in the male gaze. The mods, obsessed with clothes, pretty and precise in an "unmanly" way, were called sissies by the rockers correctly—they *were* behaving like women, they were (like the rockers themselves) dressing for men. As Bill Norman remembers:

> When you were at work, you were a nobody. So when you put on your suede or mohair suit and Desert Boots and go to the dance hall, you want to be a somebody to your mates. It's your

mates you want to impress, not the girls. You make a statement through your clothes, or your dancing, or your scooter. You had to be cool. To be chasing birds was seen as soft, a bit sentimental. You didn't want to lose face with the other guys.[11]

The convention of courting is that the girl be passive—she waits to be asked to dance and then becomes the boy's possession—but it is really the girl who is actively seeking a partner. It is she rather than the boys who will be seen as a failure if she hasn't attracted anyone by the end of the evening, and it is she who has to judge what a boy is worth, where to stop, how to let things develop. The rules of the dating game are full of practical ambiguities: What is "going steady"? When is a relationship "serious"? What sexual obligations go with what social commitments? All these questions are about the *public* meanings of sexual behavior and such meanings are still defined, primarily, by the double standard. The words of a 1964 mod continue to sum up the usual teenage situation:

> I might marry sometime if I find a decent girl. I don't think I'll bother if she's a virgin as long as she hasn't knocked around too much. Girls who're shop-worn get old before their time. Girls think boys are just out for one thing, but if they make a boy respect them it's different. Unless I really like a girl I wouldn't waste time if she doesn't want to go to bed. I think most boys are the same—it's only natural.[12]

Working-class girls in Britain go to dances in groups, prepare for them as friends, support and advise each other, dance together, help each other keep their self-respect and sense of fun. But the object of the exercise is to be picked up: girls depend on their friends to support them in the process of ceasing to be friends (and so American sororities, to use a different example, traditionally chose members not "for themselves" but according to their ability to attract the right sort of men).

Once a girl has found a boy, her activities, romantic or sexual, are essentially private; and yet crucial to a girl's marriage chances is her "reputation," which rests on the public knowledge of her private behavior (pregnancy, in this context, is the most obvious public sign of a private act). Hence, even when a girl has got a partner, there are constraints on her behavior—one convention of the British dance hall is the going-home negotiation: girls (and this is equally true in America) have always got to be "careful."

> There is a noticeable reluctance among many of the girls to accept lifts home from boys and many will make their own way home (probably by taxi) rather than go with the boys they have met during the evening. Girls are unlikely to accept a lift unless they consider the boys "trustworthy." Some evidence of the existence of the "trustworthiness" criterion employed by girls can be found in the fact that I have on occasion been asked by groups of girls to give them a lift as they had seen that I was alone in my car (and of course that I am absolutely trustworthy!). On these occasions they told me that they were not worried travelling with me because I was outnumbered (three to one)—but they still jokingly quibbled about who was getting out last.[13]

For girls, as for boys, music is background, something to kiss and make up to, but it is also background to a different set of activities and involves different sorts of commitment. Working-class girls, for example, dance more and usually better than boys who (except in specific dancing cults like mod and disco) don't actually dance much at all. Girls buy and practice to dance records (which become part of girl group life) and start dancing much younger—since the 1920s the dance hall has, indeed, been one of the few places where girls could enjoy themselves physically. Music is also a way of managing the sexual and emotional tensions implicit in a girl's role: it both expresses them and offers a release. Music and musical idols provide a focus for female fantasies just as pop and film stars did for their mothers and grandmothers.

Once girls start going steady their leisure changes drastically and most of these tensions are dissolved. As part of a permanent couple, a couple looking forward to marriage, the girl can relax from the problems of pursuit and publicity and begin to adjust to her future as wife and mother. She begins to go out almost exclusively with her boyfriend, and it's at this stage that the distinctions between respectable and non-respectable girls become most obvious. Boys take their steady girlfriends to respectable clubs and pubs, while going with their male mates to the rough ones—the reputations of the girls who enter the latter suffer accordingly. A girl with a steady boyfriend can, by definition, only go out with him—her other leisure activities must be non-sexual, even in implication.

It is during this stage of courtship that the girl also begins to break from her female friends, a separation symbolized in Britain by the pre-wedding day hen party:

> I have never yet been into the City Centre Club on a Thursday without seeing at least one hen party and on occasion there have been as many as four. The high visibility of hen parties is produced by the traditional bride-to-be's hat. I do not know the origin of the practice, but it was also common in London. When a working girl is going to be married all the other girls at work make her a very large cardboard hat which is decorated with paper flowers, tinsel, tassles and often saucy jokes about the wedding night etc. She may also have things like L-plates [signifying a learning driver] pinned on the back of her dress or coat.[14]

Because girls' leisure is not really free time, a break from work, but is instead an integral part of their careers as domestic laborers, even the most romantic expressions of girl culture are tempered by realism. There is no equivalent, for example, to the sexual fantasies of young male *Playboy* culture, and, indeed, in many ways it is boys who romanticize sex, who are most keen to distinguish "falling in love" from "fooling around," to treat love as something "true," precious, a matter of possession and jealousy. For girls such a romantic notion of love is useful (something with which demands can be made on their boyfriends—"if you *really* love me . . ."), but they themselves romanticize motherhood more than marriage. A man is financially and socially necessary, but babies mean more emotionally. Working-class girls know from the experience of their own families that women have their closest, most satisfying relationships with their children, not their husbands; this is the emotional reality of women's place in the home.

Working-class girls are also aware that they can have fun in ways their mothers can't. There are times and places when the direct sexual constraints lose their force—on vacation for example; there are people (like passing pop stars) with whom girls can risk their reputation out of community sight. (Many so-called groupies are not the professional sex-dealers of rock myth but are, rather, local girls simply enjoying a casual, impulsive sexual encounter, a passing friendship with a good-looking stranger whom they can soon forget.)

Most girls, in other words, break most rules sometime or other, and we shouldn't exaggerate the restrictions on working girls' leisure—their mothers have it much worse. "Enjoy yourselves!" they advise, because whatever the anxieties of growing up female, girls are, at least some of the time, out of the house—dancing, playing, sharing fantasies that are not yet completely cut off. Working-class cultures, black and white, have always celebrated girlhood and courtship as a brief, bittersweet memory, marriage and marital sex as simply a means of survival. The contrast—before and after marriage—remains, whatever the changing norms of premarital sex and post-marital adultery and divorce. In the 1920s, the Lynds asked Middletown women what use they'd make of an extra hour in the day. "Rest," said the working-class wives, or, blankly, "I don't know." "I'd go anywhere to get away from the house," was another frequent reply. "I've been out of the house only twice in the three months since we moved here, both times to the store." In the 1970s, Bruce Springsteen commented:

> I see my sister and her husband. They're living the lives of my parents in a certain kind of way. They got kids, they're working hard. These are people, you can see something in their eyes ... I asked my sister, "What do you do for fun?" "I don't have any fun," she says. She wasn't kidding.[15]

Marriage is still *the* female career, and it is only in cases where it is not *the* career choice for a woman that other leisure possibilities open up for her. Women *can* achieve independence through their work and earnings, through a feminist consciousness and politics. Girls *can* be just as militant in their rebellion against cultural expectations as boys, and rock has been important to such rebellion; but sexual politics, like all politics, is a matter of circumstance as well as choice. I have described the structure of girls' work and leisure in deliberately harsh terms precisely because most rock 'n' roll commentators have taken the breakdown of the structure for granted, pointing to the decline of virgin marriages, the spread of sexual experiment, the decline of parent power, the permissiveness of 1960s peer-group culture, and so forth. But sexual "permissiveness" and "liberation" have not changed the material basis of wom-

lives—their work situation, the emphasis on marriage. What's
issue, rather, is a changing sexual *ideology*. This ideology has
ised new questions for leisure, new fantasies, but these questions
ind fantasies (and rock's treatment of them) have to be understood
against the continuing realities of domestic labor.

# CHAPTER 10

# ROCK AND SEXUALITY

## YOUTH AND SEXUALITY

The girl culture I described in the last chapter is teenage culture, essentially working-class, but such leisure constraints also apply to student culture, even if the sexual differentiation of economic opportunity is less blatant for middle-class youth. Indeed it was on college campuses in the 1920s that many of the conventions of postwar teenage sexual behavior were first established: it was college girls who first decided which sex acts a respectable girl could enjoy, which were illicit; it was college boys who first organized sex as a collective male activity, turned seductions into "scores"; it was at college that petting (an extraordinary American sexual institution) was first turned into a routine. College youth culture was interpreted at the time as "liberating," particularly for the girls, but they weren't liberated from the double standard.

If girls' leisure is limited by its use as the setting for courtship, courtship itself has to be understood in the context of a particular

sort of ideology of marriage, an ideology that does give girls a freedom—the freedom to choose partners. Historians have argued that
boys had a youth, a time of transition from childhood to adulthood
as they moved from home to work, long before girls. Adolescence
as a social status is predicated on a degree of independence, and as
long as girls were protected through puberty, confined to one household until they were given away in marriage to another, they had
no youth. Girls could only become teenagers when free marital
choice became the norm, when marriage was expected to be preced-
ed by love. Only then did a transitional period become necessary for
women too, a period when they could play the marriage field for
themselves. This ideology only began to be a general norm at the
beginning of this century, as ragtime and the dance craze began.
Rudi Blesh and Harriet Janis quote the *Sedalia Times* from 1900:

> When the girls walk out evenings with the sole purpose of pick-
> ing up a young man and continuing the walk, it is time to have
> a curfew law that will include children over sixteen. The rest-
> lessness that comes upon girls upon summer evenings results
> in lasting trouble unless it is speedily controlled. The right
> kind of man does not look for a wife on the streets, and the
> right kind of girl waits till the man comes to her home for her.[1]

Lawrence Stone, in his history *The Family, Sex and Marriage
in England,* argues that the ideology of sentimental love and "well-
tried personal affection" as the basis of marriage spread from the
aristocracy to the bourgeoisie in Europe in the latter part of the
eighteenth century (the move was marked by the rise of the romantic
novel) and moved gradually down the social scale during the nineteenth century. But this was neither a natural nor an uncomplicated
change of ideas. Youthful courtship carried dangers—the threat of
sexual disorder, a challenge to parental authority.

These dangers seemed to be multiplied by the emergence of
working-class adolescents. From early in the nineteenth century, the
feature of the industrial revolution that most concerned middle-class
moralists was its apparent effect on the working-class family, as girls
worked in the new factories alongside boys, achieving with them an
"unnatural" independence from their parents. The bourgeoisie
themselves were slowly adopting the ideology of romantic love as a
way of regulating adolescent sexuality and guaranteeing their chil-

dren's orderly transition to adult respectability. Romantic love was idealized in bourgeois fiction, in love songs, stories, and poetry, and routinized in the suburbs, in middle-class clubs and sports and dances where girls could meet boys who would be guaranteed to be suitable partners for love and marriage. Peer groups began to take over from parents as the arbiters of correct sexual behavior.

By the end of the nineteenth century middle-class reformers were beginning to apply the romantic approach to the problem of working-class adolescence too—in England and France, for example, romance was promoted as a replacement for community control of working-class sexuality, and young workers were encouraged to join their own "rational" peer-group leisure associations—youth clubs, cycle clubs, sports clubs, and so forth. In the USA the most important institution for the control of adolescent sexuality was, at least after 1918, the high school. Paula Fass suggests that the 1920s, in particular, were crucial for the development of American youth culture, because it was then that the ideology of sentimental love was fused with a new kind of advocacy of sexual pleasure. It was, in her words, the "dual process of the sexualization of love and the glorification of sex that helped to anchor the twentieth-century American marriage pattern, the horse-and-carriage ideal."

The "sexualization of love" was made possible by the spread of relatively efficient contraception. Delayed small families encouraged companionate marriages; sex itself, freed from conception, was reinterpreted as a form of emotional expression, a source of mutual pleasure—from the 1920s, middle-class marriage manuals recognized female sexuality. But the other side of this process was the domestication of sex. If sexual expression, for its own sake, became one of the pleasures and purposes of marriage, so marriage itself was defined as the necessary setting for the most pleasurable sex— necessary now not in terms of traditional morality but in terms of romance: love had become the reason for sex, and true love involved a commitment to marriage. First an engagement, later going steady, became the moment in youth culture when it was morally permissible to go all the way; and from the 1920s, middle-class girls, as prospective wives, could express their "sexual personalities" publicly, could use sexual devices, like make-up, that had previously been confined to prostitutes, to "loose women."

What made this ideology initially shocking was that it legitimated youthful sexual activity as an aspect of efficient mate selection; parents lost control not only over their children's marriage choices but also over their sexual behavior. Their place was taken, once more, by peer groups, which elaborated new rules of sexuality according to which some premarital pleasure was permissible, for girls and boys alike, but not such pleasure as would disrupt the romantic transition to marriage. Paula Fass quotes a female student from Ohio State University writing in 1922 in defense of her physical enjoyment of "smoking, dancing like voodoo devotees, dressing décolleté, petting and drinking." Her point was that although

> our tastes may appear riotous and unrestrained, the aspect of the situation is not alarming. The college girl—particularly the girl in the co-educational institution—is a plucky, coolheaded individual who thinks naturally. She doesn't lose her head— she knows her game and can play it dexterously. She is armed with sexual knowledge. . . . She is secure in the most critical situations—she knows the limits, and because of her safety in such knowledge she is able to run almost the complete gamut of experience.[2]

By the 1950s, knowledge of "the limits" was an aspect of teenage culture generally, but if the task of teenage peer groups was to control teenage sexuality, the issue was, really, girls' sexual behavior. It was female morality that was defined as chastity, female "trouble" that meant pregnancy. Adults worried about boys in terms of violence, the threat to order; they only worried about girls in terms of sex, the threat to the family. And they worried about all girls in these terms, their fears weren't confined to "delinquents."

Nineteen-fifties rock 'n' roll is usually described as a particularly sexual form of expression, a source of physical "liberation," but teenage culture was already sexualized by the time it appeared. The question we really have to examine concerns the use of music not in the general expression of sexuality but in its ordering. Sexuality is not a single phenomenon that is either expressed or repressed; the term refers, rather, to a range of pleasures and experiences, a range of ways in which people make sense of themselves as sexed subjects. Sexual discourses determine prohibitions as well as possibilities, what can't be expressed as well as what can. But the most important function of 1950s teenage culture wasn't to "repress" sexuality but to articulate it in a setting of love and marriage such that male and female sexuality were organized in quite different ways. And rock 'n' roll didn't change that sexual order. Elvis Presley's sexuality, for example, meant different things to his male and female fans. There was an obvious tension between his male appropriation as cock-rocker and his female appropriation as a teeny-bop idol. Rock 'n' roll was, say its historians significantly, "emasculated," but its "decline" (from crude, wild dance music to crafted romantic ballads and spruce idols) marked not a defused rebellion but a shift of sexual discourse as the music moved from the street to the bedroom. In neither place did it challenge the conventions of peer-group sex.

The youth culture that developed in the 1960s was, in sexual terms, more rebellious: the family was part of the system under attack. Domestic ideology was subverted, sexuality separated from marriage, romantic love intercut with fleeting hedonism. In Tom Hayden's words, there was "a generation of young whites with a new, less repressed attitude toward sex and pleasure, and music has been the means of their liberation."

Rock was experienced as a new sort of sexual articulation by women as well as men. The music was, in Sheila Rowbotham's words, "like a great release after all those super-consolation ballads." Rock, writes Karen Durbin, "provided me and a lot of women with a channel for saying 'want,' and for asserting our sexuality without apologies and without having to pretty up every passion with the traditionally 'feminine' desire for true love and marriage, and that was a useful step towards liberation." At a time when girls were still being encouraged from all directions to interpret their sexuality in terms of romance, to give priority to notions of love and commitment, rock performers like the Rolling Stones were exhilarating because of their anti-romanticism, their concern for "the dark side of passion," their interest in sex as power and feeling. But the problem quickly became a different one: not whether rock stars were sexist, but whether women could enter their discourse, appropriate their music, without having to become "one of the boys."

# ROCK AND SEXUAL LIBERATION

Male sexuality is no more "naturally" aggressive, assertive, and urgent than female sexuality is "naturally" passive, meek, and sensitive. But the issue is not the nature of sex but its representations, and they work not by describing feelings, but by constructing them. The sexual content of rock can't be read off its texts unambiguously—lyrics are the sign of a voice, instrumental sounds don't have fixed connotations. The sexuality of music is usually referred to in terms of its rhythm—it is the beat that commands a directly physical response—but rock sexuality has other components too. The rock experience is a social experience, involves relationships among the listeners, refers to people's appreciation of other genres, other sound associations; and in sexual terms our musical response is, perhaps above all, to the grain of a voice, the "touch" someone has on an instrument, the sense of personality at play. The "pleasure of the text" is the pleasure of music production itself, and one reason for the dissolution of rock's liberating promises to the male routines of the 1970s was simply the inevitable translation of an open text into a closed formula: cock-rock, by definition, rules out the possibilities of surprise and delight. But the question remains: Why this formula? Nineteen-sixties rock was expressly opposed to the love and marriage ideology of traditional teenage culture; how then did it come to articulate an even more rigid sexual double standard?

The concept of youth developed in the 1960s by rock (among other media) involved the assumption that good sex meant spontaneity, free expression, an "honesty" that could only be judged in terms of immediate feelings. Sex was thus best experienced *outside* the restrictive sphere of marriage, with its distracting deceits of love and long-term commitment. This was, in principle, an ideology of sexual equality—men and women alike were entitled to set their own limits on their sexual experiences.

Such permissiveness reflected a number of shifts in the material situation of middle-class youth: an increasing number of them were at college for an increasing length of time (by the end of the 1960s more than a quarter of *all* twenty—one- to twenty—four-year-olds in the USA were in school), and they were enjoying new levels of affluence (a reflection of rising parental income), mobility, and independence. It was, therefore, increasingly possible to enjoy sex without any reference to marriage; and the pill, in particular, enabled women to manage their sex lives without reference to family, community, or peer group. Sex became just another form of leisure, and the ideology of leisure itself began to change. Free time was used increasingly impulsively, irrationally, unproductively, with reference to immediate gratification rather than to usefulness or respectability or sense of consequence. The expansion of sexual opportunity, in other words, occurred in the context of a new leisure stress on hedonism, and the result was that sex became an experience to be consumed, used up in the moment, like any other leisure good. Sex was now defined without reference to domestic ideology or romantic love, but it was still gender-bound: men were, by and large, the sexual consumers; women were, by and large, the sexual commodities, their charms laid out for customer approval in a never-ending supply of magazines and films and "spreads."

Rock sexuality developed in this permissive context, but defined itself (initially, at least) against such "plastic" consumer sex. Rock sex was bohemian sex—earthy, real, "free." The woman's place, though, remained subordinate.

Bohemian freedom, particularly in its young rebel version, is defined primarily against the family. It is from their families that the young must escape, it is through their family quarrels that they first recognize themselves as rebels, and it is their refusal to settle down to a respectable domestic life that makes their rebellion permanent. Youthful bohemia begins, then, as a revolt against women, who are identified with the home as mothers, sisters, potential domesticators. The young rebel has to be a loner, to move on, and female sexuality becomes, in itself, something repressive, confining, enveloping. In the Hollywood version of the young rebel's story (a story repeated in numerous films over the last thirty years, although James Dean remains the model for rock 'n' roll's rebellious style), the message is plain enough: the boy must get out, the girl tries to hold him back. The original middle-class youth rebels in America, the bohemians drawn to big-city life and leisure at the turn of the century, were fascinated precisely by those proletarian institutions—gambling, drinking, sports like pool—which were, in Ned Polsky's words, aspects of a "bachelor sub-culture": they were institutions for men without women, and the only intimate relationships bohemians can have are with each other, as friends.

Even rebels need sexual and domestic female services, though (one 1960s result was the symbolic hippie woman, the fleet-footed earth mother), and, traditionally, the ideal bohemian woman is the "innocent" prostitute—anti-domestic and a symbol of sex as transitory pleasure. The prostitute can be treated (as rock stars treat groupies) with a mixture of condescension and contempt, as someone without an autonomous sexuality. Sex as self-expression remains the prerogative of the man; the woman is the object of *his* needs and fantasies, admired, in a way, for her lack of romantic hyprocrisy but despised for her anonymity.

Sexual relationships involve a number of necessary oppositions. These oppositions don't have to be divided between sexual partners, aren't gender defined, but mean constant negotiation, exploration, struggle, and experiment. These negotiations are the source of sexual pleasure as well as pain, and the issues at stake—independence/dependence, risk/security, activity/passivity, movement/stability, incident/routine, creation/consumption—inform the best rock music, which deals with the sexual *frisson* of relationships, the fact that all interesting affairs are alive. But, in general (and whatever the concerns of individual musicians like Neil Young or Van Morrison or Joni Mitchell), rock performers lay claim to sexual values—movement, independence, creativity, action, risk—in such a way that female sexuality is defined (just as in working-class street culture) by the opposite values—stability, dependence, inaction, security. Women are excluded from this "rebellion" by definition; rock's anti-domestic ideology doesn't move women out of the home, but leaves them in it, as inadequates.

The issue here is sexual ideology, not sexual practice. The actual behavior of men and women is far more complicated than the ideology implies (I discussed the material constraints on working-class girls in Chapter 9). But there is one more practical point to be made. Nineteen-sixties youth culture opposed impulse to calculation, irrationality to rationality, the present to the future; but these values posed quite different problems for boys than for girls. Girls have to keep control. They can't get drunk or drugged with the same abandon as boys because to lose control *is* to face consequences—pregnancy most obviously ("I got drunk at a party . . ."), a bad reputation more generally ("She'll do *anything* . . ."). As long as female attraction is defined by the male gaze, girls are under constant pressure too to keep control of their appearance; they can't afford to let their performance go. A drunken, "raddled" woman remains a potent image of ugliness; a haggard Keith Richards retains a far more *glamorous* appeal than a haggard Janis Joplin or Grace Slick. The irrational elements of the counterculture—in other words, the sex and drugs and rock 'n' roll—could not be appropriated by girls as they were by boys without affecting their self-definitions, their relationships, their lives.

By the 1970s women were giving their own answers to the countercultural questions about sex and domesticity and love—the terms of male domination were challenged. One effect of the feminist rewriting of the sexual rule book has been a male movement to more irrational forms of sexual power—rape, violent fantasy, a neurotic inability to sustain any sexual relationship. As one male property right (as husband) is denied, another (as purchaser) is asserted; sex, and therefore women, have been commoditized. "I think," writes Lester Bangs about Debbie Harry at the end of the decade, "that if most guys in America could somehow get their fave-rave poster girl in bed and have total license to do whatever they wanted with this legendary body for one afternoon, at least 75 percent of the guys in the country would elect to beat her up." It is in this context that we have to analyze the musical forms of 1970s sexuality—punk and disco.

## PUNK SEX AND DISCO PLEASURE

Punks rejected both romantic and permissive conventions, and refused, in particular, to allow sexuality to be constructed as a commodity. They flaunted sex-shop goods in public, exposing the mass production of porno fantasy, dissolving its dehumanizing effects through shock—"Oh bondage! Up yours!" (not that this stopped the media from running numerous pictures of "punkettes" in corsets and fishnet tights). Punks denied that their sexuality had any significance at all—"My love lies limp," boasted Mark Perry of Alternative TV; "What is sex anyway?" asked Johnny Rotten. "Just thirty seconds of squelching noises."

Punk was the first form of youth music not to rest on love songs (romance remained the staple of rock lyrics throughout the countercultural 1960s), and one consequence of this was that new female voices were heard on record, stage, and radio—shrill, assertive, impure, individual voices, singer as subject not object. Punk's female musicians had a strident insistence that was far removed from the appeal of most postwar glamour girls (the only sexual surprise of a self-conscious siren like Debbie Harry, for example, was that she became a teeny-bop idol for a generation of young girls).

Punk interrupted the long-standing rock equation of sex and pleasure, though the implications of this interruption still remain unclear. British punk subculture itself hardly differed, in sexual terms, from any other working-class street movement—the boys led, the girls (fewer of them) hung on; and in the end it was probably punk's sexual effect on performers rather than on audiences that mattered—women were brought into a musical community from which they'd previously been excluded, and they brought with them new questions about sound and convention and image, about the sexuality of performance and the performance of sexuality. Whether these questions get answered we have yet to see, but at least punks opened the possibility that rock could be *against* sexism.

Disco, which between 1974 and 1978 became the dominant sound of mass music across the world, had different origins and different effects. The success of *Saturday Night Fever* simply confirmed the resonance of a genre that was already an $8-billion-per-year industry in the USA, already accounted for half the albums and singles in *Billboard*'s hot hundreds. Disco had changed the sound of radio, the organization of record companies, the status of club deejays, the meaning of a good night out, and all this has to be understood in the context of the 1970s' sexual mores. Disco was not a response (like punk) to rock itself, but challenged it indirectly, by the questions it asked about music and *dance*.

The dance floor is the most public setting for music as sexual expression and has been an important arena for youth culture since the dance crazes of the beginning of the century when Afro-American rhythms began to structure white middle-class leisure, to set new norms for physical display, contact, and movement. Dance has been, ever since, central to the meaning of popular music. Girls, in particular, have always flocked to dance halls, concerned not just about finding a husband, but also about pursuing their own pleasure. They may be attracting the lurking boys through their clothes, make-up, and appearance, but on the dance floor their energy and agility is their own affair. The most dedicated dancers in Britain, for example, the Northern soul fans, are completely self-absorbed, and even in *Saturday Night Fever* (in which dancing power was diluted by pop interests) John Travolta transcended Hollywood's clumsy choreography with the sheer quality of his commitment—from the opening shots of his strut through the streets, his gaze on himself never falters; the essence of dance floor sex is physical control, and, whatever happens, John Travolta is never going to let himself go.

Dancing as a way of life, an obsession, has a long American history. Shorty Snowden, the John Travolta of the Savoy Ballroom in the 1920s, suffered from "Sunday Night Fever":

> We started getting ready for Sunday on Saturday. The ideal was to get our one sharp suit to the tailor to be pressed on Saturday afternoon. Then we'd meet at the poolroom and brag about what we were going to do on the dance floor the next night. . . .[3]

The 1920s dance cult spread quickly to "hep" white teenagers who tried to dress, dance, move like these sharp black "dudes," and the Depression stimulated dancing among the non-hep too. Thousands of small, cheap bars with dance floors used pianos, record players, radios, and jukeboxes to fill the weekends with noise. Such working-class dance halls were crucial to the culture of courtship, but dancing meant something else even more important: it was an escape, a suspension of real time, a way in which even the unemployed could enjoy their bodies, their physical skills, the sense of human power their lives otherwise denied. Such power does not need to be rooted in sexual competition (though it often enough is); parties, Friday and Saturday night bursts of physical pleasure, sex or no sex, have always been the most intense setting for working-class musics, from ragtime to punk.

A party matters most, of course, to those people who most need to party, and, whatever else happened to mass music in the 1950s and 1960s, there were many people (black working-class Americans, British working-class teenagers, using much the same music) who never stopped dancing—1970s disco itself emerged musically from black clubs, depended commercially on its continuing white youth appeal. But, sexually, disco was most important as a gay aesthetic, and what was surprising, socially, was the appropriation of this aesthetic by the mass middle class.

Disco is dance music in the abstract, its content determined by its form. Middle-class dance music in the past, even in the 1930s, was a form determined by its content—there were still influential dance hall instructors, sheet music salesmen, and band leaders who laid down rules of partnership, decorum, uplift, and grace. There are no such rules in disco, but, on the other hand, individual expression means nothing when there is nothing individual to express. Disco is not, despite its critics, anything like Muzak. Muzak's effect is subliminal; its purpose is to encourage its hearers to do anything but listen to it. Disco's effect is material; its purpose is to encourage its hearers to do nothing but listen to it.

What do they hear? An erotic appeal, most obviously—what Richard Dyer calls "whole body eroticism." All dancing means a commitment to physical sensation, but disco expanded the possibilities of sensation. Disco pleasure is not closed off, bound by the song structures, musical beginnings and ends, but is expressed, rather, through an open-ended series of repetitions, a shifting *intensity* of involvement. And disco, as Dyer suggests, shares rock's rhythmic pulse, while avoiding rock's phallo-centrism: disco is committed to the 4:4 beat in all its implications. Disco dancing is sinous, it avoids the jerk and grind and thrust of rock; disco dancers hustle and slide, they use all their bodies' erotic possibilities.

Dancing has always been a physical pleasure sufficiently intense to block out, for the moment, all other concerns, but disco pushed such enjoyment to new extremes: the disco experience is an overwhelming experience of *now-ness*, an experience intensified still further by drugs like amyl nitrite, an experience in which the dancer is, simultaneously, completely self-centered and quite selfless, completely sexualized and, in gender terms, quite sexless. On the disco floor there is no overt competition for partners, no isolation; and disco (unlike bohemia) signifies nothing, makes no expressive claims—if bohemia suggests a different way of life, disco simply offers a different experience of it.

The disco version of eroticism and ecstasy is not, in itself, homosexual, but the aesthetic uses of these experiences did reflect gay consciousness. They were imbued, for example, with gay romanticism: disco sensations were associated with the fleeting emotional contacts, the passing relationships of a culture in which everything in a love affair can happen in a night. Disco eroticism became, too, the sign of a sexuality that was always being constructed. It was the process of construction, the very artificiality of the disco experience, that made it erotic. Disco was a version of camp: the best disco records were those made with a sense of irony, an aggressive self-consciousness, a concern for appearances. There was an obvious link between the vocal styles of disco and 1930s torch songs: Billie Holiday and Donna Summer alike stylized feelings, distanced pain, opened up the texts of sexuality (and for this reason, disco, despised by punk-rockers on principle, had an immense appeal to the post-punk avant-garde).

Mainstream disco, the Saturday night fever of the teenage working class, continued to operate according to the traditional street party line; teenagers danced in different ways, to different sounds than gays. But it was the gay disco aesthetic that middle-class dancers began to appropriate from 1974 on. If 1960s "permissive" sexual ideology had reflected new leisure and sexual opportunities, then 1970s disco culture reflected their emotional consequences. Disco was music for singles bars, sexual mobility, heterosexual cruising, weekend flings, and transitory fantasies. Gay culture reflected, in its own way, the problems and possibilities of sex without domesticity, love without the conventional distinctions of male and female. These problems and possibilities had become important now for heterosexuals too.

Disco was about eroticism and ecstasy as material goods, produced not by spiritual or emotional work, God or love, but by technology, chemistry, wealth. The disco experience (the music and the mood, the poppers and the lights) revealed the artificiality and transience of sexual feelings—they were produced to be consumed; and disco pleasure, as it moved into the commercial mainstream, became the pleasure of consumption itself. This was obvious enough in the chic appeal of Studio 54, but was just as important for the strut of the factory girls, equally chic, up the steps of Tiffany's in provincial Britain. Disco made no claims to folk status; there was no creative disco community. The music was, rather, the new international symbol of American consumer society. Chic discos sprang up around the world, each offering the secret of eternal American youth; the pleasures of consumption and the pleasures of sex became, in such settings, the same thing.

The problem with escapism is not the escape itself, but what's still there when it's over—the rain still falls when Monday morning dawns. Once something's been consumed it's gone; new goods are necessary, new experiences, new highs, new sex. As many observers commented, by the end of the 1970s disco had become a drug, but it was leisure itself that had a new desperation. In Andrew Holleran's disco novel, *Dancer from the Dance*, the most dedicated disco-goers are the most eager to escape:

> They seldom looked happy. They passed one another without a word in the elevator, like silent shades in hell, hell-bent on their next look from a handsome stranger. Their next rush from a popper. The next song that turned their bones to jelly and left them all on the dance floor with heads back, eyes nearly closed, in the ecstasy of saints receiving the stigmata. They pursued these things with such devotion that they acquired, after a few seasons, a haggard look, a look of deadly seriousness. Some wiped everything they could off their faces and reduced themselves to blanks. Yet even these, when you entered the hallway where they stood waiting to go in, would turn toward you all at once in that one unpremeditated moment (as when we see ourselves in a mirror we didn't know was there), the same look on their faces: Take me away from this.[4]

# CHAPTER 11

# ROCK AND LEISURE

## LEISURE AND WORK

It is not only in discos that pleasure is defined as the pursuit of youthful energy and grace and carelessness. As I've already suggested, since at least the 1920s, youthful styles and situations have been held up as general models for adult play. Leisure goods—clothes and make-up and sport and music and sex itself—are marketed as if they were, in themselves, antidotes to aging. Youth cultures, similarly, have been explained as leisure cultures, and the meaning of leisure itself has been taken for granted—leisure is "free time" and young people have more of it than anyone else.

Such a designation is too simple: leisure is a particular, complex organization of free time, related to the organization of work itself. Historians of leisure, investigating its emergence in the nineteenth century as an aspect of industrial capitalism, have made two points in particular.

First, industrial production was organized around the developing principles of rational work discipline: workers were subject to the social organization of the factory, to the technical requirements of machinery, and work became a matter of routine and repetition, inflexible in its use of time and space. Such work discipline could only be developed in conjunction with an equally rational leisure discipline: the traditional patterns of release and riot had to be subordinated to the timed needs of the industrial labor process. By the end of the century leisure was no longer an occasional event (a fair or carnival or harvest festival), but the routine, daily experience of "non-work."

Second, industrialization meant the increasingly sharp separation of home and work, production and consumption. Leisure became the time when commodities were purchased and consumed. By the end of the century there was a well-established market for consumer durables. Their production was central to capitalist prosperity; their consumption was made possible by new, binding arrangements of credit-and-hire purchase. Leisure meant certain commitments.

The ideology of this new society was that people worked in order to enjoy their leisure as they wished—the money they made was spent on the goods they wanted. Thus, at the beginning of the nineteenth century, the Malthusians worried that if the working classes ever became affluent enough to enjoy "idleness" they would never work again. But, in practice, work and the experience of work remained the only justifications for such idleness. In the 1930s (and today), for example, mass unemployment did not mean mass leisure, but, rather, it made more urgent the need for a job—free time without it meant shame and boredom. And postwar affluence rested not on idleness but overtime, as people worked harder and harder to buy the leisure goods they didn't have time to enjoy.

The "freedom" involved in standard accounts of leisure is, in short, deceptive. Leisure is necessary for capital, too; it is the time when labor is replenished physically and culturally, re-creation time; and it is the time when people consume, when surplus value is realized. "Free" time is structured not only by ideas but also by material forces, by the availability of goods and resources, by the effects of the labor process on people's capacities and desires. The size of their pay packet determines what resources people have; work prospects and career possibilities limit the leisure risks they are prepared to take; work discipline and the organization of workers mentally and physically on the job limit their leisure capacities. Leisure involves a tension between choice and constraint; this tension is an aspect of the general relationship between production and consumption. Leisure is, on one hand, a source of fun and freedom and pleasure, a necessary counter to alienating labor; but it must be, on the other hand, constrained and controlled and made trivial so as not to interfere with the labor process. The most obvious expression of the work/leisure relationship is the weekend: Friday and Saturday nights are party times just because there's no work to go to the next morning. Leisure, from this perspective, is not really free time at all, but an organization of non-work that is determined by the relations of capitalist production.

Young people, as we have seen, are assumed to have more leisure than anyone else, to be freer in their free time. They are not constrained, as are their parents, by economic obligations; they don't have to keep a home and family; they are more irresponsible in work and out of it. Even in physical terms they can play harder than adults. In capitalism, youth is the symbol of leisure, and, not surprisingly therefore, for anti-capitalist writers and for the mass culture critics, the young have always been seen, too, as the prime *victims* of leisure. In 1894, the socialist journalist Robert Blatchford wrote in his paper, *The Labour Prophet:*

> The young people went to dance; and I went to look at them, and I was afflicted with melancholy. And about eleven o'clock the party was over and I went home; and, as I went, I communed with myself darkly, and I said, "These poor creatures don't even know how to play."
>
> The girls at this party were nearly all Lancashire factory girls; the young men were mostly factory and colliery workers. I had seen them at work in their greasy, malodorous, sickly mills and gloomy mines, and had not felt half so forcibly as I now felt, how hard, and dull, and starved, and unlovely their lives were.
>
> There was hardly a pretty girl in the room; the best favoured were those who might have been, or ought to have been, pretty. There was not *one* girl in the room who could stand or walk with grace or freedom. They were all more or less round-shouldered. They had sickly, murky complexions and

harsh loud voices. They were dressed awkwardly and with bad taste, and they looked anxious, dull and *tired.* There was some hilarity of a rather noisy kind, but there was an utter absence of "happiness": no gaiety, no sparkle, no lightness.

The fact is these people had never been taught to be happy.

Yes; but besides that, they had never known what it is to be free.

Forty years later, in 1934, J. B. Priestley, in *English Journey,* was regretting what had happened to Nottingham's Goose Fair:

The real patrons of fairs of this kind are youngsters in their teens; and there were thousands of them pushing and cat-calling and screaming in the crowd: the boys, their faces grinning and vacant in the whirl of coloured light, sometimes looking like members of some sub-human race surging up from the interior of the earth; the girls, whose thickly powdered faces were little white masks without lines but daubed with red and black, looked like dolls out of some infernal toyshop; and the appearance of them all was fascinating and frightening. And this was Goose Fair, and Merrie England.

And thirty years later still, in 1964, Paul Johnson, in the *New Statesmen,* commented on the pop phenomenon:

Both TV channels now run weekly programmes in which popular records are played to teenagers and judged. While the music is performed, the cameras linger savagely over the faces of the audiences. What a bottomless chasm of vacuity they reveal! The huge faces, bloated with cheap confectionary and smeared with chain-store make-up, the open, sagging mouths and glazed eyes, the hands mindlessly drumming in time to the music, the broken stiletto heels, the shoddy, stereotyped, "with-it" clothes; here apparently is a collective portrait of a generation enslaved by a commercial machine. Leaving a TV studio recently, I stumbled into the exodus from one of these sessions. How pathetic and listless they seemed: young girls, hardly any more than 16, dressed as adults and already lined up as fodder for exploitation.

The assumption of all these authors is that work itself—routine, mindless, dull—destroys young people's ability to be free, to enjoy themselves in any meaningful way. Commercial leisure goods are designed, in turn, to confirm workers' cultural incapacities. The result is a concept of pleasure as debilitating: the young, in particular, are denied the chance to learn that their lives could be different. All-powerful capital, it seems, writes its version of leisure on an experience that is otherwise blank; youth is the grotesque product of commercial forces and has no cultural purpose of its own. As I suggested in chapter 3, the mass culture critics take the passivity of the mass culture audience for granted.

In fact, however, class relations in leisure are not straightforward. If nineteenth-century capitalists, at their crudest, sought to maximize surplus value by extending the working day and reducing their workers "needs" to sheer physical survival, the workers organized successfully to reduce the working day and to extend the notion of the necessities of proletarian life—the immediately obvious effect of the British Factory Acts was the free Saturday afternoon. In their campaigns the workers had support from "enlightened" capitalists, who, on one hand, believed that happy workers were more efficient and amenable than those selling their labor power only under "the dull compulsion of necessity," and, on the other hand, realized that laborers were also consumers—Marx contrasted the attitudes of capitalists to their own and to other employers' workers.

There is a tension in the capitalist organization of workers' leisure between the need to control free time (so that it does not disrupt work time) and its ideological importance as free time, the time when people experience themselves as free laborers. The control of leisure has to be indirect; leisure choices have to be limited, but they can't be determined. This isn't a simple matter of imposing bourgeois norms on passive consumers. Leisure commodities are not, in themselves, necessarily conducive to good order. Drink, for example, has been an issue of bourgeois dispute since Liberal manufacturers denounced Tory brewers; and a similar contradiction was still obvious in the commercial exploitation of punk-rock—private clubs put on the groups that town halls banned; Virgin snapped up the Sex Pistols after EMI and A&M dropped them. There are capitalists ready to market anything that is potentially profitable, whatever its effects on morality, law and order, or everyone else's profits. If pornography, drugs, weapons, or revolution will sell, then they will be sold.

In these circumstances—workers' ideological freedom as consumers, the different interests of commodity producers—the "control" of leisure is difficult. Regulation has always been more important than repression (except in brief experiments like Prohibition), and capitalist leisure has developed within a framework of licenses and licensing authorities. The modern police force, for example, was developed primarily not to fight crime but to patrol leisure, to apply the licensing laws. In nineteenth-century industrial cities the working class was isolated in its own areas and activities and it was the police who had to supervise the pubs and crowds and street corners, to enforce the regulations on drink and prostitution, gambling and performance. The emphasis was on surveillance rather than prevention; the policeman's duty was to prevent workers' leisure from becoming public disorder, public holidays from becoming political events. The policeman was, in Robert Storch's words, a "domestic missionary," bringing middle-class restraint and decency to working-class lives. He was, in his very presence, a symbol of the class *division* of nineteenth-century leisure: employers and their workers did not meet in their free time (in the ways that the landed gentry and their tenants and laborers had once met in rural feasts and sports, and that the aristocracy and lumpen proletariat still met on the race track and around the boxing ring). Policemen were thus an unwelcome street presence, whatever their effects on crime. For British music hall singers the police force was "trouble," individual policemen were the butts for endless comedy. In the USA the police became "The Man," intrusive, violent, corrupt, as they patrolled local streets and bars and dance halls, applied distant laws on drugs and liquor and sex.

The regulation of unsuitable leisure goes with the promotion of suitable leisure. Much of this process has been indirect, too—policies on housing, education, health, and the family all have their effects on leisure possibilities. But there have also been two kinds of leisure entrepreneur—moral entrepreneurs, promoting "rational recreation," and commercial entrepreneurs, churning out leisure goods with reference only to their financial proceeds.

In the nineteenth century the moral entrepreneurs saw leisure as a means to the end of self-improvement. Leisure was an educational institution; rational recreation was encouraged for its useful effects. Sir James Kay-Shuttleworth, for example, the great mid-century educator, was carried away by enthusiasm for musical instruction in schools. "Songs," he declared, "are an important means of forming an industrious, brave, loyal, and religious working class." They could, he thought, "inspire cheerful views of industry and associate amusements with duties."

Nineteenth-century leisure was defined along moral lines for the bourgeoisie as much as for the laborers (and the assumption that middle-class pleasures must also be functional lives on in the contemporary suburban culture of joggers, gardeners, and cooks). Underlying such activities is the Protestant work ethic: pleasure must be justified; leisure, too, should mean effort and self-discipline. This subordination of leisure to work has meant, at its simplest, the organization of middle-class social life around business needs—every activity chosen for its career effects; but there is an ideological distinction involved as well between improving experiences, embodied in certain forms of art and sport, and "wasteful" hedonism. By the end of the nineteenth century the distinction between rational and irrational leisure was institutionally enforced: rational leisure was promoted in schools, municipal parks, and libraries; irrational leisure was patrolled by the police. Some forms of leisure were more appropriate than others for "rationalization." In Britain there was a systematic attempt by teachers and clergymen and journalists to apply to working-class sports the moral principles embedded in public school games—discipline, effort, competition, team spirit, good manners. In the USA, to cite a different example, Negro brass bands and dance orchestras were sponsored by community clubs, put into uniforms, entered in inter-town music contests.

The problem for the moral entrepreneurs was that "rational" recreation was a contradictory concept: leisure is, by definition, a contrast to work, duty, and routine; it involves, by definition, a "sapping of moral fiber." But leisure is also, for the same reason, the setting for the non-routine experiences of love and art and ecstasy. The nineteenth-century problem had been how to combine the necessary discipline and relaxation, the necessary order and disorder; as the religious control of leisure waned, there emerged a new breed of commercial entrepreneurs, commodity salesmen, who were adept at bringing leisure "needs" into line with the leisure goods that were available.

By the 1920s, the shift from a religious to a secular account of middle-class leisure was apparent—this was an aspect of the idealization of youth. Campus culture, for example, was more concerned with hedonism than duty. The public/private distinction was redefined: leisure became the sphere of the private, play meant personal expression. What was at issue was consumption not improvement, indulgence not duty, taste not propriety.

For the commercial entrepreneurs too, however, there was a problem of order and routine; they also disapproved of "irrational" leisure, spontaneity, drunkenness, disruption, all of which was likely to affect profit as well as people. For commerce this was a problem of form rather than content. The logic of their production put a premium on the organization of leisure by notions of professionalism and predictability (which reduced commercial risk). From the beginning, British music-hall proprietors, for example, who weren't much interested in the morality of music, had their own concern for good order. In the words of *The Era*, the trade paper of licensed victuallers, in 1885:

> It is one of the greatest nuisances possible to sensible people who go to places of amusement to divert their minds from politics and business alike to have the opinions of the daily papers reproduced in verse and flung at their heads by a music hall singer. Persons who go to a place of amusement to be amused, and these, we believe, form the steadily paying class, are too sensible to care to proclaim their private opinions by applauding mindless rubbish with a political meaning.[1]

By the 1890s these music hall owners had long lists of conditions in their artist contracts: no offensive allusions to the government, no "coarse jests and rough language," comic songs were to be submitted for managerial approval at least two days in advance, no artist was to "address the audience except in the regular course of the performance." Giving steadily paying customers what they wanted had become defined as the commercial process of securing an *orderly* mass audience, and this definition was refined with the development of the mass media and their bureaucratic controls. The rise of the cinema, radio, and television meant not just the standardization of popular entertainment, but also the regulation of its spontaneous, disruptive, anarchical elements. "Professional entertainment" has rarely been improving according to the standards of nineteenth- or twentieth-century moral entrepreneurs, but it has always been, in its own way, safe; it has applied its own rules to the translation of working-class pleasures into middlebrow formulas.

So far I have been describing the various ways in which leisure has been organized and controlled—by directly and indirectly applied regulations, through the promotion of particular goods and activities; but this is still a one-sided account. The entrepreneurs and missionaries described so far have certainly intervened in working-class leisure, but they have not completely determined its shape. We need to look, too, at workers' own uses of leisure, their responses to these provisions.

In the working-class radical tradition, leisure has been, equally, a time for improvement, political education, disciplined consciousness. Socialists have been as much concerned to encourage the "rational" use of free time as bourgeois moralists (they were allied in the temperance movement, for example); and the socialist critique of escapism, commercial play and "light" entertainment, remains potent—it surfaced, for example, in the punk denunciation of disco as "mindless" hedonism.

There is often thought to be, in this context, a clear distinction between the "rough" and "respectable" working class, a distinction that refers specifically to uses of leisure. Rough leisure—drink and drugs, violence and general rowdiness, i.e., "the street"—has been the object not only of middle-class regulation but also of middle-class romanticization. In British subcultural theory, for example, the roughest youth groups are taken to be the most class-conscious, the least tainted by respectable values. But this distinction is misleading. What's at issue is not a once-and-for-all choice, rough *or* respectable, but different combinations of the rough *and* the respectable. For most young workers, honky-tonks and bars and dance halls and Saturday night fights are just part of a leisure pattern which also includes hobbies and sports and family activities. The most rowdy leisure places are, indeed, those associated with *abnormal* work situations—ports and army towns and sawmill camps and oil bases—places where people are traveling and working away from their usual leisure routes. The slumming middle-class ideal of rough leisure evades its reality: free time anarchy is only relaxing for people who don't have to worry about work the next day. Even rough working-class leisure revolves around the weekend, and if the immediate demand is escape—from boredom and a sense of failure—the real need is for a sense of control—control of one's feelings, one's physical abilities, one's life. Rough leisure—this is the socialist point—is often, in fact, the least controlled, the most desperate aspect of its participants' lives.

There is a tension too between leisure as an individual activity (the realm of choice) and leisure as a collective activity (the realm of solidarity). State leisure policies have always reflected a fear of public disorder, a concern for the dangers of dancing in the streets, class conspiracy, youthful anarchy; but the mass market depends on forms of collectivity, and leisure is associated commercially with the values of conviviality and comradeship. The resulting public/private tension has been mediated most obviously through the family: the home, as the refuge from work, has become the essential setting for mass leisure consumption. Marx suggested that in capitalist social relations the worker "feels himself at home only during his leisure." But the relationship works the other way around too—by the end of the nineteenth century workers were collecting household goods, going on family holidays, and enjoying "family entertainment." The equation of leisure and the home put women (and girls, as I have already argued) at a double disadvantage: it was their labor that made the home comfortable, but they were excluded from the usual work/leisure distinction. Women's pleasures, even more than men's, were confined to the household, but this was, in fact, their place of work.

From women's point of view, the most significant integration of the home and leisure occurred in the 1920s and 1930s as the mass production of the motor car completed the process in which leisure became a routine aspect of family life (the Lynds describe the simultaneous development in Middletown of "backyard culture" and the family barbecue). It is against such a home life that rough leisure is now defined and that youth leisure has become significant: in the last thirty years it has been the young who have preserved and developed leisure activities that are not home- or family-based. In English provincial towns, for example, the young are now the only people to use public leisure spaces at night—they dominate city center streets and pubs, cinemas, discos, and clubs. Youth culture is more clearly concerned than any other mass culture with the leisure problems of the public and the private, the individual and the community, the home and the street, dependence and independence; the young experience most immediately the regulation of play. Precisely because young people are free of the detailed restrictions of childhood (family and school) and not yet bound by adult problems (family and work), they are subject to more direct pressures on their leisure choices than anyone else—pressures from the state, from social workers, from schools, the police, and the commercial organization of teenage ideology.

Young people also have differing degrees of freedom according to their place in the labor market. The most free are unskilled young workers (the lower fifth-form culture of my survey) who are, consequently, the most trouble for youth agencies. Their casual relationship to work, their absenteeism and horseplay, go with a casual self-indulgence in leisure. In some respects such young workers are useful to employers because of their very casualness. They lack the obligations and steadiness of married men, but they also lack the commitments and conservatism and immobility. If most industrial jobs are only open to married men, over twenty-two, preferably with children and mortgages, there are some tasks which depend on casual, "free," labor—the Army is the most obvious example. Young men are, indeed, expected to wait a few years before settling down—young marriage is not encouraged. The problem then is to ensure that young men are ready and able to become respectable providers when their time does come; the young are thus kept constantly aware that their youth is temporary. Youth cultures are, by definition, impermanent. Their members "sow their wild oats" and then, inevitably, grow up, go "normal."

The lives of the young skilled, the apprentices and white-collar workers, have much the same impermanence as those of the young unskilled, even if their hedonism is indulged with less abandon. Apprentices go out less, take fewer leisure risks; they are committed to a career and can't afford an employer's doubts. They understand the limits on their freedom and know that most employers don't care what they do in their free time as long as it doesn't affect their discipline and regularity on the job. Teenage freedom is licensed equally within the obligations of family life (I have already discussed the consequences of this for girls' leisure). Most young workers live at home until they marry; they indulge themselves on the assumption of a sufficient family wage now, a solid family income in the future; and, ironically, the young unemployed are much less free than their working peers because their future is so uncertain. They are idle without choice, unable to prepare for anything, in no position to indulge themselves. They are hemmed in not just by the continuously humiliating experience of job-hunting, but also by the insecurity of having no productive purpose at all. Dole-queue rock and punk aggression express the feelings of these abandoned kids less as the articulation of group identity than as a bleat of existence.

For most teenagers, however, skilled, unskilled, and even unemployed (the expectation of a job any day now dies hard), leisure means, as it did for Craig and his friends in Keighley, having a good time—physically, irresponsibly, spontaneously. It means drinking and laughing and doing nothing and sex and trying anything once before you have to do something forever. For these young people music is the noisy and buoyant context for all their other activities. The precise difference between favorite genres—punk or heavy metal or disco—is less significant than their common purpose. Most kids move from one taste to another as they grow up and change friends, and, anyway, they spend most of their time without commitment to any particular sound at all. Teenagers know, as they always have, that they're being exploited: the thrill is that all this commercial effort is being made just for them!

In many ways students use rock just like young workers, as an aid to relaxation. But if they are engaged in much the same sort of hedonism and fun, if they are just as heavy drinkers and smokers, as sweaty dancers, students are also distinct from young workers in that the line between their work and their leisure is blurred. Malcolm Cowley even suggests that the campus culture that began to develop in the 1920s was a culture largely dominated by leisure habits—"college students inhabit an easy world of their own, except for very rich people and certain types of childless wives they have been the only American class that could take leisure for granted."

Students certainly have few direct constraints on their time. They don't have much money and they have to study, but the resulting organization of their days varies from individual to individual and is often difficult to classify: students spend much of their time desultorily reading and writing and thinking as friends drop in and the record player goes full blast—are these times of work or times of leisure?

This peculiar organization of time has a number of consequences for the use of music. Although most students have a much more intensive collective life than most young workers—living together on campus rather than scattered between parental homes—

they are also involved in a much more clearly transitory experience. Student life is bound by the years of the degree course; after it is over students are unlikely to live in the same place or even to have the same friends. Preserving their independence and identity is important not just for the immediate needs of study but also for the long-term expectations of a different life; and music can be the key symbol of an individual's tastes and style. It is not the only or even the most common basis for such identity—student groups and cults and friendships are based on a great variety of interests and activities—but when music does become important for student friendships it becomes important as the focus of attention: rock takes on an ideological purpose for students that is rarely needed in ordinary working-class youth culture.

Students' leisure is further confused by the realization that higher education is not just the grind of degree work but involves a much wider process of "civilization." Higher education gives access to culture as well as to knowledge, and "free time" activities are, in fact, part of the wider learning experience. Leisure means art as well as entertainment and insofar as students learn the conventions of traditional high culture, rock may be dragged into the argument to be given intellectual and aesthetic justification and not just casually enjoyed. Students' tastes and their ability to argue their tastes are significant; music is used as a source of value.

I've been stressing the class differences within youth uses of music and leisure because they reveal that if working-class street culture is a romantic idea for "rebel" suburban kids—a fantasy of spontaneous style and pleasure and excitement—so is student culture a romantic idea for "rebel" street kids—a fantasy of self-exploration, sexual freedom, art, and angst. These are fantasies about leisure, about different ways of life, different *possibilities*, and rock is a powerful mass medium because it puts the different fantasies together.

The point the mass culture critics miss is that rock isn't just a commodity—it is a leisure commodity. Leisure is the context of its use value, and to understand how leisure goods signify we have to refer them to meanings which have their own processes of construction and dispute: the cultural meaning of rock comes from a relationship between form and use.

Rock 'n' roll started as a working-class music not just in terms of content but also in terms of purpose—it was rooted in the music of traveling black and white dance bands, in a style of pleasure that was defined not by the criteria of professional entertainment but by the direct urgencies of the proletarian weekend. The original rock 'n' roll experience depended on a mutually nourishing relationship between the audience and the musicians, but not on shared lives. Rock 'n' roll singers weren't folk, and neither were they just *symbols* of achievement, punk signs of what anyone could do. They were, more importantly, *displaying* their mastery over their lives; they were workers whose efforts were subsumed in excitement and grace, who achieved, in Roland Barthes's terms, "the sublimation of labor by its magical effacement." And they were workers whose efforts could be judged—their dancing audiences weren't mindless. Rock 'n' roll mastery meant the mastery of movement, speed, abundance, space.

When rock became a recorded form it retained these leisure meanings but in different settings—as party music, driving music, music of the road and the street and physical sensation. The paradox of rock 'n' roll leisure, the effect of its success in intensifying feeling, was that it offered a sense of freedom that was, simultaneously, a sense of rootlessness and estrangement. This was the traditional theme of American popular music, black and white, folk and commercial, from "ain't it hard to stumble, when you got no place to fall" to "freedom's just another word for nothing left to lose," but it was focused in rock 'n' roll by the image of the youth rebel, the loner who can't settle down because he's got no place to go.

This paradox—leisure as an experience of freedom so intense that it became, simultaneously, an experience of loneliness—is rooted in the working-class experience of work, in alienation. Leisure has become the only setting for the experience of self, for the exploration of one's own skills and capacities, for the development of creative relations with other people. But this experience is, by its very nature, fleeting; and rock 'n' roll began as American working-class music—the music of a class that has rarely been symbolized as a class. American class experience is mediated through historical images of individual achievement and failure; workers remember their past in terms of mobility rather than solidarity, self-sufficiency rather than socialism. Rock 'n' roll accounts of loneliness and rebellion *celebrate* the conditions that produce them; rock's dominant value has always been tolerance.

The rock 'n' roll experience was an experience of community—

teenage community, dance hall friendships—but these were not really central to it. The music created its community by keeping other people out, and the resulting society was transient—people grew up, tastes changed, real friends and relations were elsewhere, at home and work. Rock 'n' roll made cultural sense not as an experience in itself, but in the context of specific relations of work and power. When rock 'n' roll became rock in the 1960s it was removed from these contexts and its original significance was changed. Consciousness of class became the myth of "rock brotherhood"; the rock 'n' roll experience became something that could be consumed by middle-class youth, by students; culture became commodity.

This is the process, often enough described, by which a folk culture becomes mass culture. My point is that what happened was less a change in the way music was made than in the ways it was used and interpreted; the move was not from "folk" to "mass" (both mystifying terms), but reflected shifts within class cultures (popular music, even when it is commercially made, involves a struggle for meaning—this is obvious in the history of punk, for example, or in the development of reggae). The usual way of analyzing the ideological effects of the mass media is in terms of the transformation of collective organizations of working-class culture into the fragmented sensations of passive consumption. But the development of rock as a mass medium involved a different process: fantasies of community (drawn from images of the street and lower-class city life) were sold to the suburbs, fantasies of creativity to the street.

Capitalist culture, consumer culture, depends on the never-satisfied sense of anticipation—in John Berger's words, "what-is-to-be empties what is." But this culture has a positive effect too: the dream that *everything* can be altered never dies, and this is, essentially, a proletarian dream, runs counter to the very solidity of bourgeois rule. "America," Harold Rosenberg writes, "is the civilization of people engaged in transforming themselves. In the past the stars of the performance were the pioneer and the immigrant. Today it is youth and the Black."

There are ironies in this. Blacks, the least free people in America, are taken to have the most free time—their leisure is the most "irresponsible," the most "fun," the most "cool." But black music is listened to as a way of life rather than a way of leisure; black musicians are heard to squeeze their pleasures out of even deader ends of work than those in which white youths are caught. Black music became the basis of rock 'n' roll because it expressed most intensely a commitment to change, because it depended most intensely on "free time" as the source of the sense of human worth and power denied to blacks (as, in different ways, to white working-class youth) in their "unfree time." Black music had a radical, rebellious edge: it carried a sense of possibility denied in the labor market; it suggested a comradeship, a sensuality, a grace and joy and energy lacking in work. The problem was not that the music that came out of oppression was "fun," but that "fun" itself was not a simple matter.

## LEISURE AND IDEOLOGY

If the essence of rock is fun, it is a concept strangely neglected by sociologists. Analysts of high art are obliged to respect the autonomy of aesthetic judgments, but sociologists of popular art, as we have seen, don't confront fun, but describe the "irrationality" of mass taste with aloof disgust, as if irrationality were irrelevant for popular culture instead of a vital part of it. Marxists, in particular, have interpreted the fact that people *enjoy* mass culture as a reason for gloom—Adorno, for example, valued high art for its imagination, its utopianism, but dismissed the fantasies of mass culture as psychological disorders. But the power of rock fantasy rests, precisely, on a utopianism. In *Grundrisse*, Marx comments that the capitalist, needing consumers for his products,

> searches for means to spur workers on to consumption, to give his wares new charms, to inspire them with new needs by constant chatter, etc. It is precisely this side of the relation of capital and labor which is an essential civilising moment, and on which the power of capital rests.[2]

Cultural commodities may support the contemporary power of capital, but they have their civilizing moments, and even as the most effortless background music, rock is a source of vigor and exhilaration and of good feelings that are as necessary for the next morning's political struggle as for the next day's work. My argument is that rock fun is as much a quality of the music's use as of its form. The usual theory is that the star is an extraordinary fellow who brings excitement and glamour into the lives of his fans, ordinary people, but the process works the other way around too: stars, dull professionals, are made glamorous by the imagination and wit and excitement of their fans. Rock's capitalist producers have to control use as well as form—the issue is the *ideology* of leisure. One of the reasons why rock has been the most vital form of popular culture in the last twenty years is that it has expressed so clearly the struggle involved: rock has been used simultaneously as a form of self-indulgence and individual escape *and* as a source of solidarity and active dissatisfaction.

The pleasure of rock (to refer back to chapter 3), then, is not just a textual matter, a matter of particular organizations of words and music. It reflects the wider definitions of leisure embodied in concepts like "entertainment," "relaxation," and "fun," concepts that themselves emerged from cultural struggle (and rest on a complex structure of sexual differentiation). Even the simplest of rock categories—dance music, party music—are packed with social significance: dances and parties are historically and socially specific institutions; their cultural conventions—as breaks from work, settings for sex and solidarity—are not only articulated by different types of music (disco, the Rolling Stones), but simultaneously determine those musics' effects. Rock musical texts, however sensual, however "objective," are leisure commodities, and rock musicians, whatever their sense of semiology, still have to work out what it means to be popular and to be consumed. Theories of rock have to be developed through practice, which involves relationships between musicians and audiences in particular cultural institutions. The ideology of rock is determined not just by its texts but also by its contexts. If rock is an aspect of leisure, then the "shock effect" of the best rock texts occurs in the context of a "leisure effect": "shock" is always entertaining (which is why the mass cultural critics are so dismissive of rock "politics").

The use value of entertainment derives from its intimations of fun, irresponsibility, and fulfillment—leisure is an implicit critique of work. The ideology of leisure has to strike a balance between freedom and order: the experience of freedom must be real (otherwise leisure goods would have no use) but not disruptive of work routines; leisure must give pleasure but not too much. Pleasure, in turn, is not just a psychological effect but refers to a set of experiences rooted in the social relations of production—it is defined against different situations of displeasure/pain/reality. And it is in this context that the importance of the bohemian tradition in rock (as in cultural history generally) needs to be emphasized: bohemians articulate a leisure critique of the work ethic. They are cultural radicals not just as the source of the formalist avant-garde, but also in institutional terms—they don't work (and thus outraged bourgeois moralists have always denounced successful bohemians who, it seems, make their money out of play).

This is the reason I have been stressing the importance of punk for an understanding of rock 'n' roll. British punk-rock (which, in Dick Hebdige's words, "signified chaos at every level") was both a street movement and a radical art form. Malcolm McLaren and Bernard Rhodes, who, as the original managers of the Sex Pistols and the Clash, had a crucial role in the development of punk's political style, were art school students from the 1960s, had lived on the Situationist fringe. The Situationists' concern, like the punks', was the politics of everyday life, the aesthetics of boredom. McLaren's ambition was to turn spectacle—the passively experienced structure of reality that we, as consumers, live with—into situation, the structure blown up, its rules made clear, the possibilities for action and desire exposed.

Outside London, at least, the most obvious feature of punk culture was its initial lack of straight working-class appeal. In the provinces the first punk scenes were staffed by the usual hip kids—art scholars and hippies and dropouts. Punk was a bohemian culture, and while bohemians can certainly be found on the dole queue, their lives are not determined by it. In Johnny Rotten's words, "I know it's tough on the dole but it's not that bad. When I was on it, I was getting paid for doing nothing. I thought it was fucking great. Fuck up the system the best way."

Robert Christgau suggests that

> rather than a working class youth movement punk is a basically working class bohemia that rejects both the haute bohemia of the rock elite and the hallowed bohemian myth of classlessness. Punk doesn't want to be thought of as bohemian, because bohemians are posers. But however vexed the question of their authenticity, bohemians do serve a historical function—they nurture aesthetic sensibility.[3]

The point can be generalized: a bohemian way of life has been central to British rock culture since the day that art student John

Lennon found himself in Hamburg's low life. British rockers' radical proletarianism comes, primarily, from rock's social association with lumpen leisure, and punk's cultural significance was derived not from its articulation of unemployment but from its exploration of the aesthetics of proletarian play. This was the source of punk politics; punk was not the voice of unemployed youth but a strident expression of the bohemian challenge to orderly consumption.

But punk was also the first British youth cult in which the consumption and production of music were integrated. Artists and street followers came together in their concerns, and bohemian arguments became class arguments too. Punk was, uniquely, briefly, a vanguard music for the masses, a street music that questioned street life, a pop music that challenged America, a working-class music that confronted politics. Punk was *about* the relationship of individualism and collectivism, the deprived and the privileged, survival and boredom, and, in the end, it wasn't its shock devices that shook up the record industry but its challenge to the marketing model. Punk was, from one perspective, primitive British dance music. But, on the other hand, pogo wasn't disco, and punk-rockers also claimed to make their audiences think. Punk certainly wasn't pop AM music, but neither was it rock FM music. When commentators tried to pin down its class significance, the ambiguities emerged. The question raised by punk wasn't who consumed music, but how they did.

Punk symbolized a new sort of street culture: the inner-city post-domestic young, radical professionals, squatters and communes, students, non-students living a student life, ethnic groups, gays, no one "settled down," everyone concerned to protest and survive. This street culture first emerged in American cities with the hippies; it meant the injection into bohemia and lumpen leisure alike of new sorts of responsibility and risk. Bohemia had always pretended that there should be no limits; for the lumpens there was no choice. But the questions punk focused were about leisure opportunity, about the relationships of choice *and* constraint.

If the struggle for rock meaning concerns cultural use as well as cultural form, then the ideology of rock depends not only on the relationship of producers and consumers, on a series of musical texts, but also on the effects of attempts to limit rock's significance by constraining its uses. Rock reaches its audiences via the media—records, radio, television, newspapers, the music press; for most rock consumers (and performers) these media are an important source of their knowledge and interpretations of particular rock styles and stars and sounds. The ideological work of the rock industry is not just the creation of meaning but also its regulation. The problem is how to confine music, musicians, and audiences to a particular organization of entertainment, taste, and pleasure.

# THE PROBLEM OF CONTROL

Critics of the mass media have always focused on the media's effects—the effects of television on children, newspapers on voters, advertisements on consumers, rock 'n' roll on teenagers, and so on. The problems with this approach to rock are not just methodological (how can the "effects" be measured?) but also theoretical: if the rock audience can't be understood simply as an empty receptacle for "effects," neither can the record industry be understood as a simple "cause." Indeed, my argument in this book is that the rock industry, for all its enveloping commercial machinations since the rise of rock 'n' roll, is itself an effect—an effect of postwar social changes, an effect of shifting relations of class and race and sex, an effect of new ideas of popular art and culture. The point I am making is that the central tension of rock—it is a source of pleasure that is both disturbing *and* relaxing—is not just the effect of the struggle between record companies and artists or audiences. The tension is also contained within the industry, within the audience, within the musicians, within the music itself. The resulting contradictions—order versus disorder, society versus the individual, security versus fantasy—are the contradictions of all symbolic art in all societies. What is at issue is the utopianism of art, what Marcuse called "the great refusal," the opposition of what-can-be-imagined to what-is.

The Frankfurt scholars argued that the transformation of art into commodity inevitably sapped imagination and withered hope—now all that could be imagined was what was. But the artistic impulse is not destroyed by capital; it is transformed by it. As utopianism is mediated through the new processes of cultural production and consumption, new sorts of struggles over community and leisure begin. The condemnation of consumption as "passive" is too glib. It ignores the complexity of popular culture—the "connotative richness" of rock music belies quick judgments about audience passivity: the music means too many things.

The sociology of music has usually rested on more or less crude reflection theories: the music is taken to reflect, to be "homologous" to, the society or social group that makes it. Music can then be interpreted as a particular form of ideological expression—jazz expresses the ideology of black Americans, classical music expresses the ideology of the European bourgeoisie, rock 'n' roll expresses the ideology of youth, and so on. These independently defined ideologies can then be used to account for the musical forms involved: the music is explained by reference to the social group that uses it— music is the group's "social symbol."

Marxists have converted this approach into the language of class. Different forms of music express different class ideologies, and their assessment is a matter of politics rather than aesthetics— bourgeois music is oppressive, proletarian music is liberating. Thus Marxist musicologists have argued that the essence of bourgeois music lies in its notation, its rational order; only those musical elements that can be so ordered are valued by the bourgeoisie as music. Jazz and jazz-based musics represent, by contrast, opposition to bourgeois order: they cannot be the subjects of rational control—they oppose "mutual communality" to the "hierarchy of diatonic harmony," "immediacy" to "calculation."

The conclusion from this argument is that music must be understood functionally, as a means by which social groups culturally reproduce themselves. Cultural reproduction involves the imposition of the "hegemonic discourse" of the ruling class on subordinate classes; so the ideology of rock has to be understood by reference to its role in the reproduction of the culture of capital—the contradictions of rock are thus the signs of class struggle.

I sympathize with this approach—I, too, am concerned with culture and class—but find it too gloomy, too mechanical. Class interests don't exist in the abstract, to be more or less effectively symbolized; they are themselves cultural effects. Cultural politics are about situation not intention, and rock matters because it can change the situation. The assumption of this book is that rock *is* a form of capitalist culture, but that capitalist culture is what we're trying to understand and to use, to subvert and to enjoy.

Rock 'n' roll, then, expresses in its own way (using contrasting class experiences of youth and leisure) the contradictions of capitalist culture, the problems that arise when dreams are packaged and fantasies sold. To turn dreams into commodities is not to make them any less real, but it is to confine them to certain settings—the marketplace and shopping mall, the dance hall and the cinema, the television screen and the bedroom—and to *limit* their effects. The rock industry, as a capitalist enterprise, doesn't sell some single, hegemonic idea, but is, rather, a medium through which hundreds of competing ideas flow. Commercial logic shapes these ideas, but as I showed in Part Two, efficient profit-making involves not the creation of "new needs" and audience "manipulation" but, rather, the response to existing needs and audience "satisfaction." As I've been arguing in this chapter, the primary concern of the capitalist pleasure business is *orderly* consumption—hence rock's 1970s business practices, professionalism, genre fragmentation, superstars, multimedia promotion, and so on.

In chapter 5, I argued that behind most such rock business practices lies the fear of overproduction. What is now clear is that behind this fear lies the fear of an *active* audience, whose tastes can't be predicted, whose uses of music can't be completely controlled. The record industry must always try to mold its market (this is the reality of rock-as-commodity), but this must always also involve a struggle (this is the reality of rock-as-leisure-commodity). The rock audience has its own ideas and experiences of what music is for—this is what gives the best rock performers their artistic edge. Mass culture works by draining these ideas and experiences of their edge in the very act of responding to and expressing them. What is crucial here is the capitalist control not of ideas but of cultural *practice.*

Three processes, for example, have been involved in the capitalist control of rock practice. First, there is a continuing attempt to confine rock to a particular definition of entertainment, to ensure that its leisure values are limited to a particular kind of free time, to temporary moments of relaxation. This is the use of rock made by radio, for example, which drains power from the music until even the sharpest disco rhythms, the astutest punk protests, the most stirring heavy metal sounds get heard as Muzak, cheery accompaniments to doing the dishes. A similar attitude is obvious in the music press: *Rolling Stone* developed from a magazine in which the leisure values of rock 'n' roll were the source of a critical commentary on the organization of politics and production into a magazine in which music is understood only as an enjoyable form of consumption. *Roll-*

*ing Stone,* like the rest of the music press, is now a consumer guide, an example of the way in which commercial entrepreneurs work to make leisure and pleasure *orderly.*

A second aspect of this process is the continuing effort to freeze the rock audience into a series of market tastes. Record companies themselves, radio programmers, music papers, deejays, writers, all attempt to define and categorize musical demands and so ease the processes of meeting them. If audiences can be persuaded that a precise style or genre, artist or image meets their needs, expresses the solution to their particular leisure problem, then not only is their commercial exploitation made more efficient, but rock's disturbing, challenging, and instructive elements are tamed and transformed into the (nonthreatening) confirmations of conventional taste.

This relates, thirdly, to the continuing way in which the anti-work elements of rock-as-leisure are diverted from collective forms to individual self-indulgence. The problem is the same as it was in the nineteenth century: if workers' leisure was too exciting, too inspiring, then it might become a base from which to reject work, to revolutionize it. Creative forces must be blunted and made to conform to the exigencies not just of the entertainment industry but of industry in general. The commercialization of the counterculture is usually taken as the clearest example of this process, but all fans keep a running account of the musicians who have "sold out" the rock community to their individual ambitions; and the individualization of pop performance and consumption in the 1960s was, really, a sign of the increasingly middle-class use of the music. As rock 'n' roll moved into the suburbs and onto campuses, it was routinized as a new form of professional entertainment.

## LAST WORDS

This is the rock critic's usual sour story, and I don't want to end on that note. The fact is that the music is still, above all, the source of a power and joy that are disturbing as well as relaxing—witness the contradictions of punk. Capital may or may not keep control of rock's use, but it cannot *determine* its meanings—the problems of community and leisure are not so easily resolved, and the conditions that made the music necessary in the first place haven't changed.

Rock music is capitalist music. It draws its meanings from the relationships of capitalist production, and it contributes, as a leisure activity, to the reproduction of those relationships; the music doesn't challenge the system but reflects and illuminates it. Rock is about dreams and their regulation, and the strength of rock dreams comes not from their force as symbols, but from their relationship to the experience of work and leisure: the issue, finally, is not how to live outside capitalism (hippie or bohemian style), but how to live within it. The needs expressed in rock—for freedom, control, power, a sense of *life*—are needs defined by capitalism. And rock is a mass culture. It is not folk or art but a commoditized dream: it conceals as much as it reveals. For every individual illuminating account of our common situation there are a hundred mass musical experiences that disguise it. Rock, for all the power of its individual dreams, is still confined by its mass cultural form. Its history, like the history of America itself, is a history of class struggle—the struggle for fun.

# NOTES

## CHAPTER 1: INTRODUCTION

1. The original version of this book was studded with footnotes, but as the majority of them referred to UK publications, and often obscure ones, it seemed distracting to repeat them here. Anyone who wants to follow up my empirical references should consult the original book: Simon Frith, *The Sociology of Rock* (London, 1978).

## CHAPTER 2: ROCK ROOTS

1. Richard Middleton, *Pop Music and the Blues* (London, 1972). The Alan Price quote is from an unpublished interview with David Robson in May, 1973.

2. Lester Bangs, *Blondie* (New York, 1980), p. 70.

3. From "Sinking of the Titanic," a 1918 song by Stringbeans, quoted in Marshall and Jean Stearns, *Jazz Dance* (New York, 1979), p. 240.

4. Eileen Southern, *The Music of Black Americans* (New York, 1971), p. 103.

5. Marshall Stearns, *The Story of Jazz* (London, 1970), p. 282.

6. Ian Hoare, ed., *The Soul Book* (New York, 1976), p. 152.

7. Paul Garon, *Blues and the Poetic Spirit* (New York, 1978), p. 149.

8. Southern, p. 165.

9. Daniel Kingman, *American Music: A Panorama* (New York, 1979), p. 288.

10. Quoted in Arnold Shaw, *Honkers and Shouters* (New York, 1978), pp. 322–23.

11. Quoted in Marc Eliot, *Death of a Rebel* (New York, 1979), p. 51.

12. Dave Laing, ed., *The Electric Muse* (London, 1975), pp. 78–79.

13. Quoted in Eliot, p. 93.

14. Quoted in Ronald Pearsall, *Victorian Popular Music* (Detroit, 1973), p. 47.

## CHAPTER 3: ROCK AND MASS CULTURE

1. Quoted in Pearsall, pp. 123, 199.

2. Jon Landau, *It's Too Late to Stop Now* (San Francisco, 1972), p. 40.

3. T. W. Adorno, *Prisms*, (London, 1967), p. 128.

4. *Ibid.*, pp. 130–32.

5. Quoted in Pearsall, p. 208.

6. Landau, p. 130.

7. Greil Marcus, *Mystery Train* (New York, 1976), p. 115.

8. Michael Lydon, "Rock for Sale," in Jonathan Eisen, ed., *The Age of Rock*, Vol. 2 (New York, 1970), pp. 56, 60.

9. Robert Levin, "Rock and Regression," in John Sinclair and Robert Levin, *Music and Politics* (Cleveland, 1971), p. 131.

## CHAPTER 4: MAKING MUSIC

1. Tony Hatch, *So You Want to Be in the Music Business* (London, 1976), p. 12.

2. Howard Becker, "The Professional Jazz Musician and His Audience," in R. Serge Denisoff and R. A. Peterson, eds., *The Sounds of Social Change* (New York, 1972), p. 254.

3. "Tommy Steele: 'The Story of Ambition,' " *The Listener* (10 October 1974), p. 458.

4. The Rolling Stones, *Our Own Story* (London, 1964), pp. 13, 187.

5. "Pete Townshend: 'A Bit of Dreamland,' " *The Listener* (10 October 1974), p. 456.

6. John Pidgeon, *Eric Clapton* (London, 1976), p. 43.

7. *Rolling Stone* (4 February 1971), p. 28.

8. Al Kooper, *Backstage Passes* (New York, 1977), p. 111.

9. Cliff Richard, *It's Great to Be Young* (London, 1960), pp. 199–200.

10. *Rolling Stone* (28 September 1968), p. 14.

11. Francis Newton, *The Jazz Scene* (London, 1961), pp. 199–200.

12. *Rolling Stone* (19 August 1971), p. 28.

13. *Rolling Stone* (7 January 1971), p. 32.

14. *The Listener* (10 October 1974), p. 457.

15. *Rolling Stone* (7 January 1971), p. 34.

16. Peter Guralnick, *Lost Highway* (Boston, 1979), pp. 85–86.

17. Eliot, p. 66.

18. Bruce Cook, *The Beat Generation* (New York, 1971), p. 220.

## CHAPTER 5: MAKING RECORDS

1. *Music Week* (9 June 1973).

2. R. Serge Denisoff, *Solid Gold* (New Brunswick, 1975), p. 119.

3. *Melody Maker* (4 May 1974).

4. Colin MacInnes, "Socialist Impresarios," *New Statesman* (15 June 1962).

5. Robert Stephen Spitz, *The Making of Superstars* (New York, 1978), p. 210.

6. Michael Wale, *Voxpop* (London, 1972), p. 224.

7. Spitz, p. 131.

8. Wale, p. 67.

9. *Melody Maker* (23 March 1974).

10. American independent record label boss Hy Weiss.

11. Erik Barnouw, *A History of Broadcasting in the United States*, Vol. 3 (New York, 1970), pp. 303–304.

12. Brian Savin of BRMB, quoted in *Radio and Record News*, special supplement on "ILR Success Story," 1978.

13. From an unpublished interview with myself and Charlie Gillett in 1973.

## CHAPTER 6: MAKING MONEY

1. *New Musical Express* (3 November 1973).

2. PRS, "Membership of the Performing Rights Society" (London, 1976), p. 5.

3. Quoted in Mike Jahn, *Rock from Elvis Presley to the Rolling Stones* (New York, 1973), p. 69.

## CHAPTER 7: MAKING MEANING

1. Alan Smith of *New Musical Express*, quoted in Gavin Millar, *Pop! Hit or Miss?* (London, 1963), p. 2.

2. Quoted in Chet Flippo, "The History of Rolling Stone," *Popular Music and Society*, iii (1973–74), p. 163.

3. *Melody Maker* (6 February 1971).

## CHAPTER 8: YOUTH

1. Colin MacInnes, *Absolute Beginners* (New York, 1960), p. 6.

2. Brian Jackson, *Working Class Community* (London, 1968), p. 143.

3. Paula S. Fass, *The Damned and the Beautiful* (New York, 1977), p. 14.

4. Robert S. and Helen M. Lynd, *Middletown* (New York, 1929), p. 267.

5. Dick Clark, *Your Happiest Years* (New York, 1959), p. 7.

6. MacInnes, p. 49.

7. George Melly, "Didn't I?" *New Society* (13 June 1963).

8. Harry Hopkins, *The New Look* (London, 1963), p. 429.

## CHAPTER 9: YOUTH AND MUSIC

1. Elizabeth Hardwick, "Billie Holiday," *New York Review of Books* (4 March 1976).

2. B. S. Rowntree and G. R. Lavers, *English Life and Leisure* (London, 1951), p. 282.

3. Charles Hamblett and Jane Deverson, *Generation X* (London, 1964), p. 20.

4. Fourteen-year-old girl quoted in the West Riding County Council Education Committee's *Schools Bulletin*, 1971.

5. Jock Young, *The Drug Takers* (London, 1971), p. 147.

6. Richard Mills, *Young Outsiders* (New York, 1973), pp. 130, 138.

7. T. R. Fyvel, *The Insecure Offenders* (London, 1963), p. 240.

8. Penny Reel, "The Young Mod's Forgotten Story," *New Musical Express* (14 April 1979).

9. Peter Willmott, *Adolescent Boys of East London* (London, 1969), pp. 175–76.

10. Clark, p. 70.

11. Quoted in Richard Barnes, *Mods!* (London, 1979), p. 15.

12. Quoted in Hamblett and Deverson, p. 132.

13. Coventry City Centre Report, 1980, p. 5.

14. *Ibid.*, p. 7.

15. Quoted in Dave Marsh, *Born to Run* (New York, 1979), pp. 154–55.

## CHAPTER 10: ROCK AND SEXUALITY

1. Rudi Blesh and Harriet Janis, *They All Played Ragtime* (New York, 1950), p. 33.

2. Fass, p. 307.

3. Marshall and Jean Stearns, p. 322.

4. Andrew Holleran, *Dancer From The Dance* (New York, 1978), pp. 38–39.

## CHAPTER 11: ROCK AND LEISURE

1. Quoted in Peter Bailey, *Leisure and Class in Victorian England* (Toronto, 1978), p. 165.

2. Karl Marx, *Grundrisse* (London, Penguin ed., 1973), p. 287.

3. Robert Christgau, "We Have to Deal With It," *Village Voice* (9 January 1978).

# BIBLIOGRAPHY

Rock 'n' roll has had remarkably little academic attention. This has, from a researcher's point of view, advantages as well as disadvantages. The disadvantages are obvious: most of the important discussions and analyses of rock appear in transient issues of magazines and in fleeting conversations. Rock books do appear, but they disappear quickly and they don't *look* like serious studies—university libraries buy few of them. Collecting rock documents can be as obsessive a hobby as collecting rock records, but the advantage of this situation is that so much of the writing about rock is fresh and challenging—nonsense and insights are mixed up in equal measures. People write about rock for love not degrees (and certainly not for money—rock book deals have to be *prized* out of publishers); rock analysis is not bogged down in academic cross references and methodological paranoia. In short, rock books are hard to find, but fun to read.

In this bibliography I've included all the books that were necessary to produce my own. There are good books I haven't read or haven't found (my reading reflects my UK base), and most of the books I have read are now out of print. But it is important to list them, if only to honor the people who, without the benefits of research grants (and with the pressures of deadlines and cautious editors) have *worked* to make sense of their and my obsessions.

## ROCK CULTURE

The first person who made me think about pop music was Nik Cohn. He wrote a column for *Queen* magazine in the mid-sixties and seemed to have a direct line to my own pleasures. His *Rock from the Beginning* (New York, 1969), ostensibly a history of rock 'n' roll, is still the best account of the 1960s British rock aesthetic. Cohn was an exceptional writer in Britain (I don't remember any of his contemporaries on the music papers themselves), for rock writing as culture criticism has been almost exclusively an American concern. Most of this writing is lost in back numbers of *Rolling Stone, Creem*, and *Village Voice*, in the early *Crawdaddy, Who Put the Bomp*, and *Cheetah;* but the best critics can also be found in books. Robert Christgau's *Any Old Way You Choose It* (New York, 1973) is a collection of his pieces from 1967–73—thanks to his political sensitivity, they aren't dated. Greil Marcus's *Mystery Train* (New York, 1976) is a wonderfully ambitious attempt to root rock 'n' roll in American literary myths—the approach triumphs in the "Presliad." Ellen Willis's best pieces are in her *Beginning to See the Light* (New York, 1981). Dave Marsh's *Born to Run* (New York, 1979) and Lester Bangs's *Blondie* (New York, 1980) are rock-star biographies (a reflection of publishers' rock concerns) that matter, in fact, as critical statements: neither book reveals much about its subject, but both are important arguments about what rock means. Lester Bangs's 1970s articles (primarily for *Creem*) should, nonetheless, be anthologized in their own right—Bangs has been, crucially, the one rock critic whose stance is not rooted in the 1960s. I've never been able to read Richard Meltzer's fake philosophy thesis, *The Aesthetics of Rock* (New York, 1970), but some of his more incidental writing was collected as *Gulcher* (San Francisco, 1972)—no one has better cut rock down to its pop size. Jon Landau's *auteurist It's Too Late to Stop Now* (San Francisco, 1972) is dated as criticism, but if read alongside Ralph J. Gleason's eagerly naive *The Jefferson Airplane and the San Francisco Sound* (New York, 1969), it remains significant as the source of *Rolling Stone*'s account of music [for a harder-headed, more historically aware version of San Francisco ideology see Greil Marcus, ed., *Rock and Roll Will Stand!* (Boston, 1969). Richard Goldstein's anthology of 1960s lyrics, *The Poetry of Rock* (New York, 1969)], captures rock's original pretensions exactly.

The only British rock books with the same degree of intelligence and controversy are Dave Laing's *The Sound of our Time* (New York, 1970), an early attempt to analyze rock in terms of Marxist culture criticism, and George Melly's *Revolt into Style* (New York, 1971), an acute outsider's description of British rock culture from 1964 to 1969.

There are several useful anthologies. Jonathan Eisen's *The Age of Rock*, Vols. 1 & 2 (New York, 1969, 1970) includes, amid much posturing, key 1960s articles like Tom Smucker's "Movement vs. Groovement" (Eisen's *Twenty-Minute Fandangos and Forever Changes*, [New York, 1971], is all posturing). R. Serge Denisoff and R. A. Peterson, eds., *The Sounds of Social Change* (New York, 1972) is an academic reader, rather dry. George H. Lewis's *Side-Saddle on the Golden Calf* (Pacific Palisades, 1972) is a collection of more playful academic pieces on popular culture generally. Greil Marcus, ed., *Stranded* (New York, 1979), a selection of critics on their desert island disc, is a useful sampler of rock cultural assumptions at the end of the 1970s. Jim Miller, ed., *The Rolling Stone Illustrated History of Rock & Roll* (New York, 1980) is patchier but useful. Phil Hardy and Dave Laing, eds., *Encyclopedia of Rock and Roll*, Vols. 1–3 (London, 1976) is a necessary (and amazingly reliable) reference book. Mark Shipper's revealing, *real* history of the Beatles, *Paperback Writer* (New York, 1977), is the funniest rock book.

## MUSICAL CULTURES
There is a mass of scholarly, semi-scholarly, and pure fan material on specific musics, and I only have space here to list the books directly relevant to my concerns.

## BLACK MUSIC
The best general introductions are Eileen Southern's historical *The Music of Black Americans* (New York, 1971) and Ortiz Walton's *Music: Black, White and Blue* (New York, 1972). Rudi Blesh and Harriet Janis, *They All Played Ragtime* (New York, 1950) is excellent on black music and the rise of Tin Pan Alley. Marshall Stearns's *The Story of Jazz* (London, 1970) is the clearest jazz overview. Francis Newton's *The Jazz Scene* (London, 1961) is the clearest jazz sociology. Sidney Finkelstein's *Jazz: A People's Music* (New York, 1948), LeRoi Jones's *Blues People* (New York, 1963) and *Black Music* (New York, 1967), and Frank Kofsky's *Black Nationalism and Revolution in Music* (New York, 1970) raise a variety of political issues. Paul Oliver's *The Meaning of the Blues* (New York, 1963) is still the soundest introduction to blues analysis, but Paul Garon's *Blues and the Poetic Spirit* (New York, 1978), a "Freudian surrealist" approach, is the most stimulating (and see Carl Boggs's review, "The blues tradition from poetic revolt to cultural impasse," *Socialist Review*, 38, 1978). Tony Russell's *Blacks, Whites and Blues* (London, 1970) is a necessary account of rural black and white musical overlaps. Tony Heilbut's *The Gospel Sound* (New York, 1971) and Marshall and Jean Stearns's *Jazz Dance* (New York, 1979) are such loving investigations of their topics that they become important general accounts of American social history.

Charles Keil, *Urban Blues* (Chicago, 1966) and Michael Haralambos, *Right on: From Blues to Soul in Black America* (New York, 1979) are important sociological accounts of the shift from blues to soul. Charlie Gillett's *The Sound of the City* (New York, 1970) and Arnold Shaw's *Honkers and Shouters* (New York, 1978) tell the story in detail and are important for their passing accounts of the music business in the 1950s and 1960s. Ray Charles's and David Ritz's *Brother Ray* (New York, 1979) is an illuminating insider's account. Ian Hoare, ed., *The Soul Book* (New York, 1976) has a brilliant chapter by Ian Hoare himself on soul lyrics.

There is not yet a good history of reggae music—Sebastian Clarke's *Jah Music* (London, 1980) is narrow in its coverage and often misleading. There are travelogues—Stephen Davis and Peter Simon, *Reggae Bloodlines* (New York, 1977) and Adrian Boot and Michael Thomas, *Jamaica: Babylon on a Thin Wire* (New York, 1977), and polemical pamphlets—Rolston Kallyndyr and Henderson Dalrymple, *Reggae: A People's Music* (London, n.d.), and Henderson Dalrymple, *Bob Marley: Music, Myth and the Rastas* (London, 1976). John Plummer, *Movement of Jah People* (Washington, D.C., 1978) is on reggae's meaning for Jamaicans in Britain; Linton Kwesi Johnson's "Jamaica Rebel Music" (*Race and Class*, 17, 1976) is an interesting analysis of reggae lyrics. Michael Thelwell's Jamaican novel *The Harder They Come* (New York, 1980) is the best introduction to the importance of music in Jamaica itself.

## COUNTRY MUSIC

Country music has been better served by academics than any other American popular music, and the basic book, Bill C. Malone's *Country Music, U.S.A.* (Austin, Texas, 1968) is scholarly in both academic and fan terms. Its approach is complemented by Douglas B. Green, *Country Roots* (New York, 1976), Bill C. Malone and Judith McCulloh, eds., *Stars of Country Music* (Urbana, Ill., 1975) and Patrick Carr, ed., *The Illustrated History of Country Music* (New York, 1980). The most important of the numerous country-folk articles is Archie Green's "Hillbilly Music: Source and Symbol" (*Journal of American Folklore*, 78, 1965). Paul Hemphill's *The Nashville Sound* (New York, 1970) and John Grissim's *Country Music: White Man's Blues* (New York, 1970) are solid journalistic accounts of the Nashville scene as country became big business. Alanna Nash, *Dolly* (New York, 1979), Christopher S. Wren, *The Life and Legends of Johnny Cash* (New York, 1974), Tammy Wynette, *Stand by Your Man* (New York, 1979), and, especially, Loretta Lynn and George Vecsey, *Coal Miner's Daughter* (New York, 1977) are revealing country biographies. Richard Peterson is doing important sociological work on country music production and consumption. See "The production of cultural change: the case of contemporary country music" (*Sociological Research*, 45, 1978) and, with Paul Di Maggio, "From region to class, the changing locus of country music" (*Social Forces*, 53, 1975). But the best country book of all is Nick Tosches's *Country: The Biggest Music In America* (New York, 1977)—a witty, startling, revisionist history of all those aspects of country music (sex, race, drugs, money) that its bland Nashville salesmen conceal (Tosches's research down the back alleys of black and white musical history continues in the pages of *Creem*).

## FOLK MUSIC

The standard British text on folk music is A. L. Lloyd's *Folk Song in England* (New York, 1967), but this should now be read in conjunction with Dave Harker's research into the history of British folk ideology. Harker's only book so far, *One For The Money* (London, 1980), unfortunately buries this folk work in a trivial, Trotskyist theory of pop. The most illuminating account of the American folk movement is still R. Serge Denisoff's cynical analysis of folk and radicalism, *Great Day Coming* (Urbana, Ill., 1971). Joe Klein's *Woody Guthrie* (New York, 1980) is illuminating about the man himself but has little of interest on the folk scene. Dave De Turk and A. Paulin Jr., eds. *The American Folk Scene* (New York, 1967) is a useful collection of articles and arguments from the 1960s New York folk scene. But Marc Eliot's life of Phil Ochs, *Death of a Rebel* (New York, 1979), is the best description of the shift to folk-rock (much more illuminating than Anthony Scaduto's life of Dylan). For folk and rock in Britain see Dave Laing, ed., *The Electric Muse* (London, 1975).

## POP MUSIC

The best treatment of nineteenth-century popular music is Ronald Pearsall's *Victorian Popular Music* (Detroit, 1973). The best books on British music hall are D. F. Cheshire's *Music Hall in Britain* (Cranbury, N.J., 1974) and Colin MacInnes's *Sweet Saturday Night* (New York, 1967). There are useful overviews of British popular music in Edward Lee, *Music of the People* (London, 1970) and Frances Rust, *Dance in Society* (London, 1969).

Writers about American popular music fall rather easily into a nostalgic lack of analysis, and there is no good history of Tin Pan Alley. The best is Ian Whitcomb's *After the Ball* (New York, 1972), just for its rash generalizations. The standard texts, detailed and rather dull, are Isaac Goldberg's *Tin Pan Alley* (New York, 1930) and David Ewen's *The Life and Death of Tin Pan Alley* (New York, 1964). Eddie Rogers's *Tin Pan Alley* (London, 1964) is an interesting inside account of the British pop song business. Arnold Shaw's *Sinatra* (New York, 1968) is a useful description of the institutionalization of the American popular singer. Charles Hamm's *Yesterdays* (New York, 1979) is a well-researched musicological history of American popular music. Alec Wilder's *American Popular Song* (New York, 1972), Henry Pleasants's *The Great American Popular Singers* (New York, 1974), and Ira Gershwin's *Lyrics on Several Occasions* (New York, 1973) are sparkling, intelligent analyses of the *art* of the American song. Joel Whitburn's Record Research, Inc. (Wisconsin) provides a continuing analysis of pop music, based on the *Billboard* charts of "Top Pop Artists and Singles" since 1955.

## THE MASS CULTURE DEBATE

The mass culture debate has been going on too long to need a bibliographical guide here. The crucial American arguments from the 1930s to the 1950s are in B. Rosenberg and D. M. White, eds., *Mass Culture* (New York, 1957)—this includes David Riesman's article on youth and music. The Frankfurt School dominated Marxist discussions of mass culture, and there is a useful collection of the key 1930s arguments—Ernst Bloch, et al., *Aesthetics and Politics* (New York, 1979)—this includes an excellent updating afterword by Fredric Jameson. One of Adorno's last pieces, "Culture Industry Reconsidered" (*New German Critique*, 12, 1977), confirms his 1930s stance. But the most important Frankfurt statement for rock ideologists themselves was Herbert Marcuse's *One Dimensional Man* (Boston, 1964). For its influence, see John Sinclair and Robert Levin, *Music and Politics* (Cleveland, 1971).

British mass cultural critics temper their Marxism with arguments taken from the literary critic F. R. Leavis; see, for example, Stuart Hall and Paddy Whannel, *The Popular Arts* (New York, 1965). The Marx/Leavis arguments have been applied to rock in particular by folk ideologists; see Trevor Fisher, *We're Only in It for the Money* (Birmingham 1972), Charles Parker, "Pop Song: the Manipulated Ritual," in P. Abbs, ed., *The Black Rainbow* (London, 1975), and the debate between Leon Rosselson, Gary Herman, and Ian Hoare in Carl Gardner, ed., *Media, Politics, and Culture* (Atlantic Highlands, N.J., 1979).

The pluralist defense of mass culture is, by and large, rather feeble. See, for example, Herbert Gans's unsatisfactory account of "taste cultures" in *Popular Culture and High Culture* (New York, 1975). I am more convinced by theories of cultural struggle. The most interesting (and least orthodox) Marxist mass cultural theorist is Walter Benjamin. See his *Illuminations* (London, 1970), *Understanding Brecht* (London, 1973), and *Charles Baudelaire* (London, 1976). Benjamin's approach was applied influentially to 1960s cultural politics by Hans Magnus Enzensberger's "Constituents of a Theory of the Media" (*New Left Review*, 64, 1970). For an unusual and fascinating empirical account of music and American mass media see Neal and Janice Gregory, *When Elvis Died* (Washington, 1980).

## MUSIC AND MEANING

For the musicology of rock see Henry Pleasants, *Serious Music—and All That Jazz!* (New York, 1969), Richard Middleton, *Pop Music and the Blues* (London, 1972), and Wilfred Mellers's study of the Beatles, *Twilight of the Gods* (New

York, 1974). None of these books quite gets the point of the music it discusses—each isolates texts from contexts and drifts into anthropological cliché when discussing what popular music means to its listeners. John Shepherd, et al., *Whose Music? A Sociology of Musical Language* (New Brunswick, N.J., 1980) and Graham Vulliamy and Ed Lee, eds., *Pop Music in School* (Cambridge, Mass., 1980) add general interactionist accounts of musical language and class categories.

Andrew Chester and Richard Merton's debate, "For a Rock Aesthetic" (*New Left Review*, 59, 1970), and Iain Chambers's "It's More Than a Song to Sing" (*Estatto do Annali-Anglistica, Naples*, 22, 1979) are dense attempts to make sense of rock itself as an ideological form. Roland Barthes's brief, stimulating comments on music can be found in *Image-Music-Text* (New York, 1978) and *The Eiffel Tower* (New York, 1979). They should be read in conjunction with Susan Sontag's *Against Interpretation* (New York, 1967).

The best accounts of the roots and rise of British punk are Caroline Coon, *1988: The New Wave Punk Rock Explosion* (New York, 1978) and Fred and Judy Vermorel, *The Sex Pistols* (London, 1978). Julie Burchill and Tony Parsons, *"The Boy Looked at Johnny"* (London, 1978) is a shoddy, compulsive, and infuriating punk history that captures the necessary spirit in the *way* it is written. The best analytic treatment of punk as music is Dave Laing's "Punk Rock" (*Marxism Today*, April, 1978).

## MAKING RECORDS/MAKING MONEY

The few sociologists of rock have focused attention on its production, and I am indebted, in particular, to Paul Hirsch's work, *The Structure of the Popular Music Industry* (Michigan, 1970), "Sociological Approaches to the Pop Music Phenomenon" (*American Behavioral Scientist*, 14, 1971), and "Producer and Distributor Roles Among Cultural Organizations" (*Social Research*, 45, 1978). The theory of market competition and cultural cycles has been developed most convincingly by Richard Peterson and D. G. Berger, "Entrepreneurship and organization: evidence from the popular music industry" (*Administrative Science Quarterly*, 16, 1971) and Richard Peterson, "Cycles in symbol production: the case of popular music" (*American Sociological Review*, 40, 1975). R. Serge Denisoff, *Solid Gold* (New Brunswick, 1975) provides a general sociology of the American record industry that is better on some aspects of the business (radio) than others (record companies). I prefer Denisoff's cheerful naiveté to the knowing journalism of Steve Chapple and Reebee Garofalo's *Rock 'n' Roll Is Here to Pay* (Chicago, 1977), but the latter is the best source for the facts and figures of the rock business (the nearest British equivalent is Michael Cable's *The Music Industry Inside Out*, London, 1977). For plain guides to the music business without Chapple and Garofalo's anti-commercialism, see S. Shemel and M. W. Krasilovsky, *This Business of Music* (New York, 1964), Tony Hatch, *So You Want to Be in the Music Business* (London, 1976), and Sharon Lawrence, *So You Want to Be a Rock and Roll Star* (New York, 1976). There are now a plethora of such guides, basically indistinguishable from each other. But by far the best book on the American rock industry is Geoffrey Stokes's *Star-Making Machinery* (Indianapolis, 1976), a detailed analysis of the making and marketing of a Commander Cody LP that becomes an acute dissection of rock business practices in general. Also see Bob Greene's good book on an Alice Cooper tour, *Billion Dollar Baby* (New York, 1974).

Much of the business information I've used in this book comes from on- and off-the-record conversations with people in rock or from interviews published in the music and trade press. There are two useful collections of such interviews—Robert Stephen Spitz, *The Making of Superstars* (New York, 1978) covers America and Michael Wale, *Voxpop* (London, 1972) covers Britain. Charlie Gillet and Simon Frith, eds., *Rock File*, Vols. 1–5 (London, 1972, 1974–76, 1978) are relevant collections of statistics and argument.

For the music business in the 1950s see Dick Clark and Richard Robinson, *Rock, Roll and Remember* (New York, 1976) and for the music business in Britain, John Kennedy, *Tommy Steele* (London, 1958). For the rise of British beat see Allan Williams, *The Man Who Gave the Beatles Away* (London, 1975)—Williams managed the Beatles before Brian Epstein—and Michael Braun, *Love Me Do* (London 1964), a sharp report of a Beatles tour. For the rise of rock see Clive Davis, *Clive* (New York, 1975), an irritatingly coy but fascinating account of how CBS became a rock label, and Derek Taylor, *As Time Goes By* (London, 1972), the even coyer memoir of the Beatles' (among others') publicist. Peter McCabe and Robert D. Shonfield, *Apple to the Core* (New York, 1976) is a precise financial account of the collapse of Apple. Robert Stephen Spitz, *Barefoot in Babylon* (New York, 1979) is an exhaustive, exhausting history of the Woodstock Festival that lays to rest any lingering thoughts that it was a Good Thing. The best description of the rock business in the 1970s is Stephen Holden's sensational novel *Triple Platinum* (New York, 1979). For cultural imperialism and the multinational record business see Jeremy Tunstall, *The Media Are American* (New York, 1979) and Armand Mattelart, *Multinational Corporations and the Control of Culture* (Atlantic Highlands, N.J., 1979).

For particular record companies see Charlie Gillett's model history of Atlantic, *Making Tracks* (New York, 1974). There are, unfortunately, no other such studies, although Peter Benjaminson's slicker *The Story of Motown* (New York, 1979) has useful information. It should be read with Elaine Jesmer's *Number One with a Bullet* (New York, 1974), a Harold Robbins-esque treatment of a "successful independent soul label" that raises the specters I have avoided—Mafia involvement, gangsters, drugs, where record company money *goes*.

For record producers see George Martin and Jeremy Hornsby, *All You Need is Ears* (New York, 1980), Richard Williams's study of Phil Spector, *Out of His Head* (New York, 1972), and Edward Kealy's excellent article "From Craft to Art: the Case of Sound Mixers and Popular Music" (*Sociology of Work and Occupation*, 6, 1979). For song publishers see Alan Peacock and Ronald Weir, *The Composer in the Market Place* (London, 1975) and Ernst Roth, *The Business of Music* (London, 1969).

### RADIO AND PRESS

The basic history of American radio is Erik Barnouw, *A History of Broadcasting in the United States*, Vols. 1–3 (New York, 1966, 1968, 1970). For British radio see Asa Briggs, *The History of Broadcasting in the United Kingdom*, Vols. 1 & 2 (London, 1961, 1965), and Tom Burns, *The BBC: Public Institution and Private World* (New York, 1977). For American pop radio see Arnold Passman: *The Deejays* (New York, 1971) and Peter Fornatale and Joshua E. Mills, *Radio in the Television Age* (New York, 1980), neither of which is very satisfactory.

There is not much written on the music press, but see Roger Lewis, *Outlaws of America* (London, 1972) for the underground press, and Chet Flippo, "The History of *Rolling Stone*" (*Popular Music and Society*, 3, 1973–74). For *Rolling Stone* ideology see its own anthologies, especially *The Rolling Stone Record Review*, Vols. 1 & 2 (New York, 1971, 1974) and Ben Fong-Torres, ed., *What's That Sound?* (New York, 1976). There is nothing on the British music press.

## MUSICIANS

The pages of the music papers are filled by interviews with the stars. They are usually unilluminating, but for some exceptions see *The Rolling Stone Interviews*, Vols. 1 & 2 (New York, 1971, 1973) and Michael Lydon's sensitive conversations (mostly with black artists), *Rock Folk* (New York, 1971), and *Boogie Lightning* (New York, 1974). The best books on American popular musicians, though, are Peter Guralnick's *Feel Like Going Home* (New York, 1971) and *Lost Highway* (Boston, 1979). Howard Becker's *Outsiders* (New York, 1963) is the classic sociological account of the professional musician's life, and Robert R. Faulkner's *Hollywood Studio Musicians* (Chicago, 1971) is a good study of session music making. Al Kooper's and Ben Edmonds's *Backstage Passes* (New York, 1977) is a revealing memoir of a pop musician's life in New York in the 1960s. Pete Frame's *Rock Family Trees* (London, 1980) captures wonderfully, obsessively, the music-making history of almost every current rock star.

Music book publishing is dominated by instant biographies of the latest stars. Most of these are as banal as the music papers' interviews, but some of the stars' lives are important. The biggest stars have solid biographies (Anthony Scaduto on Bob Dylan, Jerry Hopkins on Elvis Presley, Philip Norman on the Beatles), but I find the trashy exposés more illuminating—Red West, et al., *Elvis: What Happened?* (New York, 1977) or Larry Sloman, *On the Road with Bob Dylan* (New York, 1978). The Rolling Stones have had more trashy books devoted to them than anyone else, and the hagiographies—from the Rolling Stones' *Our Own Story* (New York, 1970) to Barbara Charone's *Keith Richards* (London, 1979)—should be read against the gossip—Robert Greenfield's *Stones Touring Party* (New York, 1974) and Tony Sanchez's *Up and Down with the Rolling Stones* (New York, 1979).

For 1950s musicians see John Goldrosen, *Buddy Holly* (London 1975) and Cliff Richard, *It's Great to Be Young* (London, 1960). For 1960s musicians see David Leaf, *The Beach Boys and the California Myth* (New York, 1978) and David Henderson, *Jimi Hendrix* (New York, 1978). For a hilarious anti-biography see Fred and Judy Vermorel's *Kate Bush* (London, 1980).

The bohemian connection can be traced through Milton Mezzrow and Bernard Wolfe, *Really the Blues* (New York, 1946), Ross Russell, *Bird Lives!* (New York, 1973), George Melly, *Owning Up* (London, 1965) (on life as a British jazz musician in the 1950s), Bruce Cook, *The Beat Generation* (New York, 1971), and Jerry Hopkins and Daniel Sugarman, *No One Here Gets Out Alive* (New York, 1980). This last book is a poor biography of Jim Morrison, but it does reveal the unpleasantness of the people who hang around rock stars, and it does show how far a small talent can go if it is sold as poetry and revolt.

Ian Hunter's *Diary of a Rock and Roll Star* (London, 1974) is an interesting record of life on the road, but there is not, to my knowledge (and despite numerous attempts), a good novel about the rock 'n' roll life. For some of the mysteries involved in making music see Josef Skvorecky, *The Bass Saxophone* (New York,

1978)—about playing jazz in Czechoslovakia, and Guy Peellaert and Nik Cohn, *Rock Dreams* (New York, 1973)—fans' musician fantasies.

## YOUTH

There is a large academic literature on youth, but little of it is relevant to the analysis of youth culture and music. This is a selective guide to what is.

John Gillis, *Youth and History* (New York, 1974) is a useful historical survey. For more detailed insights see Joseph F. Kelt, "Adolescence and Youth in Nineteenth Century America," in T. K. Rabb and R. I. Rotberg, eds., *The Family in History* (New York, 1973) and Ted W. Margudant, "Primary Schools and Youth Groups in Pre-War Paris" (*Journal of Contemporary History*, 1978). Clarence Rook, *The Hooligan Nights* (1899, reprinted Oxford, 1979) is a journalist's report on London teenage life in the 1890s, and Robert Roberts's *The Classic Slum* (Manchester, Eng., 1971) is a wonderful memoir of teenage life in a northern English town at the beginning of the century. Paula S. Fass, *The Damned and the Beautiful* (New York, 1977) is a brilliant analysis of American youth culture in the 1920s, and Kenneth Allsop's *Hard Travelin'* (New York, 1967) has important material on unemployed American youth in the 1930s.

For the rise of teenage culture in the USA, see A. B. Hollingshead, *Elmtown's Youth and Elmtown Revisited* (New York, 1975), Edgar Z. Friedenberg, *The Vanishing Adolescent* (Boston, 1959), James S. Coleman, *The Adolescent Society* (New York, 1961), and E. W. Vaz, ed., *Middle-Class Juvenile Delinquency* (New York, 1967). The most penetrating accounts of British teenage culture in the 1950s are Ray Gosling's youthful autobiographies, *Sum Total* (London, 1962), and *Personal Copy* (London, 1980), and Colin MacInnes's journalistic observations, *England, Half English* (New York, 1962). Mark Abrams's market research, *The Teenage Consumer* (London, 1959) was very influential for British sociologists—see J. B. Mays, *The Young Pretenders* (New York, 1966). For British youth culture in the 1960s, see Timothy Raison, ed., *Youth in New Society* (London, 1966)—this includes Colin Fletcher's piece on Liverpool gangs and groups, Peter Willmott, *Adolescent Boys of East London* (London, 1969), and Jeremy Seabrook's angry *City Close-Up* (London, 1971). For the 1970s, see Dave Robins and Philip Cohen, *Knuckle Sandwich* (London, 1978).

The major sociological attempts to theorize on youth are Karl Mannheim, *Diagnosis of Our Time* (London, 1944), on generations, and S. N. Eisenstadt, *From Generation to Generation* (New York, 1956), structural functionalism. For right- and left-wing sociological reflections on 1960s youth culture, see Bryan Wilson, *The Youth Culture and the Universities* (London, 1970) and Richard Flacks, *Youth and Social Change* (Chicago, 1971).

For subcultural theory, see A. K. Cohen, *Delinquent Boys* (London, 1956), on corner and college boys, and H. Fineston, "Cats, Kicks and Color" (*Social Problems*, 5, 1957), on corner boys only. American subcultural theory was brought to Britain in David Downes's *The Delinquent Solution* (New York, 1966), on English corner and college boys, and Stanley Cohen's *Folk Devils and Moral Panics* (London, 1973), on mods, rockers, and the press. Stuart Hall, et al., *Resistance Through Rituals* (New York, 1976) and Mike Brake, *The Sociology of Youth Culture and Youth Subcultures* (London, 1980) show how the theory was developed by "the Birmingham School" in the 1970s.

Most studies of specific youth styles are British [though for an American study see Stephen Buff, "Greasers, Dupers and Hippies: Three Responses to the Adult World" in L. K. Howe, ed., *The White Majority*, (New York, 1971)]. For teddy boys see T. R. Fyvel, *The Insecure Offenders* (London, 1963) and Chris Steel-Perkins and Richard Smith, *The Teds* (London, 1979). For mods see Charles Hamblett and Jane Deverson, *Generation X* (London, 1964), Tom Wolfe, *The Pump House Gang* (New York, 1968), and Richard Barnes, *Mods!* (London, 1979). For skinheads see Susie Daniel and Pete McGuire, eds., *The Paint House* (London, 1972). For hippies see Richard Neville, *Play Power* (London, 1970), Jock Young, *The Drug Takers* (London, 1971), Richard Mills, *Young Outsiders* (New York, 1973), and Paul Willis, *Profane Culture* (London, 1978). For punks and post-punks see Dick Hebdige, *Subculture: The Meaning of Style* (New York, 1979) and Peter York, *Style Wars* (London, 1980).

Philip G. Altbach, *Student Politics in America* (New York, 1974) is a good general history. For 1960s student radicalism see Jeff Nuttall, *Bomb Culture* (New York, 1970), Julian Nagel, ed., *Student Power* (London, 1969), and David Widgery, *The Left in Britain 1956–68* (London, 1976). For the revolutionary youth movement see Harold Jacobs, ed., *Weatherman* (Berkeley, 1970). The theoretical argument for a youth movement was made most powerfully in John and Margaret Rowntree, "The Political Economy of Youth" (*Our Generation*, 6, 1968); also see Paul Piccone, "From youth culture to political praxis" (*Radical America*, 3, 1969).

For youth and music in the 1920s and 1930s, see Neil Leonard's interesting *Jazz and the White Americans* (Chicago, 1962). Bruce Chipman's *Hardening Rock* (Boston, 1972) and Alfred Wertheimer's *Elvis '56* (London, 1979) are photo collections that capture the place of rock 'n' roll in 1950s teenage culture. Mick Gold's *Rock on the Road* (London, 1976) does the same thing for British teenagers in the 1970s. Graham Murdock and Guy Phelps, *Mass Media and the Secondary School* (London, 1973) is a well-organized survey of musical tastes and uses among youth in a British provincial town. Morris Dickstein's *Gates of Eden* (New York, 1978) is a feeble attempt by a literary critic to make sense of youth music and "American culture in the Sixties."

In the end, the best accounts of growing up with music can be found in novels. I've drawn insights particularly from Colin MacInnes's *Absolute Beginners* (New York, 1960) and Richard Price's *The Wanderers* (New York, 1974)—on British and American street life; Ed Sanders's *Tales of Beatnik Glory* (New York, 1976)—on New York bohemia; and Andrew Holleran's *Dancer from the Dance* (New York, 1978)—on disco culture. But there are numerous other clues scattered through postwar American fiction.

## ROCK AND SEXUALITY

There is still relatively little work on the sexual divisions of youth and rock culture. In Britain I've learned a lot from Angela McRobbie's "Working Class Girls and the Culture of Femininity," in Women's Study Group: *Women Take Issue* (London, 1978), *Jackie: an Ideology of Adolescent Femininity* (Birmingham 1978), and "Settling Accounts with Subcultures" (*Screen Education*, 34, 1980). For more general descriptions of growing up female, see Sheila Rowbotham, *Woman's Consciousness, Man's World* (New York, 1974), Sue Sharpe, *Just Like a Girl* (London, 1976), Ann Whitehead, "Sexual Antagonism in Herefordshire," in D. Barker and S. Allen, eds, *Dependence and Exploitation in Marriage* (London, 1976), and Diana Leonard, *Sex and Generation* (London, 1980). For a sharp and sensitive account of working-class sexuality in America in the 1970s, see Lillian Rubin, *Worlds of Pain* (New York, 1976).

For rock and sexuality see Simon Frith and Angela McRobbie, "Rock and Sexuality" (*Screen Education*, 29, 1978–79) and the reply by Jenny Taylor and Dave Laing, "Disco-Pleasure-Discourse" (*Screen Education*, 31, 1979). Terri Goddard, et al., "Popular Music," in J. King and M. Stott, eds. *Is This Your Life?* (London, 1977) is a good analysis of rock lyrics. For two brilliant descriptions of dance and sexuality, see Geoff Mungham's "Youth in pursuit of itself," in G. Pearson and G. Mungham, eds. *Working-Class Youth Culture* (London, 1976)— on the working-class dance hall, and Richard Dyer's "In Defence of Disco" (*Gay Left*, 8, 1979)—on gay discos.

## LEISURE

Most of the so-called sociology of leisure is tedious and irrelevant to a study of rock. The books I found most helpful were written at the margins of the discipline. For the history of British leisure I relied heavily on Peter Bailey, *Leisure and Class in Victorian England* (Toronto, 1978), Hugh Cunningham, *Leisure in the Industrial Revolution* (New York, 1980), Robert D. Storch, "The policeman as domestic missionary" (*Journal of Social History*, 9, 1976), and Jeff Nuttall's life of the prewar music hall comic Frank Randle, *King Twist* (London, 1978). Richard Dyer's *Light Entertainment* (New York, 1977) is an interesting attempt to make sense of the dominant ideology of leisure media since the war.

There is still much to be learned about American leisure habits and their development this century from Robert and Helen Lynd's *Middletown* (New York, 1929) and *Middletown in Transition* (New York, 1937). For more recent insights into leisure and the American working class, see Joseph T. Howell's fine *Hard Living on Clay Street* (New York, 1973). The best introduction to leisure and American bohemia is Ned Polsky's *Hustlers, Beats, and Others* (New York, 1969) and see Ronald Morris's fascinating *Wait Until Dark, Jazz and the Underworld, 1880–1940* (Bowling Green, 1980).

The classic theories of leisure, Thorstein Veblen's *The Theory of the Leisure Class* (New York, 1899) and Johan Huizinga's *Homo Ludens* (London, 1949), are still the essential reading. I have taken many ideas, too, from three contemporary cultural critics—Harold Rosenberg (see, for example, *The Tradition of the New*, New York, 1959, and *Discovering the Present*, Chicago, 1973), John Berger (see, for example, *About Looking*, New York, 1980), and C. L. R. James (see his book on cricket, *Beyond a Boundary*, London, 1963). Each of these writers has been inspired, in his own way, by Marx, who stands, too, somewhere at the back of my understanding of rock and youth, capital and leisure.

# INDEX

## ABOUT THE AUTHOR

SIMON FRITH, born in Sussex, England, in 1946, graduated from Oxford University and the University of California, Berkeley, receiving a B.A. in Philosophy, Politics and Economics and a Ph.D. in Sociology. He has contributed to many books on sociology and youth culture in England, as well as to *New Society*, *Time Out*, and other social and music journals. In this country, he has contributed to both *Creem* and the *Village Voice*, and is a regular columnist for *New York Rocker*. Simon Frith is a senior lecturer in Sociology at the University of Warwick, in England.